P9-CDJ-816

America

BAY CITY
SAGINAW
FLINT
SYRACUSE   FITCHBURG
ELMIRA   SPRINGFIELD
MUSKEGON   NEWARK   HOBOKEN
GRAND RAPIDS   JERSEY CITY
KALAMAZOO   ANN ARBOR   LONG ISLAND
               JACKSON   CLEVELAND   BAYONNE
                                            STATEN ISLAND
                          HARRISBURG

ST. LOUIS

CATAWBA

HUNTSVILLE

BIRMINGHAM

MOBILE
PASCAGOULA
NEW ORLEANS

Magazines

BRIDE'S
CHARM
GENTLEMAN'S QUARTERLY
GLAMOUR
HOUSE & GARDEN
LIVING FOR YOUNG HOMEMAKERS
MADEMOISELLE
PARADE
SELF
VOGUE

ama,

JOHN ECCLES, 1982

Newspaperman

NEWSPAPERMAN

S.I. Newhouse and the Business of News

Richard H. Meeker

Ticknor & Fields □ New Haven and New York □ 1983

Library of Congress Cataloging in Publication Data

Meeker, Richard H., 1949-
  Newspaperman: S.I. Newhouse and the business of news.

  Includes bibliographical references and index.
  1. Newhouse, Samuel I.   2. Newspaper publishing—
United States—Biography.   3. American newspaper—History.   I. Title.
Z473.N47M43   1983   070.5'092'4 [B]   83-5008
ISBN 0-89919-200-9

Endpaper map ("Newhouse's America") by John Eccles

Printed in the United States of America

V 10 9 8 7 6 5 4 3 2 1

Book design by Ann Schroeder

To my father,
Leonard C. Meeker

"The function of the press in society is to inform,
but its role is to make money."
— A. J. Liebling, *The Press*

Contents

Introduction: Summer 1979   1

I. 1895-1924: APPRENTICE

1. First Assignment   7
2. Running the *Times*   14
3. Life Beyond the *Times*   21
4. Upstairs, Downstairs   25
5. First Acquisition   28
6. On His Own   34

II. 1924-1933: TECHNICIAN

7. Starting Over   47
8. A Lesson in Vindictiveness   54
9. The People's Champion   59
10. Acquiring the *Press*   65

III. 1934-1938: MASTER

11. Guilded   77
12. Newark   88
13. Smashing the Opposition   96
14. The Final Battle   101
15. The Chief   107

IV. 1939-1955: OPPORTUNIST

16. Syracuse   113
17. The Good Life   123

18. Jersey City 130

19. Harrisburg 139

20. Portland 149

21. Meeting the Press 156

22. Local Autonomy 164

V. 1955–1962: EMPIRE BUILDER

23. In Vogue 177

24. Coming Out 181

25. The Solid-Gold Pyramid 187

26. Striking It Rich 190

27. On Top 198

28. Disgruntled Heritors 202

29. The Living Monument 213

VI. 1962–1979: THE LAST YEARS

30. Newhouse & Sons 225

31. The Publishers of the Future 230

32. Final Exam 237

33. Last Act 244

34. Thirty 250

Afterword 255

Acknowledgments 259

A Note on Sources 261

Index 283

Illustrations follow page 134.

Introduction: Summer 1979

THE MEN FROM SYRACUSE UNIVERSITY had risen early to be in Manhattan by noon, and now that they had arrived at their destination, they took a few moments to collect their thoughts. William Tolley, chancellor emeritus, and Melvin Eggers, the university's present leader, were about to visit S. I. Newhouse, their school's greatest living benefactor as well as America's richest and most successful newspaper publisher.

Though Tolley and other university officials had met with Newhouse dozens of times before, they had never gotten around to talking with him about his last will and testament. Now, not having seen the 84-year-old billionaire for some time, they worried that they might never have an opportunity to broach the subject. Their concern was confirmed almost the moment they were ushered into his sumptuous Park Avenue apartment that bright summer day; at the far side of the room, Newhouse sat motionless on a sofa, his eyes vacant.

There was nothing for Tolley to do but launch into the little speech he had rehearsed for the occasion. "Look, Sam," he began, "you've got the money of the Rockefellers. It's time you started thinking like the Rockefellers." As he continued, the hopelessness of the situation became increasingly apparent. Newhouse's round face — remarkably pink and healthy-looking the last time they talked— was now waxen. The friendly twinkle in his clear grey eyes was gone, too. Even the bulging underlip and the eyebrows that curled devilishly upward in mid-arch no longer served to energize his expression.

Paying no attention to Tolley's remarks, Newhouse seemed entranced by the contents of a jar directly in front of him, and

■ 1

every few moments would reach out for a piece of candy, only to have his wife slap his hand away reprovingly.

Things were going so poorly that the visitors were relieved when Mitzi attempted to change the subject. She had some photos of a place they'd looked at recently in Florida and were considering buying. What did her guests think of it?

Something in the question must have gotten through to S. I., for just then the empty expression in his eyes began to dissolve. He sat bolt upright, and for a moment, as if distilled by the ravages of ill health and old age, his essence issued forth. "Mitzi, don't," he intoned. "I'd rather buy another newspaper."

Newhouse died a few weeks later, but no one ever came up with a more fitting epitaph than the words he spoke that afternoon in the presence of the men from Syracuse. He was the greatest buyer of newspapers America has ever known. Nothing gave him more pleasure, and no one — not even the legendary William Randolph Hearst — was better at it. With him, it seemed instinctive — he sensed the right time to make a move, the exact amount of money required, and the proper strategy. Moreover, he managed his "properties," as he called them, so profitably that there was always plenty of cash on hand to make still more acquisitions when opportunity beckoned.

Just two years before his death, Newhouse masterminded the biggest transaction in American newspaper history when he outbid — and outfoxed — the *Los Angeles Times*'s huge parent company, Times Mirror Publishing, and landed the entire Booth newspaper chain in Michigan for more than $300 million. Included in the deal was *Parade*, a weekly rotogravure magazine with a circulation of nearly 20 million.

After that final purchase, Newhouse owned outright some twenty-nine newspapers with combined daily circulations of more than three million in twenty-two American cities. His holdings included the *Cleveland Plain Dealer, Newark Star-Ledger, New Orleans Times-Picayune, St. Louis Globe-Democrat, Springfield Union, Syracuse Herald-Journal, Birmingham News,* and Portland *Oregonian.* Along the way, he picked up a string of magazines — *Vogue, Glamour, Mademoiselle, Self, Gentleman's Quarterly, House & Garden,* and *Bride's* — that reached millions more readers. He also acquired more than a dozen radio and TV stations, a burgeoning cable-TV network, a share in a huge pulp mill, and large chunks of valuable real estate, including an airport in Massachusetts. Altogether, his assets amounted to the greatest fortune ever amassed by an American publisher.

Behind the creation of an empire so huge lay a life filled with the stuff of American myth. The oldest son of poor East European immigrants, Newhouse dropped out of school at the age of thirteen to help support his family. A few years later, his father left home, leaving him to look after his mother and seven younger brothers and sisters. While still little more than a child, he was able, through hard work, good fortune, and ingenuity, to pull the family out of poverty. He was still in his twenties when he purchased his first newspaper and set about putting it on its feet. In all, his newspaper career spanned nearly seven decades, with his greatest achievements coming after he had reached the age of fifty-five.

At the same time, Newhouse kept his life shrouded in such secrecy that only a small fraction of the tens of millions of readers of his publications ever realized that the newspapers and magazines were his. Indeed, within his own organization, which employed 15,000, he remained a thoroughly elusive figure to all but a handful of key executives.

Obviously, the first task of any biographer is to break through the secrecy. Newhouse did not make that task easy. During his life, he developed few close friendships, rarely wrote personal letters, and did not keep a diary. Moreover, his family refused to cooperate with me. When first approached about this project in mid-1980, Newhouse's two sons, Si and Donald, seemed hesitant. Two weeks later, Si informed me by telephone that he and his brother felt their father had been essentially a private man, who would not have wished to be the subject of a book such as I proposed. Thus, Si informed me, neither he nor his brother nor any other member of their immediate families would agree to get involved. Consequently, I never got to speak to Newhouse's widow, Mitzi, at all; her only communication to me was a note written and typed by her secretary, repeating what Si had told me. Even S. I.'s cousin Henrietta, who had had a tremendous crush on him when they were young, decided, after consulting Donald, not to be interviewed.

About a year later, while in New Orleans, I spoke briefly on the telephone with Newhouse's youngest brother, Norman, who gave me a different explanation of the family's reticence. He said that he and his brother Theodore and their nephews and cousins were still engaged in running the business, and that they were concerned that a biography published so soon after S. I.'s death might cause them problems in that enterprise. "When the right time comes, and we have found the right biographer," Norman concluded, "then we'll open everything up." Given what I now know about the Newhouses and how they operate, I doubt that time will ever come.

For 18 months I interviewed hundreds of people and studied each of the newspapers and magazines carefully, just to piece together the basic facts of Newhouse's life. It took an additional year of research and writing to assemble this account. From the outset, I wanted this to be more than the chronicle of a career; I wanted to know more about Newhouse the man. What was it, for example, in his childhood, the friendships of his youth, and his family life that led him to the newspaper business in the first place, and then gave him such mastery over it?

Beyond that, my interest in Newhouse is public. For I believe he played a crucial role in reshaping one of our most important institutions — the daily newspaper. Because no individual since Hearst has made so significant and lasting a mark on American journalism, coming to grips with Newhouse means placing him in the context of newspaper publishing today — a landscape containing fewer papers, concentrated in fewer hands, and regarded with less credibility than at any time in modern history.

Part I
1895 – 1924: Apprentice

1 First Assignment

S. I. NEWHOUSE WAS NOT BORN into a life of comforts or security. He was the first child of recent Jewish immigrants. He was small for his age and was picked on by classmates/ But what made the most lasting mark on him was his family's seeming inability to capture the American dream. Years later, he was to confide in a friend that he thought he might never get over the shame he felt about his beginnings. At least one thing was certain, he added sharply. He would see to it that no member of his family would ever be poor again.

Newhouse's father and mother arrived in America in 1890 and 1892, respectively. His father, Meier Neuhaus, was the second in the family to make the long voyage from home in the Pale of Settlement in Russia, across Europe by caravan, and into steerage on a ship bound for the United States. An older sister had made the journey earlier that year, sent from home by her father, Nachman Neuhaus, a rabbi in the Vitebsk district. After Meier, other siblings arrived in rapid succession — Devorah, Becky, Louis, Joe, and Frieda.

Nachman's daughters met good men and established themselves quickly in their new country, but the sons were neither so fortunate nor so enterprising. Meier, short and frail, found his life particularly disrupted by the transition to the hurly-burly of Manhattan's Lower East Side. There, on Orchard, Hester, and Delancey streets, between Houston and Division, was a world peopled by immigrants like himself, but a world that was utterly foreign to him. The outdoors was all little shops and pushcarts, vegetables and secondhand bargains, horses and wagons; and the streets seethed with a terrifying undercurrent of corruption and criminality. The world inside the buildings that lined the streets of the Lower East Side was just as unpleasant — dingily lit, unheated, filthy rooms that served as home and working place alike to the poor people who crowded them.

When he disembarked at Castle Garden, near New York's Battery, Meier knew no English and possessed no trade with which to earn a living. He liked to talk, though, and made friends quickly among what was then the largest concentration of Jewish people in the world. Within a short time, in one of those dirty, crowded rooms, he learned to operate a machine that manufactured the leather ends of suspenders, known as "trimmings."

Of Austrian origin, Rose Arenfeldt was short, too. Somewhat stocky, with a round, determined-looking face, she had been shipped off to America by her parents while still a teenager. In 1894, she and Meier fell in love. Almost right away, Rose found herself pregnant, and the two were married in a hastily arranged ceremony that fall. There was no honeymoon; the young couple were lucky just to have a place of their own in New York City's Tenth Ward. It was there, in the rear of a shabby, five-story dumbbell tenement at 53 Orchard Street, that the following 24 May Rose Neuhaus gave birth to her first child, a son named Solomon.

For a baby boy who was to forge one of America's largest newspaper empires, it was a fitting time and place to get started. Eighteen ninety-five was the year William Randolph Hearst purchased New York's morning *Journal* and hired away — at unthinkably large salaries — many of the editors, writers, illustrators, and executives who had made Joseph Pulitzer's *World* a success. Among Hearst's acquisitions was an illustrator named Richard F. Outcault, whose drawings of "Hogan's Alley" caricatured life on the Lower East Side and featured a kid with a toothless grin, dressed in billowing, balloon-like clothes. With the installation of color presses, the kid's garb was printed in the splash of yellow that gave that period of journalism its name.

Meier and Rose needed no Yellow Kid to tell them they were miserable. The Lower East Side was an unpleasant way station, a place to leave at the first opportunity. So when a fellow worker tipped Meier off about a job making trimmings in Jersey City, he didn't hesitate to pack his family's things. After a ferry and trolley-car ride west across the Hudson, they arrived in a suburb called

Greenville. There, just north of the Morris Canal, in the center of a piece of land that jutted into New York Harbor, nice single-family houses could be found. Light and fresh air abounded, and compared with Orchard Street, it was a big park.

The Neuhauses stayed a year before the itch to move set in again. A man named Lublintz, in Bayonne, on the other side of the canal, was offering work — also in the trimmings business — and Meier took it.

For years Bayonne had been a resort for the gentry of New York City. By the turn of the century, however, it had metamorphosed from a polite retreat to a center of heavy industry, and by 1897, when Meier, Rose, and two-year-old Solomon first settled there, the town was already a smoky, smelly array of cracking towers and storage tanks.

Bayonne's midsection housed Poles, Russians, Italians, and Irish in relative harmony, and certainly in better conditions than were available in Manhattan, where most of them had started out. Jews dominated the area north of Sixteenth Street to about Twenty-fifth, and it was to this section of town that the Neuhauses moved, into a building inhabited by the Blackmans, Glucksteins, Blotkins, Seigels, Pearlmans, and Seretzes. Of Russian origin all, the heads of these families were painters, day laborers, shirtmakers, and carpenters.

The Neuhauses' initial stay in Bayonne proved a short one, though, for Meier's dreams soon got the better of him again, and the following year, he moved his family back to Greenville, where he went into the suspender business for himself.

Meier was naturalized on 10 September 1902 in Jersey City, and began signing his name "Meyer Newhouse" a year or two later. But nothing in the process of Americanization could improve his meager skills as a businessman. On 1 May 1905, his fledgling suspender company went under.

Meyer's sudden failure must have been an especially crushing blow for his children. Solomon, now known as Sammy, and his younger sister Ada and brother Louis were yanked out of Jersey City School No. 20 with less than a month to go that year. Along with their parents and two younger siblings, Theodore and Naomi, they had to return to Bayonne. Though Lublintz took Meyer back, his pay was negligible, and the family scraped by in a series of crowded tenement apartments, where they sometimes exchanged janitorial work for rent.

If poverty was the most palpable fact of Sammy's early years, his size soon came to rival it. When he enrolled in the fifth grade at Bayonne's brand new P.S. 7 that fall, he was the smallest in the class, a shrimp compared to even the shortest girls. Moreover, there were a lot of tough kids in the neighborhood between home and school, and they weren't about to leave him alone.

In the spring of 1908, Sammy Newhouse graduated from No. 7's eighth grade. A very round-faced young man with a lock of hair falling over his forehead, he delighted his teachers with a brief speech in which he spoke of himself as a tiny postage stamp taking a message out into the world. Sammy must have had a lot more on his mind that day, though. His father, head of a household then containing eight children, had developed such severe asthma that he was no longer able to work at all.

Rose had to take over, and she did the one job that seemed practical. She became a "customer peddler," taking orders for dry goods from people in Bayonne, then filling them over in Manhattan. Since she still had many friends and acquaintances on Lower Broadway and the East Side, she could strike good bargains. But when she returned from these shopping expeditions, the pack on her back bulging with sheets, towels, pillowcases, and napkins, it was all her oldest son could do to hide his embarrassment as he watched her trundle from door to door, bent over under the load.

The children helped out as best they could, Lublintz donated his kids' hand-me-downs, cousins in the Bronx sent packages, and a local physician provided free medical care. Even so, the Newhouses barely eked out a living in their crowded apartment on 25th Street. In order for the family to survive, Meyer and Rose's thirteen-year-old son would have to quit school and go to work, but they had no idea what he should do. Obviously, there wasn't much of a future in suspender ends or in continuing to run errands for people around town.

That spring, they heard about a school in New York City that offered a compelling program. The Gaffney School, located on Eighth Avenue at West Twenty-third Street, promised to locate a job for any student who could pass its courses in typing, stenography, and bookkeeping; tuition for the summer curriculum was $37.50. Every weekday that June, July, and August, Sammy took the early morning trolley north from Bayonne, over the Morris Canal, through Greenville, to Jersey City, where he caught the railroad ferry to Manhattan. To pay his way back and forth, he took his first newspaper job — helping another boy carry bundles of papers across on the ferry.

Besides training in typing, bookkeeping, and stenography, the summer of 1908 offered Sammy an introduction to the most amazing environment he had ever experienced — New York City. He couldn't believe how big everything was. The forty-one-story Singer building had been completed that year, and the even more impressive fifty-story Metropolitan tower was under construction. In Bayonne, by comparison, the tallest building was barely four stories high. Sammy's curiosity carried him well away from the short walk between the ferry docks and the school, into a maze of shops, restaurants, and offices, but these fascinations were beyond his reach. It took money to buy department store goods or to eat a meal at a sidewalk cafe, and he hadn't a penny to spare.

That August, the three months' training ended, and after Sammy passed all the courses, it was time for the school to make good on its pledge. A prospective employer was identified, and Sammy, with his ailing father as an escort, paid the man a visit. The moment the young applicant walked in the door, the man broke into laughter. "I can't hire the likes of you!" he roared. "Your head doesn't even come to the top of the desk!"

He fared little better in subsequent efforts to find a job, and soon there remained only one person to whom Meyer could take his son. A large and attractive man, Hyman Lazarus had been a great athlete in his youth, excelling at boxing. Now a prominent local lawyer with his own firm, Lazarus & Brenner, he was something of a patron of the Jewish community in Bayonne. Fathers were forever seeking his advice about their sons, and he seemed to take special interest in each family with whom he came in touch. But when Meyer Newhouse brought his son late that summer, Sammy was rebuffed again. "I don't need him," the burly lawyer said, "I don't need any help in the office."

By then, the Newhouses were desperate. "Let my son work for

you for a month for nothing," Meyer proposed. "If you find he's useful, then pay him what you think he's worth. If not, it won't have cost you anything." Lazarus relented. Sammy swept floors, typed letters, and carried messages, and by the end of the trial month, it was clear to Lazarus that he should keep his new helper.

By the end of that trial month, it was also clear that in Hyman Lazarus, Sammy had happened upon a powerful father figure. Whereas his own flesh and blood was frail and stooped, Lazarus was tall and imposing. And whereas Meyer Newhouse had become an apprehensive, hesitant man, Lazarus exuded joy and warmth. The lawyer so impressed Sammy that Meyer lost all influence over his son. Soon, even the smallest matters — like Meyer's concern that Sammy ate too many tomatoes — had to be referred to Lazarus for resolution.

Thus inspired, Sammy did everything in his power to please his employer. The following summer, when the law firm's accountant quit precipitously, Sammy asked if he could try out for the job. With the training he had received at the Gaffney School and his natural facility with numbers, he found keeping the books easy. Soon Sammy was running more important errands and taking care of his boss's real-estate holdings in Bayonne as well. He made sure the rents were paid, supervised repairs, and still managed to stay on top of his work for the law firm.

Lazarus was especially impressed with his new helper's frugality. If one of the apartments needed a skeleton key, for example, Sammy would go to Brigadier, who owned a hardware store nearby, and ask the price of a gross. Then, dividing by 144, he would attempt to pay this price for just one key.

In the meantime, Sammy's boss's interests expanded beyond the law practice and apartment buildings. He helped launch a drive for a new synagogue and took charge of Bayonne's volunteer fire department. He was a personal friend and active supporter of New Jersey Governor Woodrow Wilson. He was also appointed judge, the first Jew in the county to be accorded such an honor.

As far as his devoted helper was to be concerned, however, Lazarus's most important move was his involvement with a local newspaper that was in financial trouble. At first, he merely served as guarantor of one of the *Bayonne Times*'s loans. But in 1911, when the paper's publisher defaulted, he took complete control, soon moving the operation across town to the first floor of the building that housed his law offices. Save for dictating an occasional editorial, however, Lazarus attended very little to his new publication. As he should have expected, it continued to lose money.

When Lazarus brought up the matter of the *Times*'s financial problems during a political trip to Atlanta later that year, one of his listeners suggested what seemed the perfect cure — that he hire as editor the man's son, Octavus Roy Cohen. Cohen had already established a reputation for himself with a series of articles for the *Saturday Evening Post* on the subject of race relations in the South, and Lazarus figured that Cohen's brand of snappy, controversial writing would improve the fortunes of the *Times*.

On arrival in Bayonne, Cohen was oblivious to his boss's helper upstairs, but Sammy watched the judge's new favorite jealously. What he saw was as good an introduction as any to the world of newspapers. Cohen emphasized politics and steered his vessel on a markedly liberal course. That was about all he did with the paper, though. Early each afternoon, when the *Times* had been put to bed for the day, its new editor would drift next door to the Bayonne Opera House, where he would set about winning the hearts of a string of chorus girls. The overall effect of his activities on the bottom line of the paper's ledger was predictable; neither advertising nor circulation showed improvement.

Though Lazarus neglected the affairs of the *Times*, he could not forever remain ignorant of his new editor's after-hours activities or of the financial drain the paper continued to represent. It was not long before he marched downstairs to confront Cohen. The two had a heated argument, which Lazarus finally ended — much to Sammy's pleasure — by picking Cohen up and heaving him from the paper's offices with the admonition never to return. Another editor was appointed on the spot, and the *Times*'s publisher went back upstairs to his law office.

Lazarus had neither the time nor the inclination to take a more active role in the day-to-day operations of his newspaper, but he realized that he needed at least a watchful eye in the place, and he already had in his employ the perfect person for the job — his office boy, bookkeeper, and apartment manager.

"Sammy," he said, "go downstairs and look after the paper."

2 Running the *Times*

LIKE SO MANY OTHER Jewish immigrant mothers in America, Rose Newhouse lavished attention on her oldest boy. Her doting became so extreme that some of their neighbors wondered if she might not be overdoing it, possibly to compensate for her husband's shortcomings.

"This little son of mine is no ordinary man," Rose told her children. So while Ada first, and then Naomi, supervised the chores in their growing household, and Louis, the second son, sold papers, and Theodore and Norman scrounged daily for firewood and coal, Sammy was the constant recipient of his mother's advice. Over and over, she pressed on him her belief that if he used his brains and worked hard, he could do anything he wanted.

For his new assignment at the *Times*, Sammy needed as much of his mother's encouragement as he could get. Not only was he just sixteen when Judge Lazarus ordered him to look after the paper, but he was also totally unschooled in the ways of the trade. Still, it didn't take much to conclude that the quickest way to halt the paper's drain on his boss's bank account was to increase revenues. A perusal of the books showed that advertising accounted for nearly three-quarters of the *Times*'s gross income.

Since he didn't know the first thing about selling ads, Sammy started hanging around Bayonne's biggest newsstand, at Forty-second Street and Broadway, to see what he could learn from the big-city newspapers. Soon he was clipping out advertisements he thought particularly effective and taking them around to local retailers. "We can print something like that for you," he would say, and if a merchant wasn't too interested at first, he kept after him with regular visits. It wasn't long before the *Bayonne Times* was running ads for local men's clothing stores and furniture dealers that Sammy had copied straight out of the *New York Times*, the *World*, the *Journal*, and the *Newark Evening News*.

Sammy also noticed that the papers at the Forty-second Street newsstand routinely carried notices of special sales, which seemed to have been created solely for advertising purposes. Following their lead, he set about helping the store owners of Bayonne map their own special merchandising campaigns. Of course, he was more than willing to run the resulting ads in the *Times*.

He saw that there were other ways to attract advertising, and he soon realized that the best incentive was a price break. The key was to trade lower prices for something at least as valuable. Because a captive market was important, one of the first discounts he offered was to merchants who would agree not to advertise in other Bayonne publications. For such an assurance, Sammy would even throw in preferred placement. On the surface, all he got in return was the advertiser's promise not to use the local *Herald*, *Democrat*, or *Review*. But he sensed — correctly — that the merchants would not cut back on their overall advertising budgets. Thus, a promise not to advertise with the *Times*'s competitors often represented a commitment to place additional advertising with the *Times* itself.

Discounts for running the same ad repeatedly could also benefit the paper. In those days, a substantial part of the cost of producing an ad was tied up in making the mat from which it was printed. Multiple insertions of the same ad would thus create significant savings. If the *Times* were to offer a discount for such repeat advertising but keep it less than the actual savings that accrued, it could increase profits dramatically and at the same time lead advertisers to believe they were getting a bargain. Similar thinking applied to half- and full-page ads; the bigger they were, the less per inch each column cost to compose.

Sammy was so single-minded in his new pursuit that when he learned that stores in Jersey City, just up the peninsula, were having difficulty with credit accounts in Bayonne, he offered to help with collections. From his position in the judge's law office, it was easy to put pressure on delinquent customers in Bayonne. In return, he got the Jersey City merchants to agree to place ads with the *Times*.

Bayonne was perfect for Sammy's sales routine. Most of its stores were concentrated in a strip along Broadway that ran right down the center of town, and the *Times*'s young ad salesman could visit a great many of them in a short time as he hurried about between chores for Lazarus & Brenner.

If lesson one in the ad sales business was straightforward — keep the volume as high as possible without denting the profit margin — its corollary was even simpler: make sure you get paid. Thanks to the unfortunate example of his father's suspender company, which folded because of failure to collect from all its customers, Sammy had learned this lesson well. Soon the *Times* was offering additional discounts for ads that were paid for in advance.

But how was one to keep track of all the deals being made with advertisers? Here Sammy had a special advantage. In an age without decent adding machines, let alone handheld calculators, he had the ability to store in his mind a multitude of facts and figures. Any competent salesperson could keep track of the big advertisers' accounts — Steinert Furniture Store or Larkey's or Jacobs & Friedman's — but Sammy Newhouse could remember all the accounts, even individual classified ads. If the need arose, he could recall instantly how many lines an advertiser had purchased, what the discount was, and when the money was due.

The paper's new salesman was brutal with unpaid accounts. In the past, Bayonne's merchants had made a practice of stretching their credit at the *Times* to the limit. Now, falling behind precipitated all sorts of onerous demands, including the requirement that debtors run bigger ads until their accounts were made current. If they refused to concur, they were effectively barred from advertising in any newspaper in Bayonne. For, once a merchant had accepted the original discount, which was given for not placing ads with the competition, he could advertise elsewhere only after repaying the discount—which, in most cases, proved out of the question. It was an unpleasant way to do business, and on several occasions, Judge Lazarus had to intercede on behalf of shop owners who complained that the pressure was intolerable.

"There was something about him that was considered tough," recalled Maurice Brigadier, who became associated with Lazarus & Brenner the same year that Newhouse was given responsibility for the paper. "It came from the way he could handle big men's jobs when he was only a boy."

After less than twelve months of Sammy's attention, the *Bayonne Times* was showing a small profit. He had accomplished a minor miracle and had done so without touching the element of a newspaper generally considered the key to success or failure — its editorial content. In that regard, the *Times* was, for the most part, no better and no worse than other daily newspapers its size. It was filled with short accounts of local affairs and tended to emphasize police blotter items and bizarre tragedies. "BABY BROTHER OF LITTLE PARALYSIS VICTIM BURNED TO DEATH AT HIS HOME," read a typical page-one headline.

Though Sammy occasionally filled in when the *Times* was a reporter short, he did so only to save money and not because he was interested in the actual gathering and writing of news. He did read the *Times* carefully, however, and was always curious to see what juicy bits of gossip he could pick up at the law office.

One local figure to whom he paid special attention was Pearl Bergoff, the self-styled king of America's strikebreakers. For just three weeks' work, it was said in town, Bergoff made $700,000 for putting down a labor disturbance at the Brooklyn Rapid Transit Company. From the Erie Railway, he supposedly received a $1-million retainer. Whatever the exact amounts, Bergoff had done well enough that, upon his arrival in Bayonne in 1909, he built himself a three-story, sixteen-room, gabled house on the boulevard.

Most of Bergoff's business was conducted out of town, but in mid-1915, some 7,000 workers walked off their jobs in a wage dispute with the local Standard Oil refinery and set up picket lines in front of the plant's entrance, at the east end of Twenty-second Street. Immediately, Bergoff's services were engaged. In addition to bringing in the usual gang of sharpshooters and thugs, he arranged for five undercover men to infiltrate the picketers. Dozens of strikers were killed or wounded and their leaders jailed before the walkout was quashed. Most of Bayonne was outraged by Bergoff's tactics, but Sammy admitted to others at the newspaper — one of whom had been shot at by Bergoff's men — that he admired the Red Demon's ability to get results.

* * *

During these early years with Lazarus, Sammy Newhouse was a whirling dervish. No matter what the task, he was always on the run. Because he appeared to be a little boy in adult's clothing, people who saw him dashing down the streets of Bayonne occasionally laughed out loud. If Sammy noticed their snickers, he certainly didn't worry about them. He had to get himself and his family out of the mess they were in, and he had no time to fret over what people thought. Nor did he have time to sympathize with unfortunates, such as people from whom he collected rents or advertisers who couldn't make payments. And he had no use whatsoever for the romantic notions of socialism that were then sweeping through the working places of America.

Sammy had gone from office boy at thirteen to bookkeeper at fourteen. By the end of another year, he had become a sort of personal business manager and handyman as well. Then, at sixteen, he'd added the *Bayonne Times* to his list of responsibilities and had been a key figure in moving it back into the black. Soon he was business manager of the *Times* and office manager of the law firm, too. By 1912 he was making seventy-five dollars a week — a far cry from what he earned when his father first placed him with Lazarus in 1908.

To make up for dropping out of high school, he followed Lazarus's advice and took the New Jersey Regents' Examination. Then, he started night school at the New Jersey College of Law, which held classes in Newark and neighboring Elizabeth. It took four years of part-time study, but in early June of 1916, one week after his twenty-first birthday, Newhouse passed the state bar examination and entered a select professional circle in Bayonne. To celebrate, Judge Lazarus took his protégé to the best haberdashery in town and bought him a complete outfit — suit, shoes, overcoat, and hat.

About the same time, Sam — as he now preferred to be called — asked the judge for a bit of a raise. The seventy-five dollars he was taking home each week was handsome — heads of working-class families were considered well off if they earned one-third as much — so he didn't ask for more salary. Instead, he asked to share in the profits he was helping the *Times* earn. The judge agreed to let him have 20 percent of whatever the paper netted that year.

* * *

The *Times* became all the more attractive to Sam when he got his first true taste of the practice of law. Soon after he passed the bar exam, one of the clients of Lazarus & Brenner came to the firm for help in collecting on an eighty-dollar promissory note. The case seemed as good as any to get Sam started in court. Though the sum of money involved was small and the defense didn't seem to have much to go on, Sam went to a lot of trouble preparing his arguments for the jury. When he finally presented them in court, he was wound up tight as a spring, and his nervousness showed through his usually nasal voice, so that he squeaked when he spoke. Still, he was certain of a favorable verdict when the jury withdrew to deliberate.

He was astonished when the jurors returned a few hours later to announce that they were unable to come to a decision. His surefire client had lost, and in disgust, Sam pulled a wad of bills from his pocket and gave everything he had to the man, a sum nearly equal to the amount contested at the trial. What he didn't know then was that his opposing counsel, Jack Feinberg, who had been a law school classmate, had rigged the jury. "You never had a chance," his adversary told him years later when they met at a social function.

Notwithstanding this admission, Sam liked to tell Feinberg's two sons, who themselves became lawyers in Bayonne, how losing to their father had been the deciding factor in his choice of newspapering over law.

Actually, it wasn't until Lazarus's partner, Alfred Brenner, told Sam quite a few years later that he thought he should choose between his two jobs that Sam gave up law altogether. Brenner had made it clear that he felt his young associate was better equipped for the business downstairs.

Sam Newhouse's world was looking up, and whatever optimism he was feeling was certainly buttressed by the times. The economy had dipped in 1914, but the outbreak of the Great War in Europe that year soon spurred American trade and banking. And it did wonders for newspaper sales; people rushed to read about Ypres, the first battle of the Marne, and the sinking of the Lusitania. Sam's father, however, was outraged by the war. Though generally meek and mild-mannered, he had become a fire-breathing socialist, and unlike his son, who was fascinated by money and success, he hated capitalism. He viewed the World War as an economic proposition and was incensed that the government of his adopted country would even consider selling Liberty bonds.

"Things just can't be the way my father sees them," Sam would tell acquaintances years later. But the beginning of the war in Europe did not please him any more than it pleased his father, for he realized that if the United States were to be sucked into the conflict, he might have to fight.

At one time, a volunteer for the British Army had to be five feet, eight inches tall, but so many soldiers were killed and injured that the limit was lowered first to five feet, five inches, and then to five feet, three inches. Only one more inch, and Sam would qualify if similar revisions were made by the U.S. armed services.

In early 1917, President Wilson, long a proponent of peace, issued a call for military preparedness. Marches were held; American boys enlisted in Great Britain's army and navy; and American arms and money began to be shipped overseas.

As American entry into the war appeared inevitable, Meyer Newhouse did something that helped his son in a way that his other efforts at being a father had not. He left home, to stay with his sister Becky in Hartford, Connecticut. He thought the climate there might help his asthma, but more important, his absence would make Sam the oldest male in the family in Bayonne; as the Newhouses' breadwinner, he would be exempt from military duty. So while some 4,000 other young men from Bayonne went off to fight, Sam remained at home and in charge of the *Times*.

3 Life Beyond the *Times*

SMALL'S WORK AT THE PAPER was the Newhouses' salvation. By the end of the war in late 1918, he was earning enough that Rose could give up peddling altogether, and the family could rent a house uptown, at Twenty-seventh Avenue and Hudson County Boulevard. Sam was able to arrange work at the *Times* for the older of his brothers and sisters; and the three youngest — Norman, Estelle, and Gertrude — were able to finish high school and contemplate attending college.

In return for all he had done for them, Rose made her oldest son the undisputed head of the household, a role Sam clearly relished. He sat at the head of the dinner table and had a room of his own, where he held a Saturday night card game for some of the men at the *Times*. Though the stakes were never high, the players loved to act important, smoking cigars and pretending not to notice when small change fell on the floor.

Sam found he had little influence over Lou and Ada, who were near to his own age, but, with help from Rose where it was needed, he meted out punishments when the "kids," as he called his younger siblings, misbehaved. He checked report cards and even tried to make sure the boys with whom Naomi, Gertrude, and Estelle associated were suitable.

Little Norman was the apple of his oldest brother's eye. The most precocious child in the family, he began hawking newspapers at the age of four and quickly developed an ingenious sales pitch. Working the territory over near Avenue C at Twenty-second Street, where crowds of workers changed trolley cars on the way home, he would take a single paper from a pile stashed with other newsboys and pretend that it was all he had left. The ruse was such a success that

■ 21

he rarely had a paper in his hands for more than a minute or two.

Norman was equally adept in school, graduating at fourteen as the class valedictorian. Money from Sam made it possible for him to become the first in the family to go to college, and he enrolled that fall at New York University, where he was both the shortest and youngest new student on campus.

For years, Sam had put in long hours. Waking most mornings at five, he would work at the paper until dinner time and afterwards attend to his legal studies until ten or so. Now, having worked full-time since the age of thirteen, he took life a little easier. As soon as he could afford to, he bought a two-seater Ford roadster with a canvas top. It had to be cranked to start, but it carried him over to the Bronx to see Aunt Rose and her family and to Hartford on weekends to see his father and Tanta Becky. It also allowed him to go to Coney Island and Rye Beach with friends and to visit the Adirondacks and Atlantic City.

There were other newfound diversions, too. Sam especially loved spending Sundays in New York City. He'd get up early to meet cousin Abe Silk or Moe Zinader, who worked with him in advertising sales at the *Times*, or Leo Rifkin, who had his own clothing store in Bayonne. Then, the young men would make the trolley-ferry-subway trip to their destination.

If Leo was along, their first stop was always Carnegie Hall, at Seventh Avenue and West Fifty-seventh Street. There, instead of going to hear a concert, they listened to lectures by Rabbi Stephen Wise, a nonassimilationist whose views on such divergent topics as Zionism and civic reform horrified many of Manhattan's more proper Jews.

What Rabbi Wise was saying, though, didn't interest Sam, who was there for the sheer entertainment of the lectures. There in the great music hall, the rabbi would play his deep, resonant voice like a musical instrument, achieving extraordinary dramatic flourishes. His appearance, too, was unusual. He was tall, broad-browed, and had long hair parted in the middle of his head; it grew so thick at the nape that he looked as regal as a lion. No basket was ever passed at these services, but one Sunday the good rabbi made a plea for "a noiseless, jingleless collection," and up in the balcony, Sam's eyes bulged when he saw how many bills piled up.

Next, it was downtown to Ratner's, at 138 Delancey Street on the

Lower East Side. There they could savor a Sunday lunch of babkas and blintzes, gefilte fish and schmaltz herring, and Ratner's incomparable onion rolls. The self-styled "vegetarian dairy restaurant" had other attractions as well, for right next door was Loew's Delancey Theater, and who could tell what famous vaudevillian might step into the restaurant while the young men were enjoying their meal. After lunch, Sam and his friends would seek out one of two entertainments — vaudeville or baseball.

For girls, Sam came to rely on Leo Rifkin, who seemed to have great ease when it came to the opposite sex. Perhaps it was because Leo was big and handsome. Perhaps it was because he was in the clothing business. Whatever it was, he had a knack for coming up with girls in New York City nearly any time Sam wanted to go out. Practically every Sunday, Leo produced new dates for the two of them to take to the Palace or a baseball game, and sometimes to dinner afterwards. Unlike many young men their age, who liked to crash big Jewish weddings in the city and run around with fast girls, Leo and Sam made it clear that they didn't go in for "funny business."

With Sam supplying the car and Leo the social grace, the two also shared vacations in the Catskill and Adirondack mountains and at the Jersey shore. They even took golf lessons together. But their friendship didn't stop Sam from kidding Leo mercilessly about his religious beliefs, particularly Leo's strict adherence to the dietary laws he'd been taught at home. Despite a grandfather who had been a rabbi and his mother's attempts to keep their home kosher, Sam never took much interest in Jewish traditions — they meant about as much to him as his father's ideas about politics — and one Sunday at a Coney Island fish house, he and two girls finally got Leo to eat some oysters and crab. All the way home to Bayonne that night, Leo worried about the retribution he'd suffer, and all the way home, his best friend mocked him for his superstitiousness.

There were several girls to whom Sam paid serious attention, but he always seemed to meet with rejection. His first real crush was on Henrietta Cohn, a cousin in the Bronx. For two or three years around the time he was twenty, Henrietta was his favorite girl. On weekends in the summertime, Sam and his friend Moe Zinader would meet Henrietta and her younger sister, Stella, at the Cohn home and take them out to Coney Island or Rye Beach. After a fling on the roller coaster, they'd change into full-length bathing suits and swim for a while, but mostly Sam and Henrietta sat apart, talking quietly. Sam was very serious; his conversation consisted largely of work at the *Times*, legal studies, and baseball. He had an eye for the very best, though, and when he finally took Henrietta and Stella out for dinner, it was to one of the finest restaurants in Manhattan — Riggs, on Forty-second Street across from the Public Library.

Henrietta wrote about Sam frequently in her diary, and in one entry, she got so carried away with romantic notions that she mentioned the possibility of their getting married. But she hadn't counted on her sister's snooping, nor on Stella's wrecking the romance by telling their mother, who disapproved of cousins courting.

After Henrietta, there was Rose Belinkoff, a sensitive, tall girl who worked as a stenographer at Lazarus & Brenner. As office manager, Sam had been responsible for her training, and, though the other stenographers liked Rose, they quickly became jealous of the boss's special fancy for her. When Sam gave her a beautiful scarf, the jealousy increased, and they began referring openly to the mismatched couple as "Mutt and Jeff." All this kidding proved too much, and after a while Rose stopped seeing Sam.

Sam struck out again with Evelyn Steinbaum, an especially attractive employee of the *Times*, who was hired in 1921, right out of high school, to take classified ads over the telephone. Though Sam made a big play for her, she preferred his friend Moe Zinader, and two years later Evelyn and Moe were married.

Sam's friends — and he had only a few close ones — always suspected that his heart wasn't really in the pursuit of girls or fun. He struck them as a grimly determined young man, even when he was sitting in the stands rooting for Babe Ruth or applauding some slapstick routine on the Palace Theater stage. It was clear that he was shy when it came to socializing, and that he preferred work to play. What wasn't so clear to Sam's friends in 1923, or even to Sam himself, was where this disposition would lead him.

4 Upstairs, Downstairs

THE OFFICES OF LAZARUS & BRENNER were at 579 Avenue C in the Centreville section of Bayonne, between Twenty-fifth and Twenty-sixth streets. On the corner was the magnificent — at least by local standards — Bayonne Opera House complex. Its first floor contained a saloon, Fischler's Ice Cream Parlor, and Balinky's Drug Store. Weekdays, Sam Newhouse was seen regularly in that part of town. He was friendly with Balinky, who was a frequent advertiser in the *Times*, and he occasionally stopped in at Fischler's, which did a brisk lunch trade. The saloon he visited only to solicit ads.

Most often when he was seen, though, it was on the *Bayonne Times* building's outdoor stairway, which connected the two jobs that occupied so much of Sam's time. Upstairs, at Lazarus & Brenner, he had become the managing partner of what was already the largest law practice in the county. He supervised the bookkeeping, hired and trained the stenographers, and performed a share of the legal work by drafting wills, drawing up complaints in accident cases, and preparing contracts for the firm's clients. Sam didn't handle many clients himself; rather, he saw to it that the firm's records were kept in order, and that business ran smoothly. He was a terrible stickler for detail and could never find stenographers to his liking. Because of his gruff demeanor, many of the women in the office referred to him as "SIN" behind his back.

He was a perfectionist and was very efficient, but there was still the problem of his height. When visitors came to see the managing attorney of the firm and Sam happened to be at the door, it wasn't uncommon for them to say they were interested in seeing the office manager, not the office boy.

Downstairs, Sam was the business manager of a newspaper whose circulation and advertising had nearly doubled since he had been associated with it. When he began at the *Times*, he knew practically nothing about a newspaper's operations: how stories were assigned and written, how the Linotype and printing machines worked, or even how the business was organized. Now, in addition to supervising advertising sales, he was learning about other aspects of journalism. As he became more responsible for the overall operation and understood it better, he began involving himself in all facets of the business — from making sure the *Times* wasn't getting nickle-and-dimed to death on supplies to manning his favorite promotion: posting scores from World Series games on a big billboard in front of the *Times*'s offices. Even when the fall baseball championships coincided with the Jewish High Holidays, he was there to put up the scores, inning by inning, as they came in over the wire.

The one area in which Sam encountered great difficulties was production. To his mind, the workers were incredibly lazy and sloppy, and, now that he was taking a share of the paper's profits, these inefficient people were no longer hurting just the *Times*, they were taking money from his own pocket.

His problems with the back shop employees were not helped by the fact that most of them were big, burly he-men who were set in their ways and who definitely didn't like being told what to do by a shrimp from upstairs in the judge's office. One day the *Times*'s business manager pushed his case for efficiency a little too far with one of the pressmen, and it became like the days in P.S. No. 7 all over again. The big fellow slapped Sam with the back of his hand, sending him scrambling out the door and back upstairs to the law offices.

It had not been too many years since Judge Lazarus had won the state's heavyweight boxing championship. When he learned what had just transpired in the pressroom, he laid a hand on his assistant's shoulder, and the two of them went back down the stairway to pay Sam's insubordinate assailant a visit.

"You're fired!" the judge bellowed, before punching the man so hard that he ended up in the hospital.

When the dust from the confrontation had cleared, Sam knew that something of a truce had been reached, but he also realized that he needed more than an occasional supportive outburst from the *Times*'s proprietor to have his way. As soon as he could, he set about getting extra leverage by moving relatives, like brother Louis, and friends, like Harry Scherer, into the pressroom. It wasn't long before he had fixed things so that a majority of the workers were on his side.

The paper's editorial focus became clearer, too, once Sam finally found an editor he could trust — Herbert L. Martin. Under Martin, the *Times* moved away from sensationalism and seemed unafraid to interpret local events for its readers. Ironically, as the paper's editorial content became more worthwhile, its advertising columns began to carry an increased number of promotions for quackery, like the full-page ad that ran under the banner headline, "YOUR GLANDS WEAR OUT!" Lewis Laboratories in far-away Chicago was inviting readers to send in a coupon and money for its special treatment. "You Will Throw Away Your 'Tonics' and Your Alcoholic 'Medicines' Once You Try This Greatest Of All Health Builders," the ad promised.

5 First Acquisition

BY THE TIME he turned twenty-five, Sam Newhouse was already well schooled in the newspaper business. Not only had he seen firsthand the workings of the paper he managed, but he had watched the papers in Jersey City and Hoboken closely and had read as much as he could about the profession he had chosen.

Saturday afternoon was his special time for reading. The *Times* came out early that day, the last of the papers going by noon to newsboys waiting eagerly on the back stoop. Inside, the writers were long gone, and the mechanical people cleaned up hastily and left. On those Saturdays, Sam would walk home for a quick lunch and then return to the *Times* building for his self-taught course in newspapering.

If the weather was good, he would take a big oak chair outside and place beside it neat stacks of periodicals he'd picked up during the week. There were regular mailings from the American Newspaper Publishers Association, trade journals from the newsstand uptown on Broadway, borrowings from Walter Dear (publisher of the nearby *Jersey City Journal*), less specialized newspapers and magazines, and anything else the *Times*'s young business manager could dig up.

Newsboys who had finished their sales downtown and were headed uptown — with a stop on the way for three-cent cones at Fischler's — would see their supervisor leaning back in the chair as he returned their greetings. "Hello, Willie," he would call out to twelve-year-old William Krupkin. "Hello, Johnnie, hello, Nat. . . ." It surprised the boys that he knew their names, for he usually saw them in a crowd when they arrived to pick up their papers. At those times, Sam would be on the back stoop of the *Times* building, wearing a big change apron so that he could collect the boys' pennies.

But on Saturday afternoon, the man who earlier had seemed overly concerned with the coins jingling in his apron would appear relaxed, sitting nonchalantly at the front of the building, surrounded by stacks of reading material and chatting amiably with the boys, as if he owned the place. An hour or so later, as they trotted back past him, the boys would notice that the periodicals were no longer arranged in neat stacks but were scattered about, as if Sam had read them all in the short time they'd been gone.

Sam was fascinated by the articles he perused and could easily tell which were worthy of greater attention. Here was his introduction to the latest in printing presses and typesetting equipment, to ideas for greater office efficiency, and to grander thoughts. The publications regaled him with stories not only of Pulitzer and Hearst, but also of E. W. Scripps, Frank Munsey, Cyrus H. K. Curtis, and the Gannett brothers. All were making fabulous fortunes by owning what was then a new phenomenon — chains of newspapers. The stories he read were replete with suspensions and mergers and births of new papers, which were subsequently merged or suspended themselves. Anyone who took the trouble to read this material could tell that concentration was the future of the newspaper industry, and that those who owned these chains could make fortunes never before dreamed of in the business.

Not surprisingly, these Saturday reading sessions gave Sam the bug to buy a newspaper in the worst way. "I intend to have my own chain of newspapers," he started boasting to fellow *Bayonne Times* men. "Just like Mr. Hearst." With one of his former associates at Lazarus & Brenner, he was more specific. "The only thing I ever heard him talk about was newspapers," recalled Maurice Brigadier. "He decided that the secret to accumulating wealth was to buy newspapers."

It was by word of mouth that one usually learned of newspapers for sale, and in early 1920 Sam heard of one. Judge Lazarus was not so keen on the idea of expanding his newspaper business, though, and was downright appalled when Sam told him that the paper on which he had set his sights was hundreds of miles and nearly a day's journey away, in a town even smaller than Bayonne — Fitchburg, Massachusetts, some forty miles northwest of Boston. Still, Lazarus had profited handsomely from Sam's enterprise over the past ten years, and his young associate was doggedly persistent about "the property" in Fitchburg. Before the deal blew over or someone else intervened, Lazarus agreed that the *Bayonne Times* would back Sam Newhouse in buying the Fitchburg Daily News Company for a price of $15,000. Newhouse bought half, clearing out his savings account and borrowing from his brothers and sisters to do so. The Times Company, owned entirely by the judge, bought the other half.

Had the prospective buyers investigated a bit beyond the seller's sales pitch, they surely would have hesitated. For the *Fitchburg News*, in existence only since 1904, had stiff competition from another evening paper, the *Sentinel*, which had been in existence since 1873. The *Sentinel* had other advantages. It was Republican, whereas the *News* was Independent, and it had exclusive rights to the Associated Press wire service, giving it the beat on reports of state, national, and international news. No wonder it had a two-to-one circulation lead over its financially troubled competitor. This fact, too, was hidden, because the *News* falsified its statements to the national Audit Bureau of Circulation.

Ignorant of much of this history, Newhouse concluded the purchase on behalf of himself and the *Times* in April of 1920 and immediately arranged a schedule that would allow him to pay weekly visits to the new property. Gone were Sundays in New York. Now Sam worked Sunday through Wednesday in Bayonne before leaving on the New York and Hudson River Railroad for Fitchburg, a journey that took most of Thursday going and most of Saturday returning. Around the same time, he started to call himself "S. I.," possibly because he thought that going by his initials would make him seem more important.

In Fitchburg, he stayed at the Crescent, a well-kept brick and marble rooming house near the center of town, just three blocks away from the *News's* offices. His top-floor apartment offered a spectacular view of the Nashua River and all the commerce the river and World War I had engendered. There were textile plants, railroad-car shops, steam-engine foundries, and huge granite quarries nearby. In a lot of ways, it seemed, the town on which he had gambled his family's savings resembled Bayonne.

But S. I. had overlooked Fitchburg's most salient characteristic. It was a Yankee town, filled with raw-boned New Englanders and a smattering of Finns and old Germans, and they didn't much care for outsiders, particularly Jews. The merchants of Fitchburg weren't named Grotsky or Lublintz or Steinert. The firm of Nichols & Frost sold dry goods, and men's clothing was purchased at William C. Kimball's.

Any hope S. I. had ever had of founding a chain of newspapers with Fitchburg as the first link must have evaporated like the snow that spring. After only a few visits, he sent Leo Rifkin one of the few personal letters he ever wrote. Written longhand in small script, it covered both sides of two pages, and, according to Rifkin, "It was pathetic. Nobody liked him. The people didn't like him. The employees didn't like him. The merchants didn't like him. He felt anti-Semitism of all kinds. All in all, he said it was the unhappiest venture of his life."

There were other difficulties with the new enterprise. For one thing, whenever S. I. was back in Bayonne, Judge Lazarus kept after him not to be out of town so much. The judge couldn't see any sign that S. I.'s absences were harmful, but they caused him a good deal of concern, for he saw S. I. as the secret to his newspaper's success; and, as some of Lazarus's other business ventures were having their ups and downs, he had come to depend increasingly on the *Times* for funds.

Things weren't made any easier in Fitchburg by a fire that swept through the offices of the *News* soon after it changed hands that spring. As a result, for more than a week, the Fitchburg Daily News Company was unable to print its own paper and had to farm the work out — at great expense — to its competitor.

It took a lot to convince S. I. that he had made a mistake in buying the Fitchburg paper, for he had risked everything he and his family had and couldn't very well give it up. But after months of hearing himself referred to as "that little kike" and worse, and after seeing advertising decline and circulation stand still, he finally accepted the situation.

But how could he get his money back? Here his self-taught Saturday afternoon course in the newspaper business proved invaluable. The trade journals were filled with stories of newspaper consolidations in small- and medium-sized cities. The owner of one paper would buy out a competitor, close it down, and start charging more for his product. Case after case showed that the investment would be repaid in a short time. Hearst alone bought and then shut down or merged some fifteen newspapers during this period; Scripps-Howard closed an equal number.

So, after less than a year of owning and operating the *Fitchburg News*, S. I. went directly to his competitor, Frank L. Hoyt, and made him a compelling proposal. First, he explained, newspapers everywhere were raising their newsstand prices. In fact, he had just supervised a lucrative one-cent-a-copy increase in Bayonne. In Fitchburg, though, the *Sentinel* would surely lose subscribers were it to charge more, because they would switch over to the cheaper *News*.

S. I. then pulled out a little sheet of paper and the nubbin of a pencil. Suppose, he said to Hoyt, you bought the *News*'s subscription list, liquidated the paper, and then raised the newsstand price. Your readers would have nowhere else to go and look what you'd make. After a few quick calculations, he demonstrated how, by means of such an arrangement, Hoyt could net an extra $350 a week in circulation revenue alone. This meant that if he paid $15,000 for the *News*, he'd earn the money back in less than a year. Besides, Newhouse continued, after a while without competition, the *Sentinel* could raise its rates for advertising and profit even more.

Hoyt instantly saw the logic of Newhouse's offer, but just as quickly he saw a potential flaw in it. What if a new competitor were to start a paper in Fitchburg and charge one cent per copy and undercut the *Sentinel*'s ad rates as well? Newhouse had a reply ready. If he took the printing press and equipment out of town, and the contract for newsprint with it, wouldn't that be a sufficient barrier to new competition? It just happened, though he didn't tell Hoyt this, that the *Bayonne Times* desperately needed printing equipment and could make good use of the *News*'s eight-page flatbed Duplex. Moreover, the *Times* could save some thirty dollars a ton on newsprint if it took over the Fitchburg paper's contract with the Great Northern Paper Company in Maine.

Hoyt agreed. He borrowed $15,000 to pay Newhouse and Lazarus and then sat back to watch his new profits flow in, while the *News*'s offices on Oliver Street were dismantled, and the presses, Linotype machines, and so forth were spirited out of town.

It was an incredible bargain all around. The *Sentinel* prospered as never before. The *Bayonne Times* got its $7,500 back, as well as a favorable newsprint contract and a sound printing press. And, when all the other machinery was sold and accounted for, Newhouse and Lazarus were left with a handsome profit.

6 On His Own

BY THE TIME of the near disaster in Fitchburg, Newhouse's attitude toward his boss of the past thirteen years had changed dramatically. He was no longer a naive little boy in need of a job and a guiding hand, and the toughness that friends and associates first discerned in him during his teenage years had hardened into an increasingly single-minded, cynical outlook. Once he had positively revered Hyman Lazarus; now he looked upon him as a partner — and a none-too-helpful one at that.

One aspect of their relationship particularly grated on Newhouse. He was doing the work that made the *Times* prosper in Bayonne, yet the judge was getting most of the fruits of that labor and owned all the stock in the company. But when Newhouse asked for a share of the business, Lazarus turned him down, explaining that he wanted to save ownership of the paper for his children.

Angered by what he considered an unfair arrangement, Newhouse took things into his own hands. If he couldn't have stock, he figured that he was at least entitled to a larger salary for his efforts. So, as the *Times*'s business manager, he simply started giving himself a larger share of the paper's profits. Over the next few months, he gradually increased his cut from the one-fifth Lazarus had agreed to several years before to fully one-half of the net revenues. Though others might not have agreed, Newhouse saw nothing improper in the new arrangement. And because earnings continued their spectacular rise and the judge continued his inattentive ways, no one caught on.

Some of the money from this new salary arrangement went into buying the family its first house — on Forty-fifth Street, in one of Bayonne's more elegant residential areas. Norman no longer had to accept scholarship aid at NYU, and the youngest girls, Gertrude and Estelle, could attend good private women's colleges. S. I. celebrated his new prosperity by trading in his Ford for a Hudson roadster and resuming his travels with Leo Rifkin.

Most of all, though, he wanted to buy another newspaper — even if it meant continuing in partnership with Lazarus. The following summer, the opportunity presented itself, when he heard from a newspaper broker that the *Staten Island Advance* was for sale.

Staten Island was close by and seemed friendlier to Jews than Fitchburg, but that was about the extent of its advantages. Though it was one of the five boroughs of the greatest city in the world, Staten Island was still quite rural in 1922. On Sundays, people from Bayonne would ride the trolley down to Bergen Point to take the side-wheeler ferry over to Port Richmond, then a town of no more than 20,000 but the center of most of Staten Island's commercial life. From there, they would walk into the fields of outlying farms and up the gentle slopes of the line of hills that ran down the center of the island. Mostly, the visitors from Bayonne remarked on the wild flowers and farm animals they saw during the course of their bucolic walks and on the sea traffic spread out before them on all sides in New York Harbor and Newark Bay.

Staten Island possessed other towns besides Port Richmond, all of them smaller. There was St. George a few miles to the east and, along the island's eastern shore, a series of villages a few miles apart, connected by a trolley line. There were few streets, and most of those were unmarked, muddy, and rutted.

In Port Richmond, on Castleton Avenue, sat the little barnlike building that housed the *Staten Island Advance*. Though it had been around for decades, the paper had only begun publishing on a daily basis four years earlier. Because the island's widely dispersed population made it difficult to establish a solid circulation base and there were few local merchants to advertise in the paper, the owners of the *Advance* were having a tough time just breaking even. Nevertheless, they were demanding $98,000 for 51 percent of the stock in the company. It was no bargain, but if he wanted a second newspaper, S. I. realized he didn't have much choice; it might be years before another one close to home would come up for sale at a price he and the *Bayonne Times* could afford. And there might never be another paper in which he could interest his reluctant partner.

That October, when Newhouse and Lazarus took control of the *Advance*, it sold at two cents per copy and had a daily circulation that had averaged 10,168 for the previous six months. They got a competent publisher, Blanchard M. Preble, who maintained an ownership interest. And they took control at a time when the *Advance*'s losses, which had been on a roller coaster under the previous owners, were declining. Overall, though, it was a sorry property.

The *Advance*'s problems differed little from those of the Bayonne paper a decade before — not enough advertising and circulation, and inefficient production. Newhouse attacked the new challenge with the same zeal that he had put into the *Bayonne Times*, but this time he had nearly a decade of experience and members of his own family to draw on. Brother Louis was an expert compositor by now, and Teddy had finished high school and was working in the circulation department at the *Times*. Each morning, the three brothers rose at five o'clock; by sunrise, they were on the ferry for Port Richmond and the offices of their new newspaper.

As he had in Bayonne, Newhouse made advertising his first priority. Since there weren't many businesses on the island itself, he realized he would have to go elsewhere — to Perth Amboy on the Jersey shore, Manhattan, Brooklyn, even Newark — to find merchants who might pay to advertise in the *Advance*. Day after day, he called on the best prospects, telling them what potential for growth Staten Island had, and what a great untapped market its 160,000 inhabitants represented. Then, when he got ads from these off-islanders, Newhouse clumped them together by town in the *Advance*, to give the merchants of the various communities the sense that they were competing with each other. He hoped this placement would be an incentive to advertisers to make their ads even bigger or to run them more frequently. It would also serve to goad the few merchants on the island to fight back with ads of their own.

It wasn't long before each edition of the *Advance* carried a half page of ads touting shops in Perth Amboy, a second half page for New York City, yet another for Brooklyn, and the ultimate coup — a full page from Macy's. Since many of the ads ran in the *Bayonne Times* as well, Newhouse could offer all sorts of discounts that the former owners of the *Advance* hadn't even thought of. The mat for the Macy's ad, for example, could be used first in Bayonne and then taken down to Port Richmond first thing the next morning by one of the brothers. This meant a substantial savings for the *Advance*, hence a discount for Macy's. But there was more: it was a full-page advertisement, hence a second discount; and it was on a contract to run regularly in the *Advance*, hence a third discount.

As a result of this combination of savings to the Staten Island paper, the *Advance* could offer Macy's priority placement on page three and charge for the full page about what the various merchants of Perth Amboy paid for half of page five. Not only did the Macy's ad produce as much profit as the Perth Amboy half page; it also served to make the *Advance* more credible in the eyes of other potential major advertisers. Soon Abraham & Strauss was taking out a full page of its own for a store in Brooklyn, and the *Advance* was no longer an anemic ten- or twelve-page paper but regularly ran editions of eighteen, twenty, and twenty-two pages.

Throughout 1922 and 1923, the *Advance* was its own best ally. Issue after issue praised Staten Island's business and real-estate potential and promoted newspaper circulation. The paper touted itself as "The Home Daily With Three Times The Circulation Of All Other Island Papers Combined," and encouraged the notion of "Staten Island As A Homesite."

There were also the front-page exploits of "Home Trade Harry." "KEEP THIS PAPER," huge banner headlines announced. "IT'S WORTH $5 TO YOU IF HOME TRADE HARRY CALLS." Harry rode all over Staten Island — fifty to sixty miles per evening — to see if people had the *Advance*. If they did, they received a crisp, new five-dollar bill. In addition, Harry made notes about families that liked to "home trade" — buy goods on the island — and reported on them in the paper.

In August 1922, a few months before the *Advance* was sold to Newhouse and Lazarus, its editors had stated their "aim": "To publish a good newspaper, clean, truthful, and fearless; without prejudice as to race, creed, or politics; standing always for justice and fair play; working for the growth of the nation, state, and community." The new owners kept the motto but operated under quite different principles. The real purpose of a newspaper, Newhouse was discovering, was to sell ads and make money. The editorial product with which a publisher surrounded the advertising was a means toward an end, not an end in itself.

So in 1922 and 1923, the *Advance*, when it wasn't busy promoting itself and Staten Island, did what came easiest editorially. It splashed banner headlines across the front page to flag racy wire-service material; it carried whatever harmless items local people sent in; and, above all, it tried its best not to offend anyone. Newhouse's efforts soon bore results. The *Advance*'s circulation rose from an average of 10,168 for the six months preceding the purchase in late 1922 to 15,645 during the last week of September 1923 — a gain of fully 50 percent. During the same period, the paper doubled its number of pages as a result of extra advertising. What would happen, Newhouse must have wondered, if he could get his hands on a more solid operation?

Newhouse continued to supervise operations at the *Bayonne Times*, with his friend Moe Zinader running the business end and a new editor, St. John McClean, supervising copy. He worked mornings on Staten Island, then ate lunch on board "The Bayonne City" or "The Englewood" as he ferried back to Bayonne for the afternoon. Frequently, he made another trip to Staten Island at night.

In the meantime, Judge Lazarus was becoming increasingly preoccupied with other activities, both political and commercial, and was thus more isolated than ever from his newspaper ventures. He was involved with Jersey City Mayor Frank Hague in a series of real-estate deals and had gone in with a cousin on the operation of a group of women's-wear shops. He had also become quite a ladies' man. Clerks in his law office complained of the sentry duty they were called on to perform when any of a succession of young women visited the senior partner of Lazarus & Brenner.

On top of all this, Lazarus still had his judgeship to attend to. He was so busy, in fact, that during his first year of half ownership of the *Advance*, he was involved in its operation only once, when Staten Island's tough Democratic leader, John Lynch, tried to pressure the newly arrived Newhouse into endorsing a slate of candidates. When Lynch threatened to have supportive merchants withhold advertising from the *Advance*, Newhouse had Lazarus, who was equally well connected in Democratic circles, tell the pol in no uncertain terms to lay off.

* * *

On Friday, 2 November 1923, a few days after the first anniversary of Newhouse and Lazarus's purchase, the *Advance* announced that Blanchard Preble was leaving to acquire and operate a newspaper in Montclair, New Jersey. The following Thursday, S. I. Newhouse's name went on the masthead in the publisher's position. It was the first time his name had ever appeared in one of his newspapers.

Newhouse's first year in charge of the *Staten Island Advance* involved a tremendous amount of work and energy, yet it left him restless. He had at least obtained security for his family, but there, too, was another nagging reminder. He was now twenty-eight years old. At an age when most men of his acquaintance were already married and providing for families of their own, he didn't even have any prospects.

Leo Rifkin was still single, though, and now he and S. I. approached their weekend jaunts with new zeal, even venturing to Montreal, where they got a couple of girls to bootleg booze back into New York for them under their clothes. Compared with others of their generation, S. I. and Leo weren't wild, but their spirits reflected an uncertainty that had come over the country after the Great War. Still, what they each hankered after was a steady girl, and after a while, even the drives to the Catskills and the Adirondacks began to lose their freshness.

Then good fortune intervened. In the fall of 1923, S. I. and Leo took a long weekend off to go to Atlantic City. Soon after they checked into their rooms at the Breakers Hotel, Leo ran into an attractive young woman in the lobby and struck up a conversation with her. She'd be very happy to go out with him that evening, she said. Things were going smoothly, until Leo remembered his pal back in his room. "Wait a minute, Blanche," he said. "I have a friend with me, and I've got to get a girl for him, too. But he's very short. Please see what you can do."

Earlier that weekend, Blanche had been introduced to a young woman who would fit the bill perfectly. Dark-haired and somewhat plain-looking, Mitzi Epstein was most remarkable for her size — she was just under four feet, eight inches tall and was skinny as a rail. But, despite her doll-like appearance, Mitzi was in no danger of going unnoticed — her vivacity had taken Blanche by surprise. She also seemed a little out of Blanche's league, what with all her talk of the fashion world, the Parsons School of Design — where she was a student — and her many beaux. Still, people came to the Breakers to meet other people, and Blanche figured that if she wanted a date with Leo, she'd better fix his friend up with Mitzi.

S. I. and Mitzi's evening together was not a great success. Unable to direct her energy, Mitzi struck S. I. as rather flighty, and he didn't help matters by boasting about his and Leo's exploits in Bayonne — among other things, he told Mitzi he'd paid his way through law school with winnings from card games.

Still, she was the first girl he'd ever gone out with who was shorter than he was, and, as the four of them seemed to get along, they made a date to meet the following Sunday in New York. Later that evening, S. I. confided to Leo that Mitzi was different from any other girl he'd ever met. Her sense of style and taste in clothes definitely appealed to him. However, she also seemed a bit in the clouds, and that put him off. "I'm just not so sure about her," he told Leo. "I'm just not so sure."

Sam and Judith Epstein weren't so sure, either. Both were immigrants — she from Austria, and he from Bohemia — and they had started their own business and were prospering at it. They ran a factory that manufactured specialty clothing for women, in particular a scarflike item called a "guimpe." They catered to the fanciest clothing stores in New York and elsewhere, so the idea of Mitzi going out with a fellow who worked on newspapers in Bayonne and on Staten Island was not especially appealing to them. That Sunday, when Leo and Sam called for Mitzi, Mrs. Epstein got the idea that perhaps her daughter might be better off with the taller, handsomer fellow who had his own clothing business.

But that Sunday night was the night that cinched it for S. I. and Mitzi. She was terribly impressed by the brand new Cadillac in which he and Leo showed up and was even more excited by his plans to own lots of newspapers. For his part, S. I. was smitten by the fact that she actually seemed to like him.

Mitzi was also great fun. S. I. had always been shy and reserved, but Mitzi seemed to have enough zest for both of them. As he got to know her better on that second date, he came to believe that she was not so flighty after all, and that she shared his very considerable dreams. On the drive back to Bayonne that evening, Leo couldn't help but sense his friend's excitement. "Leo," S. I. announced, "now, I'm very sure."

It was a marvelous time for a courtship. With the war over, New York was livelier than ever, its glamour only enhanced by prohibition. S. I. and Mitzi plunged right in, flying through the gauze and glitter of Manhattan like a couple of chosen children. They would meet at Mitzi's parents' house on Ninety-second Street and head off immediately for exciting evenings that started in the Village and ended up in Central Park after visits to clubs like 21 and Monaco, where S. I. enjoyed peering through peepholes and bribing sinister-looking doormen to let them in.

Soon the Epsteins accepted their daughter's feelings toward her new beau, and not too much later, Mitzi accepted from him a showy five-carat diamond engagement ring. The wedding date was set for 8 May 1924, to be followed, S. I. promised, by a honeymoon in Europe.

That winter, Newhouse heard of another newspaper for sale, the *Elizabeth Times*, in a town midway between Newark and Perth Amboy. Flush with romance and business success, he was interested immediately and took the proposition to Judge Lazarus. But this time Lazarus balked. "Sammy," he said, "I just don't think I'm going to go along with newspapers any more." The judge's change of heart was a blow, for without Lazarus's backing, there was no way Newhouse could gain control of the paper in Elizabeth or of any other decent-sized publication in the vicinity.

But if the judge had lost interest in the newspaper business, perhaps he could be persuaded to sell his share of the *Advance* — for if there was one thing Newhouse wanted more than to buy more newspapers in partnership with Hyman Lazarus, it was to have a newspaper of his own. He approached the judge with the proposition and was elated when Lazarus accepted. Immediately, S. I. set about scraping together the money Lazarus wanted for his part of the paper and forming a corporation to run it.

Newhouse's biggest concern was to get all this accomplished before his marriage to Mitzi. Plans for the honeymoon in Europe were scrapped, and articles of incorporation for the Staten Island Advance Company were hurriedly drawn up. S. I. raided the *Times*'s staff of editor St. John McClean and found an advertising manager elsewhere in the person of William Wolfe. Both could have received better pay in Bayonne but were lured to Staten Island by Newhouse's promise to make them his partners.

On 7 May 1924, the three men appeared before a notary public in Richmond County, New York, to register their new corporation. Newhouse was to have 60 percent of the stock of the new company; his partners, 20 percent each. The language of the corporate papers clearly portended more than ownership of a simple island newspaper. In the documents it filed with the county, the new corporation stated as its purpose: "To engage in, conduct, manage, and transact the business of publishing, selling, binding, and distribution of books, journals, magazines, newspapers, periodicals, and all other kinds of publications . . . collecting and distributing news and press reports and dispatches and information of every sort and kind by any and all means whatsoever. . . ."

The following day, Sam had another, equally significant engagement. He and Mitzi and their families and a few friends met in the afternoon at the Commodore Hotel, on Forty-second Street in Manhattan, next to Grand Central Station. Leo Rifkin was best man, and Rabbi Abraham Burstein, who was related to the family by virtue of his marriage to cousin Stella Cohn, performed the ceremony. After the wedding and a brief reception at the hotel, S. I. and Mitzi hopped into a car and headed for Niagara Falls; the European cruise would have to wait.

That summer and fall, S. I. was so preoccupied with his new bride and his newspaper ownership that he seldom saw his former boss and partner, Hyman Lazarus, whose newspaper he continued to manage. He didn't even notice the onset of a gradual chill in their relations. The judge had been chided by business associates that he had been taken by Sammy on the *Advance* deal, and he had also begun to suspect that his protégé was getting more than his share of the profits of the *Times*. Lazarus did not raise these matters with Newhouse but was sufficiently upset that he held onto a grandfather clock that he had planned to give him as a wedding present.

Nor did Newhouse know about the personal difficulties the judge was encountering at the hands of a woman who had borne him a child out of wedlock years before and who was suddenly demanding steep support payments. To make matters worse, Lazarus had been called on to preside over the notorious "Pig Woman" case, against a Secaucus woman accused of murdering her husband as he slept, by beheading him with a hatchet. She was convicted of the crime, and it was left to Lazarus to pronounce the sentence. He agonized dreadfully, for he knew that he would have to sentence her to death. When the trial was over, he retired to his place in the country to try to calm his frazzled nerves. There, he contracted a terrible case of poison ivy, and on the morning of 14 November 1924, died of complications at the age of fifty-two.

The funeral the following Sunday was the largest observance of its kind ever held in Bayonne. With Newhouse and two dozen other honorary pallbearers in the lead, the sad procession marched slowly from the Lazarus home, through town, to the Hebrew Free School, where bleachers had been erected for Rabbi Plotkin's eulogy. Afterwards, the throng trudged down to Bergen Point to watch as Hyman Lazarus was ferried to his final resting place, the Baron Hirsch Cemetery on Staten Island.

Aboard the boat he had ridden so many times over the last year, Newhouse felt the unseasonably warm November day revert to winter. As the air cooled, the view grew clearer, and he could see laid out before him a panorama that was to shape his life and that was to be the keystone for an empire of newspapers beyond even his wildest imaginings.

Straight off the bow of the ferry were the hills of Staten Island, rural and inviting. To the east, beyond Brooklyn, were the rapidly filling spaces of Queens. To the northeast loomed Ellis Island and the Statue of Liberty, and, silhouetted in the background, the growing skyscrapers of Manhattan.

Part II

1924 - 1933: Technician

7 Starting Over

NEWHOUSE REMAINED VISIBLY SHAKEN for weeks after Hyman Lazarus died. But it was not grief alone that plagued him; he was concerned that the judge's untimely passing might create additional problems for himself and his family.

He had good reason to worry. The woman whose demands for support had troubled Lazarus throughout most of 1924 now tried to halt the administration of the judge's estate. In a caveat filed with the probate court early that December, she declared that Lazarus was the father of her son, and that, therefore, the boy was entitled to a share of the judge's estate — including ownership of the newspaper. Were she to succeed, Newhouse would be stripped of control immediately.

The woman's timing could not have been worse. All Newhouse had to his name at that time was a share of the *Advance*, and it was still struggling. Consequently, he was relying on earnings from the *Times* to underwrite his venture on Staten Island. If the judge's paper were taken away from him just now, the results would be disastrous. Not only would the *Advance* suddenly be under the gun, but Newhouse would no longer be able to keep the "kids" in college. Nor would he be in a position to continue to make payments on two houses — the fashionable two-story place for himself and Mitzi on Lincoln Parkway, over near Newark Bay; the other, equally pleasant, for the rest of the family uptown.

According to New Jersey law, however, illegitimate children could inherit only through their mothers, and since the woman herself held no valid claim against the estate, Lazarus's partner, Alfred Brenner, was able to make quick work of the caveat.

But that only opened the door to more serious problems. Under the judge's will, all of his property was to pass to his widow, Margaret Connolly Lazarus, a strong-minded woman who had never disguised her distrust of Newhouse. Determined to save the *Times* for their children, Sydney and Herman, she had been against the judge allowing his office boy to take control of the paper in the first place. The fact that Newhouse had then packed its payroll with relatives only fueled her resentment.

With Mrs. Lazarus now the owner, Newhouse knew it was inevitable that he would be relieved of his duties. All he could hope for was the chance of buying some time to prepare the *Advance* to support him and his family when the dread moment arrived. In that regard, at least, he was fortunate. The Lazarus boys were still teenagers, hardly ready to take full responsibility for the *Times*. So, even though the idea was distasteful to him, Newhouse offered to become the boys' teacher. He promised to show them how the business worked, and when they were ready, to hand control of the paper over to them.

Margaret Lazarus saw through his ruse, and so did her cousin, Sam Lerner, who urged that she get rid of Newhouse immediately. Lerner, however, would not agree to take over the paper himself, leaving Mrs. Lazarus no choice but to accept Newhouse's offer.

Meanwhile, although S. I. and Mitzi continued to live in Bayonne, almost all of Newhouse's attention was directed toward Staten Island, where his most immediate concern was circulation. Without more subscribers, the *Advance* could not hope to raise its advertising lineage rapidly, and without additional income, it would be in no position to support his family.

Yet, circulation was the very area of the *Advance*'s operations over which Newhouse exercised least control. Home delivery and newsstand sales were both handled by independent news dealers. The dealers, in turn, looked at the *Advance* as just another newspaper — a rather insignificant one at that. Their stock-in-trade, even on Staten Island, were the big Manhattan dailies — the *Times*, *Herald*, *World*, *Tribune*, and *Journal*. Moreover, because they operated on a strict commission basis with all their customers, they had no incentive to push the *Advance*. As far as they were concerned, any increases in that paper's circulation could come only at the expense of the other papers they carried.

The independent dealers' very existence had created similar problems in the other outlying boroughs of New York City. But in Brooklyn, Newhouse soon learned, the local *Times* had devised a means of controlling its own circulation. The *Times*'s method was so simple and so successful that within a decade or so, it would revolutionize the entire newspaper delivery business. The *Brooklyn Times* had established a private home-delivery system by hiring dozens of schoolboys and assigning them territories. Though the arrangement was still something of an experiment, it was just the sort of solution Newhouse needed, and he hired Danny Smith, one of the *Times*'s circulation assistants, to establish a similar carrier-boy delivery system on Staten Island.

For a time, the dealers fought the new arrangement by refusing to carry the *Advance* at their newsstands. But, again following the lead of the *Brooklyn Times*, Newhouse had a response. He had Smith and some of the new carriers set up makeshift shacks next to the newsstands of recalcitrant dealers. The shacks carried the *Advance* and, more important, cigarettes at cut-rate prices. It was not long before the dealers relented and Newhouse dismantled his jerry-built cigarette shops.

Because they were young and energetic and had only one paper to promote, Danny Smith's carrier boys generated new readers in droves for the two o'clock "Home" edition of the *Advance*. But the paper published an early edition as well for the island's substantial ferry traffic to Manhattan, and that was having problems of its own. One look at the news racks in the ferryhouse at St. George showed why: the *Advance* was buried in a jumble of out-of-town papers and local weekly and semiweekly publications. Once again, the independent news dealers were the problem — but this time, because of the dispute over home delivery, Newhouse had even less leverage.

He had made the acquaintance, however, of a newsboy eight years his junior who worked at one of the stands in the terminal building. Less than five feet tall, with a slight build and a freckled face framing large brown eyes, Henry Garfinkle came from a background remarkably similar to Newhouse's. The oldest of eight children born to immigrant Russian Jews on Manhattan's Lower East Side, he had supported his family from the time he was thirteen, when his father died. He had tried all sorts of jobs — from peddling fruit to loan sharking — but selling newspapers, he eagerly informed the *Advance*'s publisher, was the job he liked best. Someday, he said, he hoped to become the greatest newsboy in the world.

Newhouse took an immediate liking to Garfinkle. He enjoyed his quick sense of humor and realized that he was as energetic as he was ambitious. Moreover, he could sense in him a toughness he admired. It was apparent, too, that the newsboy's dreams were made to order for dealing with the *Advance*'s difficulties with commuter sales in the morning. With encouragement from Newhouse — as well as a secret, interest-free loan of $3,000 — Garfinkle bought his first stand in the St. George ferryhouse. Thereafter, he simply outhustled everyone else in the building, and his was soon the largest concession in the terminal, containing not one but several newsstands. It went without saying that he displayed the *Advance* prominently at each of his locations.

Back in Bayonne, what training the Lazarus boys were receiving from Newhouse took the form of frequent criticism, involving little in the way of helpful suggestions or support. Syd, in particular, bristled at being reminded that he was too soft on advertisers. He was even more upset when S. I. told him it was a terrible waste of time to flirt with the young women who worked in the *Times* building.

By late spring, Mrs. Lazarus had become openly impatient over her arrangement with Newhouse, complaining about the situation whenever she saw him at the office. Finally, in May, when Newhouse felt the *Advance* was strong enough, he called her hand. "All right, Mrs. Lazarus," he said during a particularly heated exchange, "if you don't approve of me, I'll get out." She accepted his resignation on the spot and in almost the same breath dismissed all of his relatives as well.

The separation from the *Times* brought an abrupt end to the Newhouse family's life in Bayonne. S. I. and Mitzi moved their belongings across the Kill van Kull into a model home the *Advance* had constructed as part of a real-estate promotion in Randall Manor, between Port Richmond and St. George. They also terminated most of their relationships with friends and acquaintances in Bayonne, including Leo Rifkin, who had recently married.

"We took his Mitzi and my Rose to a baseball game that summer," Rifkin recalled. "I remember Babe Ruth was playing, and

Mitzi and Rose talked stores all the time. That day, S. I. said he didn't think we'd be so close anymore, and I didn't see him much after that."

During those first years on Staten Island, Newhouse practically lived at the *Advance*. He would arrive at the office at half past five in the morning, before most of the clerical workers; and if a call for a classified ad came in at that early hour, Newhouse would take it himself. From six until ten he was production room foreman; only afterwards did he wear the publisher's hat, and even then he could not relax. For the rest of the day, he would wander around the building, poking into everyone's affairs, and doing his best to save the paper money wherever he could.

The classified department, for example, was next to the credit department, and Newhouse habitually scanned the classified pages for ads that looked dubious. "Is this one paid up?" he would yell over to the credit people. If it wasn't, he would pull the few lines of type himself. Nothing escaped his attention — not even negotiations for $1.50-a-week syndicated features. And if extra hands were needed to stuff two-section papers, he always pitched in.

Whatever time Newhouse had left during those long days went into supervising his brothers and sisters, with whom he was an especially harsh taskmaster. Naomi, who took charge of the classified department when Theodore became business manager, was the most frequent object of her brother's demands for perfection. "He'd bawl the hell out of her," recalled a man who worked in the *Advance*'s advertising department at the time. "She regularly came out of his office crying."

Newhouse's single-minded pursuit of building up the *Advance* did not sit so well with his partners, either. William Wolfe wanted a larger share of the stock so that he could become Newhouse's equal in making decisions. St. John McClean was impatient to have some of the profits they were making. But Newhouse was opposed to both demands; he saw no reason to hand over control of the paper to someone else, and he had even less interest in declaring dividends when he knew his newspaper had more important uses for the money.

Initially, Newhouse may not have intended to squeeze Wolfe and McClean out, but it wasn't long before he realized that if he stuck to his plans for building up the *Advance,* eventually he'd have the paper all to himself. The way Newhouse was running things, the only chance his partners would have to get anything out of their share of ownership would be to sell their stock back to its treasury. By 1927, they both gave in, leaving him total ownership. The price worked out to about $198,000, but more than half of that came from the *Advance* itself. Most of the rest represented profits Newhouse had taken out of the *Bayonne Times.*

Though not planned, Newhouse's move to Staten Island had been timed perfectly. By mid-1925, the place was booming with the prosperity that hit all of America during the Roaring Twenties. Land speculation, in particular, ran rampant, and with the buying and selling of undeveloped property came newspaper advertising of such volume that the *Advance* began to run special twenty-eight- and thirty-two-page real-estate sections.

The paper's sudden surge of profits made it possible for Newhouse not only to acquire new printing equipment (ending, among other things, stuffing by hand) and to buy out Wolfe and McClean, but also to obtain specialized help in those areas of the *Advance*'s operations where his own family members were not properly qualified.

After McClean's departure, the most immediate need was for an editor, and Newhouse again raided the *Bayonne Times.* Polish-born Phil Hochstein had come to the United States when he was six and had taken an early interest in journalism. Working first for a series of socialist publications in Manhattan while still a teenager, he had later been hired to edit the *Times.* At the time of his move to Staten Island, "Hoch," as Newhouse was to call his new editor, was most conspicuous for his sloppy dress and bohemian ways. "He was," one of his colleagues later explained, "the original hippie." But behind that facade was a strikingly handsome, intelligent young man who was no longer out to save the world. Hochstein was to serve as Newhouse's chief editorial adviser for nearly half a century.

Equally pressing was the *Advance*'s need for additional legal and financial expertise; the paper's operations had expanded to the point where it desperately needed a lawyer and an accountant. Newhouse filled the former position in a curious manner. In late 1924, he became embroiled in litigation over a real-estate deal on Staten Island

and was terrifically impressed by the presentation of a young man from Manhattan who represented one of the other parties. Though still in his twenties, that man, Charles Goldman, possessed a great deal of self-confidence and was quite articulate. (Newhouse later learned that as a boy he had memorized pages from the dictionary to improve his vocabulary.) Goldman's hair grew in wild shocks and had grayed prematurely, but his most noticeable appendage was an old-fashioned, outsized hearing aid that he would turn down when he wanted to filter out distracting conversations or to ignore someone. Once during a trial, when the appliance's battery went dead, Goldman told the court, "Could we take a recess, your honor? I'm afraid I've lost my hearing."

"He was a marvelous writer and a very capable negotiator," recalled Thomas Newman, who practiced in Goldman's firm for several years. "In the practice of law, he was skilled at everything." The moment the Staten Island real-estate matter was resolved, Newhouse put Goldman's firm, with offices in the Woolworth Building at 233 Broadway in Manhattan, on a regular retainer.

The *Advance* found its accountant in a different, but equally fortuitous way, when Newhouse's father-in-law introduced him to a man whose name he had picked out of the telephone directory because it meant "lucky man" — Louis Glickman. Shrewd and pragmatic, Glickman possessed special expertise in tax matters. In appearance, though, he was by far the most nondescript of Newhouse's key men. "He ate and slept his work," recalled Glickman's widow, Florence. "Once he woke up at three o'clock in the morning, saying, 'I have it! I have the solution!' That was what his job meant to him."

Newhouse, Goldman, Glickman. "They were a triumverate," said Florence Glickman. "It wasn't long before they met every Monday and Thursday for lunch at the Lawyers Club downtown [in Manhattan]." Hochstein and Garfinkle, too, would play major roles.

8 A Lesson in Vindictiveness

IN BAYONNE, HYMAN LAZARUS'S SENSE of fair play and compassionate nature had served to temper his protégé's toughness. On Staten Island, there were no such restraining influences.

The experience of a real-estate salesman named William Quigley illustrates just how ruthless Newhouse could be, left to his own devices. Though by no means a mogul, Quigley was well regarded and, like most in his position, he relied heavily on his good reputation. One day he arrived at the offices of the *Advance* beside himself and demanded to see the publisher right away. A few moments later, he was in Newhouse's office, pouring his heart out. He confessed that he had done a terrible thing — propositioning a woman who had then complained to the police. He said he'd be ruined if the story was made public and begged to have the matter kept out of the *Advance*. Newhouse made no direct reply; instead, he walked the man down the hall and left him in the advertising manager's office.

Before his visit to the *Advance* was over, Quigley was signed up for more than 10,000 column inches of advertising — more than he could ever hope to pay for, but enough of a tribute to black out coverage of his subsequent arraignment on morals charges. Unfortunately, Quigley fell behind on his payments, and when he went to trial, the *Advance* played the story prominently.

If Newhouse needed any additional incentive for such harsh practices, it was quick in coming. In mid-1927, Michael Kane, editor of the *Staten Islander*, a local semiweekly newspaper of superior journalistic and typographical quality, announced plans to publish his paper daily by year's end. Had Newhouse not already taken stern measures to fortify the *Advance*, Kane's new, expanded publication would have posed a distinct threat. Instead, Newhouse was in a position to make life unbearable for the newly arrived competition.

That fall, as the *Staten Islander* was gearing up to expand, the *Advance* quietly relaxed its credit policies with major advertisers. Newhouse had instructed his credit manager, Ed Jones, to encourage large accounts to run up sizable debts. Then, rather than cut these advertisers off when they got into such positions, as the *Advance* had done in the past, Jones was to let them continue to advertise — provided, that is, that they signed demand notes for the amounts due.

What the advertisers saw as a respite was actually the central mechanism of a powerful trap, for these were the same advertisers Kane was counting on to help him get the daily *Staten Islander* on its feet. During the week before 16 December, when Kane's paper was to publish its first daily edition, the jaws of the trap snapped shut as the *Advance* informed the merchants that it would foreclose on the demand notes the moment any of them advertised in the rival paper. Even Seymour Sander, owner of the large Meadowbrook Dairy and one of Kane's closest friends, found his firm prevented from advertising in the *Staten Islander*.

With smaller merchants, Newhouse used another tactic. Before 16 December, the *Advance*'s composing room had shared advertising mats with the *Staten Islander*. Thereafter, the arrangement was canceled, and the *Advance*'s composing room simply held on to many of the mats. Those that it agreed to pass on were cropped so closely that they were no longer serviceable.

The area of the business in which Kane least anticipated trouble was distribution. Ignorant of Newhouse's interest-free loan to Henry Garfinkle, Kane was distressed to find that, also starting 16 December, his publication no longer appeared on the newspaper racks inside the ferryhouse. For a while, the *Staten Islander* combatted the problem by stationing newsboys outside the terminal. But that proved ineffective, and Kane pleaded with Garfinkle to get his paper back on the stands. Finally, after the *Staten Islander*'s commuter sales had been decimated, Garfinkle relented. He said he would carry the paper. What he didn't say was where he would put it — under the counter, and thus available to only those passersby who asked for it specially.

Even the independent dealers found themselves having to support Newhouse. Unless they gave the *Advance* a better position on the newsstands than the *Staten Islander*, he told them, he would bring back his own makeshift stands and cut-rate prices on cigarettes. And this time, he said, he wouldn't take the stands down if the dealers later decided to cooperate.

The battle was over almost before it began. In a month, the *Staten Islander* was in deep trouble. In three months, it was unable to make payments on a $3,000 note for one of its printing presses. And in six months, it had shut down almost completely.

It was an extraordinary outcome, all the more remarkable because the new paper had been much more attractive and informative than the *Advance*. But against an existing publication with superior business leadership, Kane realized, he never had a chance.

Adding insult to injury, the moment the competition went under, Newhouse offered Kane's son Walter, formerly the *Staten Islander*'s best advertising sales representative, a job in the *Advance*'s ad department. "Walter," Newhouse said in his first words to his new employee, "your father didn't succeed, because he wasn't vindictive enough. I want you to remember that."

It wasn't long before the younger Kane got a taste of what his new boss meant. The local district attorney, Albert Fach, was up for re-election. "You get a quarter page out of him," directed the *Advance*'s ad manager, Gilbert Piersall. But when Walter arrived at the DA's office to solicit the advertisement, Fach was brusque: "Kane, I don't need to advertise. The nomination here is a virtual election." Walter reported the politician's response to Piersall, who would hear none of it. "You get that ad," he demanded and then provided him with extra ammunition.

"I hate to say it," Walter told Fach on a second visit later that day, "but I'm expected to get a quarter page, or they'll bring up the Solomon case on you." The name had a magical effect. "Now, w-wait a minute, W-Walter," Fach stuttered. "I w-want a picture taken. I'll have to get a shave."

The *Staten Island Advance* gladly ran Albert Fach's photo in his quarter-page ad, and not a word did it print about the district attorney's failure to prosecute an old friend who had committed homicide while drunk.

Newhouse could be brutal with the likes of Quigley, Kane, and Fach. But with Mitzi, he was a pushover. Even so, their abrupt move to Staten Island was not easy on her. She had no friends there; the pace of life was slower than in Bayonne; Randall Manor was a significant step down from Lincoln Parkway; and, because her husband was always at the office, she was alone most of the time. For a woman with her energy and expectations, it was not a happy situation. Yet, despite all these disappointments, she was sustained by S. I.'s promises that things would change.

She did not have to wait long. One day in mid-1926, after they had lived in the model home for about a year, S. I. took her for a drive to the top of a high bluff behind the main section of St. George. He stopped the car in front of an empty lot that looked out over the harbor below and Brooklyn beyond. Mitzi fell for it on the spot and couldn't wait to start planning the house they would construct there, at 25 Ward Avenue.

The Tudor design they chose, with its fine slate roof, was in vogue at the time, and the heavy, dark Jacobean furniture Mitzi selected seemed to her luxurious and sophisticated. Out back, on the steep hill that ran down toward the harbor, she created an immaculate rock garden.

S. I. reserved one aspect of the interior decorating for himself. He attached a great deal of significance to the fact that his initials were the same as those of the island to which they had moved and insisted that the banister railings in the new house be shaped accordingly — I's inside of S's, like dollar signs, on the main staircase.

Newhouse wanted 25 Ward Avenue to serve as Mitzi's castle. Consequently, he deferred to her judgment unhesitatingly on any matter that affected the tone of their life there. In turn, Mitzi, who had been heavily influenced by popular magazines, shaped her new household around the image of a warm, inviting hearth. She completed her cozy domestic scene with the addition of two dogs — "Laddie," an old Airedale, and "Michael," a more active, wire-haired terrier.

It was not long before their home became fuller — and S. I.'s absences less troublesome. Almost as soon as they settled in, on 8 November 1927, Mitzi gave birth to a son, whom they named Samuel I. Newhouse, Jr., ignoring a Jewish tradition of not naming children for the living. A second son, Donald Edward, was born less than two years later, on 6 August 1929.

To an even greater degree than most fathers of his generation, Newhouse left the rearing of his offspring to his wife. In fact, it wasn't until the boys were old enough to accompany him to the office on weekends that he began to pay them any real attention.

Around the time of the younger son's birth, S. I. and Mitzi received a double dose of bad news. First, doctors told Mitzi she could have no more children, though she wanted at least four. Both S. I., Jr., and Donald had been delivered by cesarean section, and the physicians thought it unwise for her to submit to the procedure again.

Soon after, Mitzi's parents' business failed, and her father died. She and S. I. insisted that her mother move into an empty room in their house. There, mother and daughter consoled each other and, together with the Epsteins' Hungarian cook, set about spoiling the boys terribly.

Though the *Advance*'s demands on him were substantial, Newhouse always set aside some time each week for his vivacious wife. Occasionally, they were seen at Rigali's, then Staten Island's most fashionable night spot, but, almost from the start, their new base was inadequate for Mitzi. At her insistence, she and S. I. would take the ferry to Manhattan to spend Saturday afternoons shopping and visiting galleries and museums. On occasion, they even took in an opera performance — something S. I. tended to enjoy more than their other activities, which he found a bit frivolous.

One aspect of these excursions made Newhouse especially uncomfortable; Mitzi had a penchant for tea dancing at fancy hotels. He had never learned to dance as a youth and must have known how ridiculous the two of them looked as they waltzed and foxtrotted among people who danced with elegance and precision. "Gosh, they were funny," remembered an acquaintance who saw them go through their routine at the Pierre Hotel late one Saturday afternoon. "They looked like a couple of kids at their first dancing class."

9 The People's Champion

WHILE THE NEWSPAPERS of Newhouse's childhood were dominated by the excesses of yellow journalism, those of his own first years in publishing were informed by an entirely different spirit. Instead of relying on scare headlines, faked pictures, and interviews with imposters, newspapers now assumed the role of "the people's champions" and took after graft and corruption in an earnest, yet exciting, fashion that mirrored the reformist spirit that had taken hold in society at large.

If ever an American community needed such a champion, it was Staten Island during the nineteen twenties. The borough's affairs were dominated by two political bosses, Public Works Commissioner David Rendt and Borough President John Lynch, both of whom were party to extreme graft and corruption.

During his first years on the island, however, Newhouse adamantly refused to use his paper to challenge the status quo. Though registered as a Democrat, he harbored few strong convictions with regard to the major social and political issues of the day, and until the *Advance* was stronger, it was his plan to avoid all political entanglements. To that end, he kept a healthy distance from local political "club" meetings and from Borough Hall, where much of the wheeling and dealing went on. He even shunned party boss Rendt, who was practically a next-door neighbor on Ward Hill.

There was one area, however, in which Staten Island's rampant graft and corruption directly affected him and his newspaper — the realm of legal advertisements. These notices, which lawyers published on behalf of their clients in such matters as probating estates, dissolving marriages and partnerships, and letting contracts out for bid, were required by New York statute and were highly prized by newspapers.

To qualify for such business, the law required only that a newspaper establish itself as being "of general circulation." The determination of whether a newspaper met that requirement, however, was the responsibility of a local judge by the name of Tiernan, who, in turn, was one of Rendt's many pawns. Because the *Advance* wouldn't perform favors for any politician — such as printing campaign fliers without charge — Tiernan had been instructed to direct the majority of the island's legal ads to papers like the Democratic *Herald*, a small party organ that would do practically anything the boss requested.

The business with the legal ads drove Newhouse to distraction, but for his first few years on the island there was nothing he could do about it. In fact, it wasn't until the end of the fight with the *Staten Islander* that he felt free to act. His chance came early in 1929, when Staten Island's two main political bosses had a falling out — over, among other things, Judge Tiernan. Borough President Lynch wanted him removed, while Rendt insisted on keeping him in office.

Though Newhouse knew nothing about the other candidate, Thomas Cosgrove, he directed his paper to support him. Moreover, he had his youngest brother, who had become the *Advance*'s political reporter soon after graduating from NYU, dog Tiernan. Whenever the controversial judge made a false step or said something foolish, the *Advance* reported it in detail.

That November, Cosgrove beat Tiernan. It was a remarkable upset and left Newhouse so excited that he gave every one of his employees an extra day's pay to help celebrate. His neighbor on Ward Hill, however, shared none of his jubilation. Next time, Rendt informed him, you and your newspaper support my men, or else. Buoyed by his newspaper's surprising political clout, Newhouse shot back, "Years from now, no one will remember your name around here, Mr. Rendt. But there will always be a *Staten Island Advance* on this island."

Thanks in part to this exchange, Newhouse took pleasure in the subsequent formation of a strong anti-Rendt faction in the local Democratic Party. Encouraged by his newspaper's ability to oust Tiernan, he ordered the *Advance* to take the side of the opposition. Led by Lynch, this group waged a strong campaign against the

Commissioner of Public Works, aiming much of its attack at his longstanding practice of leasing local parks to political cronies.

Late that summer, Lynch went a step further and announced that he planned to challenge Rendt directly for the position of party boss in the upcoming elections. Right away, Newhouse gave prominent display in the *Advance* to accounts of the activities of the anti-Rendt group, burying reports of pro-Rendt gatherings.

On Tuesday, 9 September, with only a week to go before the election, the *Advance* began a series of strongly worded front-page editorials — all of which Newhouse had carefully screened. "Rendt's every action," said the first, "has been the action of a narrow-minded political boss determined to rule or ruin. Rendt is willing to sacrifice everything and everybody in his greed for power.... Enrolled Democratic voters ... must choose next Tuesday between a ticket that is the personal choice of an obstructionist and a ticket that pledges to cooperate with the Borough President."

The next day's front-page editorial struck an even tougher note: "Lawlessness and corruption are today the most vital issues in American communal life.... Isn't it autocratic leadership, such as Rendt is seeking to impose upon the majority of the members of the Democratic County Committee, that is responsible for the entry of the criminal elements into politics? ... The Advance KNOWS that the racketeering elements have solidly thrown their lot with Rendt's political fortunes.... If Rendt is maintained in power, he will owe his success, in large measure, to racketeers who are taking so active a hand in his campaign."

In the face of these attacks, party boss Rendt filed a complaint in Police Court, on 12 September 1930, charging criminal libel against the Staten Island Advance Corporation. He timed the action so that no trial of the charges could be scheduled until well after the election. Meanwhile, the complaint provided him with plenty of ammunition during the waning days of the campaign. Rendt's lawsuit also served as a first warning to the *Advance*'s publisher that perhaps he had tackled more than he could handle in this, his second foray into Staten Island politics.

With little time to counterattack, Newhouse ordered his newspaper's attorney to do whatever was necessary to get Rendt under oath and on the witness stand before the election. There they could cross-examine him about his stewardship of local Democratic Party affairs and the Public Works Commission. Then they could use the *Advance* to spread his responses all over the island. A local magistrate acceded, and a subpoena was served on Rendt later that evening by a reporter from the *Advance.*

Rendt had to appear in court on a Saturday morning, but the last thing he wanted to do was to answer hostile questions planted by Newhouse. His attorneys asked for — and obtained — a delay until Monday. At the same time, they informed the magistrate that they intended to subpoena him as a witness when the matter resumed, thus disqualifying him from the case.

The "Home" edition of the *Advance* came out a little later than usual that Saturday afternoon, with a huge headline on the front page: "RENDT IN COURT TODAY." "Answer NOW, Mr. RENDT!" demanded an editorial on the upper left-hand side of the page.

Headlines and last-minute legal maneuvers were not the only elements of the battle. That Saturday, Mitzi and her mother, who had hardly seen S. I. during the past week, were rattled by a series of menacing phone calls. If your husband and the *Advance* don't lay off Rendt, one threatened, your home will be bombed. Newhouse, who received similar threats at his office, requested that special details of the police be stationed outside his home and the newspaper building.

The challenge to David Rendt had drawn so much local attention that a crowd of 500 was on hand to see him testify at West Brighton Police Court the following Monday morning. Magistrate Bridges entered the crowded chamber a few minutes late and announced, as the parties had expected, that he would be unable to hear the case. His next announcement, however, caught nearly everyone off guard. Because Bridges had been unable to get hold of Chief Magistrate Joseph Corrigan over the weekend, the matter would have to be heard in county court, where a judge was available. A huge crowd followed the parties to St. George by automobile, bus, and street car, arriving at the Richmond County Courthouse around quarter to eleven — just in time to watch Rendt's attorneys unveil their final delaying tactic. They directed that a subpoena be issued against the new judge, disqualifying him, too, and thereby exhausting the island's supply of judges for the day.

"RENDT WON'T TESTIFY," screamed Monday's "Home"

edition. The center of the front page carried a large photograph with the caption: "SMILES AT DELAY. David S. Rendt, Commissioner of Public Works, smiles as he leaves court after delaying proceedings in which he will have to take the witness stand to answer questions regarding his income and methods of electioneering."

"Silence is Guilt!" declared the headline of the accompanying editorial. "Rendt IS Guilty!"

The campaign was over. At Newhouse's direction, the *Staten Island Advance* had stood up for what its owner and publisher thought was right in local politics. It had presented as strong a case as could be made against Rendt; now it was time to see how the island's voters would respond.

The results were a profound humiliation for Newhouse: Rendt's ticket had captured every office for which there had been a contest.

Nor did the matter end at the polls. The *Advance* still had to face the grand jury on Rendt's charges of criminal libel. There, however, Newhouse was confident that his paper would receive a more favorable hearing, for the inquiry was to be conducted by none other than Thomas Cosgrove, the anti-Rendt judge he helped elect in the first place.

Several weeks of testimony were held, during which the grand jurors investigated not only Rendt's charges against the *Advance* but also the *Advance*'s charges against Rendt. Numerous public officials and the *Advance*'s political reporter, Norman Newhouse, were called to testify. And on 3 October 1930, the grand jury presented its report to Judge Cosgrove. It could find no criminal acts by either side and, thus, had voted no indictments.

The report represented the final defeat in Newhouse's campaign against David Rendt. Yet, on the front page of that afternoon's edition, his paper put the grand jury's action in an entirely different light: "No Basis for Indictment Found in Criminal Libel Charge Against the *Advance*." Neither the headline nor the story that followed made even passing mention that the investigation had delved as well into the newspaper's charges against Rendt, or that the grand jurors had found them lacking.

"I began with the idea of having a newspaper of my own and being its spokesman," Newhouse once told an interviewer. If Thomas

Cosgrove's victory had encouraged that inclination, the outcome of Newhouse's attacks on David Rendt had the opposite effect, extinguishing once and for all any political aspirations he might have harbored for himself or his newspaper. That experience, all too similar to his single courtroom appearance as a lawyer in Bayonne, altered his thinking dramatically.

From then on, with but one exception many years later, he was to concentrate his energies solely on the business side of newspapering. Though it was a major about-face from the established role of newspaper publishers, the new policy would serve him well. For the moment, however, since Newhouse owned but one newspaper — a small one at that — no one paid attention to his change in outlook.

10 Acquiring the *Press*

JUST BEFORE THE FIGHT with Rendt, Newhouse had received an unexpected late-night caller at his home on Ward Avenue. One of his top admen had come to explain that he would not be at work the next morning, because he had been offered a job on Wall Street that required him to start right away. Though it was customary at the *Advance* to give two weeks' notice, he hoped Newhouse might understand; a chance to work at the stock market was just too good to pass up.

Newhouse listened politely, then responded in a quiet, sure voice. "You're making a mistake," he said. "I'm going to own a lot of newspapers. I take broken-down papers and make them pay. If you stick with me, you'll be a lot better off." The man was not swayed and headed off for Manhattan the next morning, unaware that he had made a very big mistake indeed.

Though 1928 inaugurated Wall Street's golden era — that year, for the first time in history, more than a billion shares of stock changed hands — the market's giddy expansion was actually a rerun of the land rush that had fizzled just a few years before. And though Newhouse was as hungry for wealth as anyone, he harbored grave doubts about anything connected with the stock market. During Wall Street's upward surge during 1928 and 1929, his feelings on the subject became so strong that he advised his brothers and sisters not to put their money in stocks and warned his top employees that, hard as it might be to imagine, bad times lay ahead.

Newhouse possessed no mystical powers of prediction; he simply believed that profits had to come from somewhere — from greater efficiency and increased output — in sum, from something tangible. Yet, Wall Street's boom existed only on paper. Even worse in

Newhouse's eyes, the paper profits were built on a foundation of borrowed funds.

Newhouse had another, more practical reason for not being swept up in Wall Street's fever. It took money to buy stock, and all his money was in his newspaper. If he were to have the Staten Island Advance Corporation declare dividends for him to invest, he'd have to pay income taxes on those dividends. Then, if his investments proved shrewd and he managed to sell for more than he'd paid, he'd be taxed again. In effect, he might earn more money for Uncle Sam than for himself, yet he alone would have shouldered the risk.

A discussion with Louis Glickman reinforced his instincts. His accountant informed him that Congress had just changed the rules concerning taxation of corporate profits, and that the changes could be made to work to his advantage. Previously, large surpluses had been treated as dividends and taxed as income to shareholders. Recently, however, at the urging of Treasury Secretary Mellon, Congress had cancelled the rule. Now, no matter how much money the Staten Island Advance Corporation made, its owner would not have to pay taxes on excess profits, so long as he kept them in the company's bank account.

Newhouse's new accountant was well aware of his boss's desire to have his own newspaper chain. If he kept his money in the *Advance*, Louis Glickman advised him, he could buy new publishing ventures without having to pay any additional taxes.

When the Depression came, it lasted longer and was more devastating than anyone, even Newhouse, could have predicted. By 1932, nearly one-third of New York City's manufacturing firms had shut down, shoving 1.6 million workers out of their jobs. Those who weren't let go suffered huge reductions in pay.

The effects of the Depression on newspapers were almost as devastating, alleviated only by the fact that the absence of work gave people more time to devote to reading. Advertising revenues fell precipitously. Papers that had consisted of 65 and 75 percent advertising in the first part of 1929 were lucky if they got 50 percent three years later.

Though the nation's sour economy meant marginal existences for some papers and a lot of red ink for others, relatively little changed at Newhouse's *Staten Island Advance*. Not a single employee was laid off or even had to take a cut in pay. Newhouse weathered the storm and was so pleased that he kidded his mother-in-law mercilessly about the fact that, back in 1924, she had urged Mitzi to take an interest in his friend with the clothing store in Bayonne. Leo Rifkin's business, Newhouse now pointed out with cold satisfaction, had been one of the Depression's earliest casualties.

America's economic nightmare taught Newhouse that newspapers could survive anything, if properly run. In fact, the *Advance* was doing so well that by mid-1932, when the effects of the Depression were most devastating, its bank account contained deposits close to $400,000 — enough, perhaps, to buy another paper.

The Borough of Queens, on Long Island to the far side of Brooklyn, was where he wanted to make his next purchase. Having begun to boom during the late twenties — as a new home for people who worked in expensive, overcrowded Manhattan — the area bore a surprising resemblance to Staten Island.

That summer, Victor Ridder, who was to head the Works Progress Administration in New York City, invited Newhouse to ride with him on the train to Syracuse. Ridder was one of three brothers who owned newspapers in the metropolitan area, including *Der Staats Zeitung Und Herold*, a German-language daily; the *Daily Journal of Commerce*; and the *Long Island Press*, in the heart of Queens. The two had become acquainted through business and played bridge together on occasion.

Ridder had taken upon himself the task of pushing a piece of newspaper-related legislation. Though the bill in question concerned legal advertising and would affect New York City publishers more than others in the state, Ridder knew he had to present a unified front before the state legislature in Albany. Hence the trip to Syracuse, where Jerome Barnum, publisher of the morning *Post-Standard*, lived. Not only was Barnum an upstate power, but that year he was president of the American Newspaper Publishers Association, whose endorsement was essential to the success of Ridder's bill.

On the way up the Hudson River to Albany and Schenectady, then west along the Mohawk River to Syracuse, Newhouse and Ridder discussed their businesses. Quite casually, Newhouse wondered aloud if the Ridders might be interested in selling the *Long Island Press*. Ridder, in the same vein, wondered what Newhouse might be willing to pay. Newhouse replied that he had no idea; he'd have to look over the paper's plant and books. And that was that. Conversation drifted back to the matter of the bill and what to say to Barnum, until the train reached Syracuse.

Jerome Barnum, it turned out, couldn't have cared less about his visitors' pet bill. Furthermore, he was rabidly anti-Semitic, and when he saw that Ridder had brought a Jew with him to Syracuse, he did his best to be rude. Feet up on the table, face buried in a copy of the *Saturday Evening Post*, he appeared so distracted that neither Ridder nor Newhouse could tell if he were even listening.

Thoroughly disappointed, the two men retreated to the bar car of the New York Central's Limited for the long trip back to Manhattan. However, their ensuing conversation led Newhouse to think the trip to Syracuse might have been worthwhile after all.

Ridder wanted to know if he was serious about buying the *Press*, because he and his brothers, Bernard and Joseph, were definitely interested in selling. They had purchased the paper in 1926 and had installed the *Staats Zeitung*'s circulation manager, William Hofmann, as publisher. The Ridders had provided Hofmann, a former Park Row newsboy, with a special incentive by giving him 49 percent of the stock in the Long Island Daily Press Publishing Company in return for running the paper. According to Ridder, the arrangement had produced healthy growth in circulation and advertising revenues. At the same time, though, the Ridder brothers had expanded their holdings too quickly elsewhere, with the result that they had a big debt outstanding at the Chemical Bank — a note for $600,000, whose balance the bank insisted they bring down. Newhouse could have the Ridders' 51 percent share of the *Long Island Press* for the amount of the loan.

The two talked some more, with S. I. expressing a desire to buy. There was one obstacle, though; he had only $400,000 in cash. Would Ridder accept a note for the remaining $200,000? He would — provided it was made payable to the Chemical Bank and the *Press* was pledged as collateral.

Ridder's willingness to sell came as a surprise, but Newhouse immediately prepared to act on it. The trade magazine *Editor & Publisher* regularly published listings of advertising lineage and circulation for all newspapers in the country, and a few minutes' research told him that the *Press* was a ripe property. Subsequent visits to the plant on 168th Street in the town of Jamaica, and a couple of chauffeured rides through the surrounding area convinced him that $600,000 was, if anything, too low a price.

Jamaica, especially, caught his eye. The elevated train clattered right to the middle of town from Manhattan, past a long row of shops that seemed to be doing remarkably well, considering the state of the economy. The side streets, too, were heavily populated by merchants.

Newhouse's accountant pored over the *Press*'s books and reported that they were in order, while his attorney drafted a purchase agreement that included an option on Hofmann's stock, though it retained him as the newspaper's publisher. That November, the deal was consummated.

Having two papers again was like the old days with the *Times* and the *Advance*. S. I. chose to have brother Theodore spend a good part of each day with him at the *Press* building in Jamaica. They'd work on Staten Island in the morning and then be driven to Queens for the afternoon. At the *Press*, S. I. moved right in with Hofmann, sharing his office and going over the business aspects of the paper's operations with him. He wanted all the details he could get. Ad salesmen were ordered in to discuss their accounts; Ted would report on printing costs; and Hofmann would keep him informed of the latest circulation figures.

Ted and S. I. would finish each day in Jamaica by half past three or so and then drive back to Staten Island to confer with Norman and do other chores at the *Advance* before dining together around seven at S. I. and Mitzi's. In the evening, the chauffeur took them back to 1267 Castleton Avenue in Port Richmond to clean up the day's loose ends.

The newspaper Newhouse had bought from the Ridder brothers was a curious proposition. Founded in 1821 as the *Long Island Farmer*, a weekly farm journal for the 2,500 or so families who lived in what was then a very rural area, it covered crops, recipes, livestock, fashions, and parties. What news stories the *Farmer* carried were liberally spiced with editorial comment. Typical was this item: "Five Jamaica youths went up 500 feet in a balloon. They should have been spanked by their parents and probably were." The poet Walt Whitman occasionally wrote for the paper, contributing, among other articles, a piece describing a trip he took in the summer of 1841 across the Great South Bay to Fire Island. In 1912, the *Farmer* absorbed Jamaica's other daily, the *Democrat*; and in 1921 it became known as the *Long Island Daily Press and Farmer*. The latter part of the name was dropped when Hofmann and the Ridder brothers took over.

By that time, many new homeowners had arrived in Queens, bringing with them a healthy assortment of swindlers, con men, and crooked politicians. Many of Jamaica's neighboring townships lacked sewers, public transportation in the region was woefully inadequate, and homes and lots quickly became overpriced. The new residents obviously had plenty to complain about, and it wasn't long before civic protest groups had formed all over the borough.

Having been trained years before at Joseph Pulitzer's *World* in the art of drumming up new readers, Hofmann saw how easy it would be to capitalize on the situation in Jamaica. He had *Press* photographers cover the protesters' meetings and made sure his newspaper ran the resulting photos alongside texts of the groups' complaints. Beyond that, however, Hofmann did very little. He was basically a very fat, very lazy man, who liked to sit in his office listening to sporting events on the radio. He was also quite amiable, and it was fine with him if some of the older male reporters joined him at his favorite pastime, instead of looking into the substance of the protesters' complaints or even editing them before they appeared in the *Press*. So long as the number of papers he sold went up, Hofmann was content, and by January 1931, the *Press*'s circulation had exceeded 37,000. At the time of the sale to Newhouse the next year, it had grown another 9,000.

Most newspaper owners would have been excited about these achievements. If circulation was up and the financial picture was improving — as was happening at the *Press* — that was usually sufficient. But Newhouse was far more perceptive. He, too, knew that circulation was the key to attracting advertising. But a newspaper's readership also had to be stable to assure long-term success, and in this regard, he was troubled by what he saw at the *Press*.

It wasn't the amateurishness of Hofmann's product that bothered him, though he could certainly recognize a second-rate newspaper when he saw one. Rather, he was troubled that his new paper's circulation was dependent on the allegiance of so many civic protesters. Their attachment to the paper struck him as fickle at best. Should the *Press* fail to print a couple of complaints or stop running their pictures so prominently, it might lose most of these new subscribers in short order.

It was also obvious to Newhouse that the paper's editorial department was incapable of doing much more than reprinting the protesters' remarks, for the reporting staff consisted of aging incompetents. Housewives covered society events, and the regular reporters had long ago quit trying.

Thus, though the 31 October 1932 announcement of Newhouse's association with the Long Island Daily Press Corporation had contained the promise that "there will be no change of policy or personnel," in the next few months, the newspaper underwent a thorough housecleaning. Newhouse assigned Phil Hochstein to take over as managing editor, replacing him at the *Advance* with brother Norman, who had continued there as a reporter and editor after the Rendt fiasco. Hochstein, whose former bohemian ways had been transformed by an interest in good clothes, brought in friends, like Eddie Gottlieb and Mike Liebowitz, to run the city desk. When annoyed by the managing editor's new highfalutin ways, Liebowitz would mutter a refrain that became a favorite of the newsroom: "I remember him when. . . . I remember him when. . . ."

Frank Bausch took over the sports page and hired a group of new, younger sports writers, including George Vecsey and Clayton P. Knowles. The society editor, a Mrs. Webster, was ordered to jettison her corps of housewives and get new blood into her part of the operation. Lots of younger women were hired, and soon Mrs. Webster herself was replaced, by Emily Brown Fine, the wife of an old socialist friend of Hochstein, Nathan Fine.

Because Hochstein and Newhouse worried that the sudden infusion of reporters with Jewish names might upset the *Press*'s non-Jewish readers, who were by far the majority, they instructed Mrs. Fine to use her maiden name in her byline; "Liebowitz" became "Lee"; and one reporter recalled that Hochstein occasionally signed the name "Highstone" to articles he had written.

Hochstein and Newhouse's basic strategy in revamping the paper was to make the *Press* itself, and not the various civic protesters, the spokesman for the people of Queens. Whenever they heard of a situation they felt the paper could remedy, they went all out to get results. When a homeowner was having trouble with his mortgage, for example, a *Press* reporter negotiated directly with the bank and then followed up with an article describing how the *Long Island Press* had solved the problem.

There were other innovations: a daily quote from the Bible was placed atop a redesigned editorial page; page one became bolder; and soon, solid local investigative reporting was competing with wire-service reports of famine and death for banner headlines.

There was a terrific risk inherent in the changes Newhouse made at the *Press*. The trade publications he received stressed how readers could resist even the slightest alteration in their daily newspaper. Moreover, on the surface at least, the *Press* had been doing just fine. Why make any changes at all? Publisher Hofmann raised that issue almost daily in the spring of 1933. Though he was too lazy to do anything about it, he complained that Newhouse's tactics would amount to throwing away readers.

At first, it looked as though Hofmann was right; circulation dropped off. Newhouse, however, did not become alarmed. In his mind, there was no choice about what to do; in order for the *Press* to prosper in the long run, it had to take the medicine he'd prescribed for it. By the end of a year, his program was vindicated. Total paid subscriptions were up by more than 2,000.

The new regime carried with it another, subtler implication. Before Newhouse had taken over the *Press*, a few of the paper's larger advertisers had begun to worry about where all the civic protests might lead. Sooner or later, they imagined, the protesters would take after one of them, and the next day the front page of the *Press* would carry a photograph of several angry citizens standing outside a local store, complaining about shoddy merchandise, high prices, or overbearing credit policies. Now that the protesters no longer had a direct line to the *Press*'s front pages, that threat had been eliminated, and the advertisers showed their appreciation.

*   *   *

In less than a year, Newhouse accomplished in Queens something few publishers have ever achieved — he turned a second-rate rag into an ideal vehicle for the commercial messages of Long Island's merchants. But the relative ease with which he had taken control at the *Press* was no guarantee for the future. During the next four years, his Long Island property was to provide him with some of the most difficult tests of his career.

Part III
1934 – 1938: Master

11 Guilded

UNBEKNOWNST TO NEWHOUSE, members of the editorial staff of the *Long Island Press* began to meet secretly during the spring of 1934. Gathering at Gelwick's News Agency, just across Jamaica Avenue from the *Press* building, these reporters — mostly young and idealistic — had no idea they were setting the stage for a labor dispute that would last for years and create unprecedented unrest and divisiveness in their newsroom. Nor did they imagine that their banding together would serve as the catalyst that would move their employer to the front lines of his profession.

The most important figure at these meetings was someone who had had no previous connection with Newhouse or the *Press*. He was Heywood Broun, one of America's most widely read and highly paid columnists. A large man of bohemian tastes, whose attire was usually so rumpled that acquaintances often described him as "an unmade bed," Broun was the driving force behind the single most important development to occur in the newspaper business between the Depression and World War II. Just the summer before, one of his columns in the *World-Telegram* had galvanized reporters all over the country into forming the American Newspaper Guild, the first national union of editorial workers.

Instead of calling a general strike — as Broun had envisioned in his *World-Telegram* column — the new newspaper writers' union was dominated in its first year by such fierce internal dissension that, by early 1934, it was on the verge of falling apart. Up to that point, the Guild had concentrated its efforts on big-city dailies, where it hoped to establish itself with a few major victories. But when that approach backfired, some more militant members — including Broun — decided to infiltrate newsrooms at smaller papers in the New York City area, where they believed opposition from publishers would be weaker.

It was this new tactic that resulted in the secret meetings in Jamaica. The initial goal of Broun and his followers was to enlist every *Press* reporter in a local chapter of the Guild. Once that was accomplished, they could put together a list of demands — for shorter hours, higher pay, and greater job security — to take to Newhouse.

Yet, to talk to people who worked for him on Staten Island, Newhouse was a most unlikely target for union organizers. Despite his ruthless business practices, he was a paternalistic boss, and commanded almost total loyalty from his people. Whenever one of the *Advance*'s workers got sick or had an accident, Newhouse saw to it personally that the proper treatment was administered, and that the man's family was looked after as well. And though the pay was low, the paper's owner and publisher ensured that when an employee needed help with the down payment on a car or some other major purchase, the *Advance* provided it.

An exchange that occurred between Newhouse and a compositor named John Bruno in 1931 typified Newhouse's style in such matters. Bruno had been with the *Advance* since graduating from high school in 1924. Seven years later, at the height of the Depression, he decided to get married but worried that if things got any worse he might lose his job. "So," he explained, "I went to S. I. about it. He said, 'Go ahead and get married, John. You'll never have to worry about your job if you stay with me.' " Sure enough, Bruno was still a compositor at the *Advance* nearly fifty years later.

At the *Press*, too, Newhouse's ownership meant improved working conditions. Almost the moment he took control, he increased the number of reporters on the paper's payroll, raised salaries, and put an end to so-called "space rates" — by which reporters were paid according to how much of their work appeared in the paper, not how long it had taken them to produce it. Even with these improvements, though, in early 1924 the average *Press* reporter received just twenty dollars for a work week that usually lasted six days and took up sixty or more hours. There was no such thing as a retirement plan or health benefits. Nor was there even assurance of continued employment.

The Guild's promises of greater job security, shorter hours, and higher pay were a powerful attraction. After just a few secret meetings at Gelwick's, the union had signed up all of the new reporters brought in by Newhouse and Hochstein and nearly half of the twenty remaining older ones.

"We were all so young and gung ho about our so-called careers," recalled Carol Morrissey, then a nineteen-year-old society reporter and the last of the younger group to sign on with the Guild. "Our basic interest was higher wages. But when I finally went to a meeting, I spoke up: 'If we lose our jobs, how will we manage?' Heywood Broun was there. He took a $100 bill out of his pocket and put it on the table. That seemed to convince everybody it would work out."

Press reporters planned to keep their meetings quiet until they were ready to act, and as late as 1 July, Newhouse had no idea that his newsroom had been organized by the Guild. Instead, he had Hochstein's assurances that there was nothing to worry about — it was still the Depression, and reporters at the *Press* were grateful for the chance to work. The notion that they might unionize was unthinkable. Hochstein was so sure of himself that one weekend that month, at a cocktail party of newspaper people in Manhattan, he asserted, "At our place, we don't need the Guild, and we don't have it."

"Oh, yes, you do!" interjected a Guild member from another paper.

The news hit Newhouse like a thunderbolt. He couldn't believe that his own people would be so foolish as to pay heed to Heywood Broun. Nor did he appreciate the fact that the Guild had obviously chosen to pick on him because his Long Island newspaper was small and far enough outside Manhattan that he would not get support from the city's biggest newspapers if he tried to resist. Most important, there was the matter of finances. The Guild wanted to install a formal system that would insure higher wages, shorter working hours, and greater job security. Such an approach obviously ran counter to Newhouse's paternalistic management style. Worse, it would cost money — lots of it — and could seriously hamper his plans to buy still more newspapers.

Just how much of a threat to Newhouse's pocketbook the Guild was, is illustrated by an encounter that came on the heels of the disclosure. For much of that year, Norman Newhouse had been dating one of the *Press*'s society reporters. They went out to dinner frequently, and Norman even loaned the young woman his car to take on a vacation, but they never discussed the union. The day after Norman's older brother found out about the Guild's infiltration of the *Press*, they had another date, but this time Norman wasn't so pleasant. He demanded to know why he hadn't been told what was going on and informed the young woman that she had already cost them more than $1,000 by not letting him and his brother know right away. According to the woman, the clear implication of Norman's remarks was that Guild activities would cost the *Press* at least that much every week until they were halted.

Whatever the exact combination of reasons, Newhouse was determined to teach his people — and the Guild — a lesson they would not soon forget.

Three times during the week that followed the uncovering of Guild activities in Jamaica, the leader of the *Press*'s chapter, Clayton Knowles, was called into the *Press*'s front office to discuss "outside influences on the staff." At each meeting, he was threatened with dismissal for inefficiency.

At the same time, Newhouse issued instructions that on 6 July all nine women in the society department be informed that their jobs would end in two weeks. In addition, the staff was notified that the dreaded space rates would be resumed as soon as the society reporters departed. Newhouse let it be known that there was only one way he could be dissuaded from taking these harsh steps. That was if the Guild chapter disbanded immediately. Meanwhile, Hochstein urged male reporters at the paper "to protect the innocent lambs . . . they had led to the slaughter." Obviously, management was counting on chivalry — as well as a few romantic entanglements on the staff — to carry the day.

"It was a mean thing," recalled Carol Morrissey. "The boys were young and impressionable, and they didn't want to be blamed for the girls losing their jobs." Morrissey was so upset about the way things had been handled that she refused to wait around to see what happened. The day she got her notice, she stormed into the managing editor's office at the *Press*. "I talked loud because everybody in the newsroom was listening," Morrissey recalled. "I called him a 'G.D. communist' and I said, 'You and Newhouse would hang your grandmothers for one dollar.' Then I turned around and slammed the door. That was the end of my career at the *Press*."

Most of the others, it turned out, were more timid. On Tuesday, 10 July, just four days after the termination notices had been issued, the *Press*'s chapter of the Guild voted to disband. Newhouse, it appeared, had subdued his ungrateful editorial department and could now magnanimously rescind the orders to fire the young women in the society department.

Things were not to be so simple, however; he had won too complete a victory. He had not even been forced to respond to any of his reporters' concerns about wages, hours, and job security, and that evening, at a meeting in Manhattan, the Guild's leaders decided to challenge Newhouse in court and on the streets of Jamaica. "This," Guild members all over the city were informed, "is the fight we all knew we might expect. . . . It is directed at the life of the Guild." Beginning the following morning, sympathetic reporters from the entire metropolitan area descended on Long Island to picket.

The demonstration that began outside the *Press* building the morning of 11 July marked the first time in American history that editorial workers had picketed a newspaper. Adding to the excitement, a procession of automobiles toured Jamaica, carrying banners attacking Newhouse and the *Press*. Similar messages were broadcast by a sound truck. Overhead a biplane that had been turned into a flying billboard carried additional anti-*Press* slogans. And on foot, an army of canvassers went door-to-door to discourage readers and advertisers alike from using the *Press*. "Do you want to read a paper that . . . intimidates its writers, favors sweatshop conditions in its editorial offices, and prevents white-collar organization?" asked one flier. To advertisers, the Guild's message was equally strong: "Do you wish to advertise in a medium that is incurring the enmity of all those who work for their living?"

All this commotion threw Newhouse off stride, but later that day he tried to acquit himself to a reporter from the *New York Herald-Tribune*. "We have no objection to our men joining the Guild," he said disingenuously. "What we are trying to do is to reorganize our editorial department and hire a high type of man who will measure up to New York standards, instead of boys fresh out of college."

As for the historic picketing action that had taken place that day:

"Personally, I see no justification for it. However, we're satisfied if they think it will improve anything."

When did he expect a settlement? "We have nothing to settle."

Despite Newhouse's bravado, picketing continued outside the *Press* building. To make matters worse, Guild members at other newspapers produced their own accounts of the demonstrations. According to the *Herald-Tribune*, for example, "The pickets, marching to and fro with militant banners, enjoyed the work and considered that they were making history, this being the first time, to their knowledge, that a newspaper office has been picketed by editorial workers. The Guild idea . . . now claims a membership of . . . 1,700 in New York City."

As if all this wasn't trouble enough for Newhouse, the charismatic Guild leader he so despised, Heywood Broun, regularly stationed himself outside the *Press* building alongside the other pickets and offered all sorts of encouragement. Later, when police attempted to halt the leafleting, Broun called in his attorney to talk them down. When the men seemed dispirited, he bought them drinks in nearby watering holes. And when it appeared that the picketing was getting no results, Broun offered to contribute 10 percent of his salary to a strike fund.

As far as Newhouse was concerned, this latter course would lead to disaster. He had been in charge of the *Press* less than two years and was still in the process of remaking it. Should he be forced to shut down — even for a couple of days — the whole process could be damaged, perhaps beyond repair. Readers and advertisers would be lost — some forever — and the *Press*'s lifeblood, its cash flow, would be halted.

In this instance, however, Newhouse had an ace up his sleeve. As a teenager, Phil Hochstein had been active in a garment-worker's union that involved the short, fat, cigar-chomping little man who had become New York City's mayor. They were still friends, and the populist "Little Flower," as Fiorello La Guardia was called, was always eager to get involved in disputes when he could pose as their mediator. At Hochstein's request, La Guardia arranged a meeting of the principals.

On the morning of 14 July, Newhouse and several associates joined Broun and others at City Hall to negotiate. Three hours later, La Guardia announced that a settlement had been reached. The

Guild, he said, had made several minor concessions. It would not expect the *Press* to match the salary demands it made of the larger Manhattan papers; it would submit to arbitration in the case of further disputes; and it would end its picketing activities in Jamaica.

On the other hand, Newhouse had agreed to what seemed major concessions. First, he would recognize his reporters' right to form a Guild chapter. Second, those employees who had been discharged would be reinstated. Third, he would deal directly with a grievance committee. And fourth, he would begin negotiations on a detailed contract with the Guild.

At the conclusion of La Guardia's announcement, reporters listened eagerly to a few parting words between the principals. "You've made a guinea pig of the *Press*," Newhouse told Broun.

"Well," Broun responded, "you walked right into our laboratory."

By all appearances, the Guild had won an impressive victory. Coming at a time when the union seemed about to collapse under its own weight, this settlement proved essential to its continued existence. Newhouse, however, paid little heed to the historical significance of his first encounter with the Guild. All he wanted was to thwart it at his own newspaper, no matter what happened elsewhere. By making concessions in the mayor's office, he had succeeded in getting Broun and the other activists from Manhattan to leave the *Press* alone. That was essential if he was to do what he'd set out to do in the first place — eradicate all Guild influences at the paper.

Within a week, *Press* reporters received their first indication that the 14 July settlement was not a settlement at all. Newhouse had Hochstein post a brief announcement on the newsroom bulletin board. With "regret," the *Press* had canceled all summer vacation "for Guild and non-Guild members." However, the memorandum noted, "Those who think they can go away without the routine of the department being upset should see Mr. Hochstein, the managing editor." It was perfectly clear who would get time off with pay from the *Press*'s hot and stuffy newsroom that summer, and who would stay.

Refusing, by means of this subterfuge, to give Guild members summer vacation was only the first step in Newhouse's planned dissection of the reporters' union. At his direction, Guild sympathizers were given late-night shifts and bad story assignments and were made to understand that promotions would not be granted to them. Those few Guild members who dared to oppose the new policies were simply fired — allegedly for incompetence and insubordination.

In less than six months, the new program of intimidation and harassment had eliminated all but three members of the Guild. A few would continue to practice journalism with distinction. For most, however, it was the end of a dream.

"We were so naive," recalled a *Press* reporter who never set foot in a newsroom after 1934. "We thought we were entitled to form a union. And we never believed that one man — for whom we had been willing to give everything we had, because we were so entranced with the romance of journalism — we couldn't believe that same man could treat us so insensitively, so viciously. Do you think I'll ever forget what he did to me and my friends?"

Newhouse, too, had learned a lesson he would not soon forget. The way to attain mastery in labor relations, he now knew, was through smoke screens and indirection. In fact, he was already using those very tactics to thwart a potential Guild uprising at the *Staten Island Advance*. There, a hard-working, personable editorial writer by the name of Alexander Crosby called a meeting on 18 July to attempt to organize the newsroom. Heywood Broun and others would be on hand to offer encouragement. Rather than simply order his people to stay away from the meeting, however, Newhouse hit upon a more subtle method of stymying Crosby and his Manhattan backers. He had the *Advance*'s city editor direct that all newsroom employees attend the meeting.

The real meaning of the instruction became clearer when they all arrived at the gathering, only to notice the same city editor sitting silently off to the side of the room. After much speechifying by Broun, Crosby, and some of the others from Manhattan, an open vote was conducted. Only then did the *Advance*'s renegade editorialist get a sense of the true measure of the man whose paper he was attempting to unionize. Four reporters abstained from voting. Fourteen were opposed. And just one — Crosby himself — voted to establish a Staten Island chapter of the Guild.

The vote was a terrific setback for the Guild and put an end to whatever slight chance it might have possessed of organizing the *Advance*. But Newhouse wasn't through with Alexander Crosby. He meant, in his words, "to isolate his chief editorialist from his payroll," though he knew it would be too risky simply to fire Crosby because he supported the Guild. In the new game of wits and power in which Newhouse was engaged, he would need a better pretext.

It just so happened that earlier that year, the zealous Crosby had published several rather radical editorials in the *Advance* without consulting his superiors. Though his activities violated normal procedures, neither S. I. nor Norman Newhouse could have been too upset at the time, since they meted out no sanctions, and Crosby continued to write editorials. As of July, however, the matter of the unauthorized editorials assumed new significance, for even the most rabid Guild activist would be hard pressed to take the position that Crosby had been correct in publishing them the way he did.

Newhouse's deviousness did not stop there. Even though he figured he already had sufficient justification for letting Crosby go, he twisted the knife a bit first, ordering that Crosby be taken off editorials altogether and be transferred to the staff of the *Long Island Press*, where he was to receive the special treatment reserved for other Guild sympathizers. Then, when Crosby refused to accept the transfer, he had him fired for insubordination. Even the way Newhouse conducted the firing was shifty — he waited until Crosby had left for vacation in late July and he himself was on his way to Europe with Mitzi, on the trip he had promised her as a honeymoon more than a decade earlier. Then he cabled the orders to Norman.

Undaunted, Crosby went directly to the New York Newspaper Guild's leadership with the news of his dismissal. They, in turn, voted to take bold action. As a result, that 14 August, Newhouse, who only a month before had become the first newspaper publisher in America to be picketed by editorial workers, now became the first to be struck by them as well.

Picketing was instituted all over the island — at the municipal ferryhouse in St. George, at the *Advance*'s offices, in the island's various business districts, and even at the home of Norman and Theodore Newhouse, at 183 Davis Avenue. Special editions of the *Guild Reporter* were published. Car caravans toured St. George and Port Richmond. And local radio stations gave the Guild free time to broadcast readings of propaganda plays.

Everywhere, the message was the same: Boycott Newhouse's *Advance*.

Showers met the Cunard White Star liner *Aquitania* as she entered New York Harbor on 24 August 1934. On board were S. I. and Mitzi Newhouse, returning from their European cruise. During their weeks aboard the sumptuously appointed ocean liner, they had mingled with the highest class of people, and on the other side of the Atlantic, Mitzi had indulged another of her passions — scouting the latest fashions.

But on this last day, as the *Aquitania* pulled into the harbor, there was trouble. From somewhere out in the drizzle, Newhouse heard his name being called over a megaphone. For a moment, he couldn't understand what was being said, but then the message became clearer. ". . . Unfair to workers," shouted the voice, ". . . anti-Guild . . . fired a man illegally. . . ." Then, even more ominously, a small plane buzzed the *Aquitania*, giving her shocked passengers a close-up view of the message painted in bold letters on its sides: "BACK THE GUILD." Newhouse understood immediately that this was the upshot of his decision to fire Alexander Crosby.

All the unwanted attention threw Mitzi into a terrible state. What would the other people on board — people she had tried so hard to impress during the cruise — think of them now? And what about her mother and her two boys, waiting for them at the pier? S. I., too, was embarrassed by this noisy demonstration, but his discomfort soon turned to anger as it became apparent that the Guild was not going to stop at bombarding the *Aquitania* with anti-Newhouse messages. Coming toward them through the drizzle was a pilot's boat, on its way out to meet the ship, where it sat in quarantine. The special greeting crew on board had been assembled in Newhouse's honor, and it included his least favorite Guildsman, Heywood Broun, just as rumpled and unshaven as ever. Though their meeting was polite, its tone was definitely frosty. If you don't reinstate Crosby, Broun threatened, there will be serious labor trouble on Staten Island.

When the *Aquitania* finally docked, it did so amidst a crowd of curious onlookers and vehement Guild members carrying placards and shouting angrily. S. I. and Mitzi dashed past the throng to Judith Epstein and the boys, then grabbed two taxicabs and raced from the scene, only to find a half dozen Guild cars following them up Ward Hill.

That night the harassment continued. A street-corner rally held outside the Newhouses' house was soon joined by a sound truck, whose anti-Newhouse and pro-Guild messages reverberated in the thick evening air. Finally, a huge spotlight was trucked up the hill and stationed directly in front of 25 Ward Avenue, where it played across the Newhouses' front windows until the early hours of the morning.

The Guild's roisterous greeting, however, turned out to be more of a last hurrah than anything else. That is, by attempting a boycott, it had played right into Newhouse's hands. Between Henry Garfinkle's newsstands and the paper's network of carrier boys — and the fact that there was no longer a competing daily on the island — the *Advance* was up to any challenge to its circulation. Besides, the more ruckus the Guild made, the more reason Staten Islanders had to pick up copies of the *Advance* in order to find out what was going on. The Guild's attempt to create a boycott backfired totally — in fact, circulation figures for the first three weeks of August, usually the worst time of year, showed a marked improvement over the same period the previous year, and even a small increase over the figures for that July.

Thus it was that the day after the Guild had confronted him on the *Aquitania*, Newhouse could issue a formal statement to the press that showed not the slightest concern about the union's actions on Staten Island. He was brief, to the point, and a trifle melodramatic: "I will not be intimidated by picketing, hippodromizing or ballyhooing." As far as Newhouse was concerned, business at the *Advance* would go on as usual, and in a short time, picketing was restricted first to weekends only and then to just Saturdays. By mid-November, both the demonstrators and Alexander Crosby were gone, never to return. And though Newhouse now had added to his record the dubious distinction of being the first newspaper publisher ever to be struck by editorial workers, this time he also had the exquisite pleasure of seeing Guild activism work to his benefit.

12 Newark

IT HAD TAKEN A GENERATION more than Nachman Newhouse had hoped, but by the mid-1930s, there could be no doubt that the Newhouse family had escaped the clutches of poverty for good. Nor could there be any doubt that their improved circumstances emanated from S. I.'s vision and direction. The other siblings — especially Louis, Teddy, Naomi, and Norman — had worked hard, but it was their oldest brother whose seemingly unerring way with newspapers had made the prosperity possible.

And were the newspapers ever paying! Though small compared to the big-circulation dailies of Manhattan, the once-ailing *Advance* and *Press* were about to become two of the most profitable newspapers in the country, now that the obstacles posed by the Guild were out of the way. From a business standpoint, autumn was the best time of year for newspapers, and with a combined circulation that reached almost 80,000, Newhouse's papers were having a banner fourth quarter. When 1934 was over, the books showed that they had netted him nearly a quarter of a million dollars — more than three dollars per subscriber.

Moreover, the newspapers were providing the family generous stipends. Norman was earning $22,670 as editor of the *Staten Island Advance*; Naomi got $17,000 for her work in classified advertising and circulation; Louis made at least as much for supervising the composing room; and Theodore earned $16,280 as the *Advance*'s general manager, and probably as much again for supervising advertising sales at the *Press*. S. I.'s own salary exceeded $40,000.

Not surprisingly, this sudden wealth only made the thirty-nine-year-old Newhouse hunger for more newspapers, especially when he considered what William Randolph Hearst had accomplished during the preceding twenty years. If Hearst had been a giant when Newhouse first announced his intentions to emulate him, by the mid-thirties he had assumed mythical proportions. Majestically ensconced in San Simeon, he then owned daily newspapers in nineteen cities and commanded more than an eighth of the total number of newspapers sold in America. On Sundays, nearly a quarter were his.

Hearst also published the immensely popular *American Weekly*, a Sunday supplement printed in color. He operated America's largest newspaper features syndicate (King). He had his own wire service (Universal) and his own photo service (International News). In addition, he owned and operated thirteen magazines, eight radio stations, and two moving-picture companies. If Newhouse really wanted a chain of newspapers of his own, just like Mr. Hearst's, he had a lot of catching up to do.

An increased appetite, though, could do little to make additional publications available. By the mid-thirties, the number of newspapers for sale, even desperately sick ones, had diminished to the point where they were harder to come by than they had been in 1920, when Newhouse's craving had led him far, and disastrously, afield in Fitchburg. However, in January 1935 a lead surfaced while S. I. and Mitzi were on a winter cruise in Latin American waters. There, Newhouse ran into Emanuel P. Scheck, a lawyer from Newark, New Jersey, who said he knew of a newspaper for sale in his city.

Only someone with Newhouse's determination to add to his holdings would have taken on such a venture. The unlikely enterprise was the *Newark Ledger*, a newspaper beset by a bad reputation and worse financial difficulties. Its founder and publisher was Lucius T. Russell, a big, handsome man whose matinee-idol looks failed to compensate for an utterly erratic personality. Russell had begun the *Ledger* in 1917, printing editions around the clock to give readers the impression that they were always getting the most up-to-date news. When that ploy proved too costly, he tried publishing a morning and an afternoon edition each day, but it soon became apparent that the *Evening Ledger* could not compete with Newark's other afternoon papers, and Russell cut back to one edition in the morning. No matter when it was printed, the *Ledger*'s bread and butter remained coverage of scandal and corruption, produced in an incredibly unprofessional fashion.

In the mid-twenties, Russell made another radical change in his paper; he copied the format of the tabloid papers that had become so popular in Manhattan. The result was a "magazine-size" *Ledger* that proved even more sensationalistic than its predecessors — provoking frequent libel charges, touting select parcels of real estate that happened to belong to Russell, and crusading for law and order in a city not known for adherence to such principles.

There was apparently no end to Russell's contradictions and eccentricities, most of which sooner or later found their way into his paper. He was an ardent prohibitionist, for example; yet, he obtained substantial financial backing from a local brewery and also made a practice of packing his newsroom with alcoholic drifters whose services could be engaged for a pittance. Nonetheless, every once in a while, a genuine spirit of journalism would stir inside Russell, prompting him to charge into his shabby editorial offices and shout at reporters, "Get out of here and dig up some news!"

Not surprisingly, in both circulation and advertising, the *Ledger* ran a poor third in a three-newspaper town. The Scudder family's *Newark Evening News*, at the time one of the most respected newspapers in the country, was the leader, with a circulation of 120,000. Paul Block's *Newark Star-Eagle* was second, selling 80,000 copies a day. It was a rare edition of the *Ledger*, however, that sold more than 40,000 copies.

Moreover, Russell had burdened his paper with heavy personal borrowings, and in the fall of 1934, his unpredictable, bullying behavior precipitated a strike by the Newark Newspaper Guild that proved to be the straw that broke the *Ledger*'s back. The paper was already losing money, and it hit rock bottom the following spring, just as Newhouse and Scheck began discussing the possibility of a sale.

After months of wrangling in bankruptcy court, on 20 May, a deal was consummated. Newhouse would pay $310,000 for 51 percent of the stock in the company that published the paper, and five days later he would list his name as publisher on the *Ledger*'s masthead.

Long before the May closing, Newhouse had begun to spend his afternoons in Newark at the run-down *Ledger* building at 80 Bank Street. He would rise each day at six, put in a few hours at the *Advance*, have his driver run him over to Jamaica by mid-morning, and then shuttle to Newark later in the day. In all, he and his chauffeur covered sixty-two miles each day. Despite the rigorous schedule, Newhouse seemed to draw added energy from the fact that the *Ledger* suffered from practically every newspaper problem imaginable. He must also have sensed that the paper would be an ideal arena in which to show his skills.

Circulation was the area of the *Ledger*'s operations most urgently in need of Newhouse's attention. The paper's readers were the dregs of Newark, and the city's big merchants — Hahne's, Bamberger's, Hearns', Michaels Department Store, Ohrbach's, Baumann's — had little interest in buying advertising space for an audience that couldn't afford to shop in their stores. Besides, most *Ledger* readers who did make decent livings read the afternoon papers as well.

Clearly, if Newhouse's new paper continued to compete directly with the *Evening News* and the *Star-Eagle* for readers and advertisers in downtown Newark, the situation would be hopeless. No amount of investment in promotion could dislodge the other two from their positions of dominance; eventually, the *Ledger* would fail, eating up the hard-earned profits of the *Advance* and the *Press* as it went. But Newhouse had already devised a way around the difficulty.

During the preceding decade, tens of thousands of people had left Newark to live in nearby townships like Hillside, Bloomfield, the Oranges, Nutley, and Belleville. In the process, a large new group of potential newspaper readers had been created — the thousands of housewives who were left alone at home each morning when their husbands commuted into town. Curiously, the *News* and *Star-Eagle* had made little effort to reach this new audience. A good deal of chauvinism was involved, for most suburban breadwinners still worked downtown and bought papers there. But there was also a surprising amount of complacency. Because the papers' publishers, especially the publisher of the *News*, felt they had it made in Newark, they paid woefully little attention to the changing demography of their city.

Newhouse, on the other hand, had a wealth of experience with suburban and rural readers on Staten Island and Long Island. In an era that predated huge suburban shopping malls, he knew full well that the middle- and upper middle-class families who could afford to leave town were some of the most prized customers of big downtown merchants. Moreover, he understood another obvious, but nonetheless overlooked, fact. It was the housewives — the women the *News* and *Star-Eagle* had chosen to ignore — who did most of the shopping. The newspaper that first captured them as readers would be able to obtain a big share of Newark's advertising. Based on this assessment of the market, Newhouse's strategy for the *Ledger* was almost a foregone conclusion. He would direct his new paper's attentions to the suburbs.

Arranging to have the *Ledger* delivered to this new audience was relatively easy. All Newhouse had to do was bring in Danny Smith to duplicate for Greater Newark the carrier-boy networks he had established earlier for the *Advance* and the *Press*. But what should the *Ledger* cover in order to sell in Nutley and Belleville?

Here Newhouse borrowed an idea he'd read about in his trade publications. Recently, big New York City dailies had begun to use a new device — the market survey — to help with circulation. He moved his all-purpose editorial adviser, Phil Hochstein, over to Newark, and the two of them set about commissioning one.

Years later, the results of this extremely rough and unsophisticated analysis of suburban Newark would hardly raise an eyebrow, but in 1935 they were quite a surprise. For where it was generally assumed that life in a big house on a quiet, tree-lined street was all a woman could ask for, the surveys disclosed that the housewives of Nutley and Belleville were anything but content; they were desperate for relief from the monotony of their days at home. The key that would unlock suburbia to the morning *Ledger*, the surveys indicated, was material that would serve to distract or entertain — puzzles, romantic stories, movie gossip, comics. Almost anything would do, even household hints and discussions of dress and etiquette.

Soon the *Ledger* was carrying Dorothy Dix's advice for the lovelorn and dozens of items on Hollywood — including Jimmy Fidler's column and syndicated features like "Star Flashes" and "Screen Oddities." There was a short story every day, as well as something called "The Case Record of a Psychologist," a juicy column written by members of the faculty at Northwestern University. Household tips abounded in regular features with titles like "What To Do," "My Lady Beautiful," and "Home Cooking." Squeezed in between all this fluff was the North American Newspaper Alliance's package of puzzles and games.

But where the *Ledger* really got carried away was in the realm of comics. Every day, a reader of Newhouse's new paper could follow the antics of a cast of characters that included Little Abner, Tarzan, Ella Cinders, Joe Jinx, Fritzie Ritz, Bronco Bill, Jasper, Dixie Dugan, Joe Palooka, Pop, Tailspin Tommy, and Mutt and Jeff, and on Sundays, fully twenty-four pages of the *Ledger* were devoted to the comics.

Newhouse's market survey also indicated that hard news was not high on the average suburban housewife's list of priorities. She wanted coverage of social events, especially weddings, teas, and club meetings; the national and international reports that were the *Evening News*'s strong suit would command little of her attention. Once again, Newhouse and Hochstein made sure the *Ledger* delivered what the readers wanted. They printed verbatim announcements of social events sent in by people who participated in them, and filled the remainder of the news hole largely with material from the wire of the Associated Press, whose Newark offices were conveniently located in the same building as the paper. Frequently, the *Ledger* did not even bother to run the AP's slug with its copy, creating the false impression that the material had been written by the *Ledger*'s own reporters.

Soon after its takeover by Newhouse, the *Ledger* hired a columnist in the state capital and established a part-time bureau in Elizabeth. For the most part, however, it was devoid of journalistic enterprise. In fact, during Newhouse's first four years of ownership, only one member of the paper's staff was given a regular travel allowance, and that was to pay expenses involved in covering the Newark Bears baseball team. Instead of actively seeking out the news, Hochstein later explained, "We get the other Newark papers and out-of-town papers, and when we find anything of interest to us, we often rewrite it, sometimes seeking additional information to supplement the original story."

This new *Ledger* was fluffy and unprofessional, but the circulation figures soon suggested that it was just what Newark's suburban housewives wanted. In the short space between 1935 and 1938, the paper's circulation jumped from less than 40,000 to more than 60,000. Advertising increased at an even faster rate, reflecting the economic drawing power of the paper's new readers.

* * *

As usual, every aspect of the new paper's operation was subject to Newhouse's scrutiny. The situation in the ad sales department was typical. Prior to his takeover, a manager and four or five assistants had been attempting to sell space in the paper in a haphazard fashion. Possessing no overall plan and no fixed rate structure to show potential advertisers, they would wander aimlessly around Newark trying to negotiate one-time placements of ads. Obviously, they understood none of the tricks of the newspaper advertising trade that Newhouse had learned two decades before in nearby Bayonne, and, just as obviously, the paper's new publisher had no use for them. By early 1936, all were gone, replaced by more aggressive salesmen.

Newhouse also brought an extraordinary cost-consciousness to the *Ledger*'s operations. As a central mechanism of efficiency, he had his accountant, Louis Glickman, produce weekly statements summarizing the performance of each department at the paper. Soon, Newhouse could see immediately how any part of the enterprise was doing compared with the week before or the same week the previous month or even the same week the previous year. Though businesses of other kinds routinely employed such bookkeeping devices, most newspapers had not even considered using them.

Newhouse had been under no illusion that the *Ledger* would soon become as profitable as the *Advance* or the *Press*. Rather, his plan was to build up the paper as much as possible, with new people and new programs, but to do so incrementally, as and when it could afford the changes. Aided by Glickman's weekly reports, Newhouse could see just how much could be done each year before the *Ledger* would go into the red. Operating this way, he was able to push improvements to the limit, doubling administrative costs, raising salaries in the business department to attract better employees, instituting the new carrier system — with an expensive promotion scheme to back it up — and even spending $16,579 for structural improvements to 80 Bank Street.

All this time, the Scudders and Paul Block and others who followed the newspaper business in Newark thought Newhouse was losing his shirt and assumed he must be drawing funds from his other newspapers in order to continue his odd suburban publication. Had they known the true picture, these skeptics would have been astonished by the near miracles their competitor was performing.

For while Newhouse was patiently rebuilding the *Ledger*, he was also making a small profit from it. And he was able to pay himself a third salary — $20,800 a year on top of the $40,000 he was earning already.

That Newhouse would even try to save the *Ledger* was itself remarkable, given the precarious condition of the American newspaper industry in the mid-1930s. Not only were labor costs rising uncontrollably, but the Depression was dragging on. Worse, for the first time in history, a new means of mass communication — radio — was seriously challenging newspapers for advertising. Among the mass media (radio, magazines, newspapers), only radio's revenues increased during the decade following the Depression.

Adding to these concerns was the realization that newspaper publishing had become a mature industry. Instead of being characterized by new ventures and innovation, the business was dominated by the less healthy process of consolidation and merger. But while other newspaper publishers had come to doubt the worth of their businesses, Newhouse's faith in newspapers persisted. They were all he knew. They had made him and his family prosperous. And they remained his only avenue to still greater wealth and security.

13 Smashing the Opposition

THERE WAS MORE TO RESCUING the *Ledger* than the specific editorial and business remedies Newhouse prescribed. Throughout the rebuilding process, he also had to contend with two powerful forces — former owner L. T. Russell and the local chapter of the American Newspaper Guild.

From the outset, Newhouse realized that Russell would be impossible to work with. So, while bargaining to buy the *Ledger*, he had made a bribelike agreement designed to force Russell out. To entice Russell to retire to California, Newhouse consented to keep his name on the *Ledger*'s masthead as Editor, and to make his son Edwin, then a student at Princeton University, Associate Publisher. He also provided Russell with a do-nothing consulting contract worth $20,800 a year.

But Newhouse soon discovered that a man like Russell couldn't be bought off quite that easily. Always mercurial and often out of sorts with the world, the *Ledger*'s former publisher just was not the sort to hand over a newspaper he had created and walk away for good. He still owned 49 percent of the stock, and after a year's reflection, his misgivings about selling the other 51 percent to Newhouse grew to immense proportions. More and more, he came to see the deal as a swindle. Worse, letters from his son outlined major changes Newhouse was making in the paper to which Russell had dedicated eighteen years of his life. So in the late spring of 1936, L. T. returned to Newark from Beverly Hills, determined to get the *Ledger* to revert to its former ways. He began by threatening to call shareholders' meetings to correct mistakes he believed were being made by the paper's new management. No meetings were ever held, however. Then he made noises about suing Newhouse and his associates; again, the threats proved idle. Finally, he arranged a private meeting with Newhouse and made all sorts of wild charges — that too much was being spent on administrative salaries, that delivering papers to the suburbs was a waste of time, and that the *Ledger*'s new editorial focus was a disaster.

Confident that the changes he had instituted were saving the *Ledger*, not harming it, Newhouse simply ignored this unsolicited advice. The meeting with Russell convinced him that his predecessor had completely lost touch with reality.

Things between the two men were at a standstill until the following May, when sheer frustration with the situation led Russell to make a tragic miscalculation. He determined that his only recourse to save the *Ledger* was to take it back. A few days later, he climbed the front steps of the *Ledger* building and addressed a group of mailroom employees who happened to be out on strike at the time. "Newhouse stole this paper!" he yelled. "Don't settle with him! If you'll help me, we'll drive him out of town!"

This dramatic performance was reinforced a few weeks later by the publication of a special newspaper Russell personally designed and wrote. Called the *Newark Leader*, but looking for all the world like a twin of the *Ledger*, the paper carried a full-blown attack on everyone connected with the present management of the *Ledger*. According to the *Leader*, the lawyers who arranged the paper's sale were swindlers and the new managers had been falsifying circulation reports and advertising contracts, as well as engaging in bribery and mail fraud. To spice things up some more, the *Leader* described Newhouse's appearance as that "of a small, squat animal."

Paying no mind to the unsupportable nature of the bulk of his charges, Russell had 60,000 copies of the *Leader* published and saw to it that each of the Newark *Ledger*'s advertisers, shareholders, and employees received a complimentary issue. He also sent copies to neighboring newspapers, U.S. postal officials, and the Audit Bureau of Circulation.

As soon as he saw the *Leader*, Newhouse called a special meeting of the board of directors of the Newark Morning Ledger Publishing Company. There was but one piece of business on his agenda — a motion to cancel L. T. Russell's $20,800-a-year, lifetime employment contract. That contract had become all the more important to Russell when Newhouse had discontinued payment of dividends on

Ledger stock — an action he invariably took when he assumed control of a new property.

Though Russell still owned 49 percent of the paper, there was nothing he could do to prevent the termination of his contract. The *Ledger*'s board of directors had three members, and Newhouse's 51 percent gave him outright control of two of their votes, his and William Hofmann's. The third, though belonging to L. T.'s younger son, Edwin, also leaned toward Newhouse.

Newhouse had made a smart move in hiring Edwin as Associate Publisher and giving him a seat on the board of directors. Though he'd initially planned to retain Edwin for only a few years, Newhouse found him surprisingly helpful, especially in dealing with his erratic father. By the time Edwin turned twenty-one, Newhouse had raised his salary from $7,500 a year to $17,500, and now, with Edwin's vote, the motion to strip L. T. of his income passed unanimously. A day or two later, Edwin F. Russell, acting as corporate secretary, dutifully affixed his signature to the minutes of the meeting that severed his father from the *Ledger*'s payroll for good.

L. T. challenged the board's action in court and lost. The matter should have ended at that point — with the elder Russell stripped of the greater part of his income and exiled once again to Beverly Hills — but, as many who fought with him were to discover, Newhouse was no ordinary adversary. Once provoked, he would not let go. The way to handle a problem, he believed, was to eliminate its source.

In the case of L. T. Russell, the means he used were extraordinary. Newhouse had his attorney draw up a special contract stating that, should Russell ever return to New Jersey, New York, or Pennsylvania, he would be required to sell his remaining 49 percent interest in the *Ledger* to Newhouse for the ridiculously low sum of $60,000. Then, Newhouse enlisted Edwin and Mrs. Russell to help him get the piece of paper signed.

A few years later, when Russell breached the agreement and returned to Newark, Newhouse unleashed his lawyers with a vengeance. By the time their final encounter was over, Newhouse had not only stripped Russell of all his remaining newspaper stock but had also helped to have him committed to a mental institution.

*   *   *

The second major problem Newhouse had to contend with in Newark was the *Ledger* unit of the Guild. Here he began with a decided advantage, for the winter-long strike that had cost Russell his newspaper had also cost the Newark Guild all of its strike funds and undermined its morale. The *Ledger* reporters were a beaten group, and Newhouse intended to see that they remained that way.

First off, he and Charles Goldman arranged a four-month truce with the *Ledger*'s Guild unit. At the time, that concession seemed harmless enough to Guild members. Its effect, though, was to allow Newhouse to take full charge of the paper. By 1 October 1935, when formal contract discussions began, Newhouse was in a far stronger position than the Guild. Then, as the negotiations dragged on, he obtained concession after concession until the document they were producing looked as if it had been dictated by Newhouse himself. On only one point could he not get his way — the Guild would not budge from its position that it be recognized as the sole bargaining unit for all editorial workers at the *Ledger*.

When he determined that the Guild would not give in on this final matter, Newhouse simply broke off the talks and appealed directly to the entire staff of the *Ledger*. The occasion for this extraordinary gesture was a special Christmas dinner for reporters and their families at the Hotel Robert Treat in downtown Newark. After the meal was served, Newhouse rose to give his first public address since graduating from the eighth grade in Bayonne.

Carefully written in advance, the speech contained no holiday expressions of good cheer or gratitude for work well done; it dealt instead with the contract negotiations he had done so much to sandbag. Newhouse assured the *Ledger*'s editorial staff that he did not "wish them to suffer from any uncertainty as to the question of economic security or Guild recognition." For the period of one year, he said, he would abide by all terms of the contract to which he and the Guild had agreed before negotiations were suspended. Among other assurances given that day, Newhouse promised that management would make no "individual contracts" with members of the staff; it would do nothing to prevent its employees from taking part in Guild activities; and it would fire editorial workers only on grounds of "gross" incompetency, "flagrant" violation of professional ethics, or "extreme" insubordination.

These "guarantees," Newhouse declared, would hold good whether or not a contract was consummated with the Guild. "Your minds may be at rest," he stated emphatically. "From now until January 1, 1937, you may stand on all the guarantees."

Nevertheless, by the end of February 1936, Newhouse had personally seen to it that ten active Guild members — nearly a quarter of the *Ledger*'s entire editorial department — had been dismissed. At his direction, those Guild supporters who were not fired outright were singled out for other forms of harassment. And by April, Newhouse was, in fact, offering individual contracts to his reporters. The explanation given for this final breach of faith was that he wanted to be able to raise salaries in the *Ledger*'s newsroom and could not do so unless he had the reporters' assurance that they would not band together to make new demands at a later date. The few Guild activists who remained at the paper were offered neither raises nor contracts.

14 The Final Battle

AFTER A BRIEF NATIONAL REVIVAL, sparked by its apparent victory over Newhouse at the *Long Island Press* in the summer of 1934, the American Newspaper Guild had been on the verge of collapse. During this period, no newspaper owner had proved more effective than Newhouse at subduing the Guild. Not only had he succeeded in eradicating Guild influences from his newsrooms by means of a concerted program of harassment and firings, but on Long Island, he had even managed to establish a special spy network.

Without the knowledge of their co-workers, the *Press*'s spies reported to management whenever talk of re-forming the Guild surfaced in the newsroom. On at least three occasions, secret organizational meetings were held, and each time, it took less than twenty-four hours for the ringleaders to be called on the carpet by managing editor Hochstein or by Ed Sterne, who took over when Hochstein went to Newark. If they persisted, the Guild sympathizers were informed, they would be fired for insubordination and impertinence. The spies, on the other hand, received secret bonuses, easier hours, and better story assignments.

Throughout 1935 and into the next year, morale in the newsroom was low. But then, on 13 July 1936, one day short of the second anniversary of Newhouse's original City Hall "settlement" with the Guild, the U.S. Court of Appeals in New York issued a ruling that upset his control all over again and brightened the Guild's spirits. At the center of the case was Morris Watson, a Manhattan reporter for the Associated Press who was also a vice-president of the American Newspaper Guild, having been active in the organization since its beginning in 1933. Under his leadership, the Guild unit of the Associated Press had succeeded in achieving a five-day workweek for wire-service reporters in Manhattan. But in the fall of 1935, the AP announced that it was reinstating the old six-day workweek. Watson was fired when he demanded formal talks with management. He immediately filed a complaint with the National Labor Relations Board (NLRB, for short) and a few months later obtained an order calling for his reinstatement.

The Associated Press had no intention of doing any such thing. Moreover, its officers and lawyers were well aware that President Roosevelt's New Deal legislation had not withstood a series of court challenges. So they took the matter up, confident that they could convince the New York Court of Appeals of the unconstitutionality of the Wagner Labor Relations Act, which had created the NLRB in the first place.

The court's eventual ruling — upholding both the Wagner Act and the NLRB's order reinstating Watson — was an astonishing victory for the reporters' union. At Newhouse's *Press*, where harassment of Guild supporters had become a fact of life, the effect of *AP v. Watson* was electric.

"When Morris Watson was reinstated," recalled George Vecsey, then a sports writer at the paper, "that was the impetus for the Guild reorganizing." By the following December, fifty-six out of a possible sixty-five *Press* newsroom employees had joined. At the same time, one of the spies — Maurice Singer — was found out and expelled from the Guild.

Newhouse responded to all this renewed activity by sending brother Norman to take over from Ed Sterne as managing editor. Newhouse knew that Sterne's savage treatment of Guild sympathizers was a major bone of contention in the newsroom, and he was also aware of the fact that his youngest brother was the only member of his family with a friendly, outgoing personality. Whereas Lou Newhouse struck acquaintances as sullen and withdrawn, and Ted was universally disliked by people who worked with him, Norman was a warm person. He was also the only Newhouse to take a direct interest in the editorial side of the business.

On arrival at the *Press*, Norman met with each department head in the newsroom to ask for "time to correct our past mistakes. We want to prove that the Guild is not necessary here." However, his conciliatory approach did not win many converts. "When Norman first came," explained Jackie Gebhard, who worked in the society department, "he was too hail-fellow-well-met, always slapping people on the back. He really overdid it. This made everybody suspicious. Besides, we felt we were paving the way for other newspapers. It wasn't just a matter of us against management at the *Press*."

There was a reservoir of pent-up ill will at the *Press* that inevitably aided the Guild's cause. So, too, did a chart that was passed around the newsroom that fall, comparing *Press* reporters' salaries with what was paid for comparable work in Manhattan. At the *Press,* the highest starting wage was paid to deskmen who rewrote reporters' stories and edited wire-service copy. Their minimum was $27.50 a week — a little more than a third what the same job paid at the *Times, Daily News,* or *Herald Tribune.* Comparisons with the same papers made the average salaries of *Press* reporters look even worse.

One very important salary comparison was not included on the chart — how the pay of *Press* reporters stacked up against that of their paper's owner. Had the information been available, it would have shown that Newhouse was earning more than all sixty-five members of his Long Island newsroom put together.

That December, in its first concerted action against Newhouse in nearly two and a half years, the Guild demanded that formal contract negotiations be initiated. Publicly, Newhouse insisted that he was willing to consider improved working conditions for the *Press*'s editorial workers. But when it came time to hold those meetings, his position was utterly inflexible — he would not shorten hours or raise wages, nor did he even appear willing to recognize the Guild formally.

"He was just impossible," remembered one guildsman. "He was polite, all right, but he wouldn't say anything. And his lawyer, Goldman, was worse. When he didn't like what you were saying, he'd just turn his hearing aid off. You could never tell if he was listening or not.

"We weren't asking for the moon. We made it clear we didn't want what other papers paid in Manhattan. We just wanted a decent, living wage, and they made it clear in every way that they simply had no use for us."

In late March of the following spring, the Guild raised the ante. If better faith was not shown at the bargaining table, the great majority of the *Press*'s reporters would strike. Still, Newhouse refused to give the Guild representatives their due. Instead, he had Hochstein send letters to each of his editorial employees, offering pay increases to those who would abandon the strike effort.

"I was getting $27.50 a week when I got my letter," recalled one deskman. "I could have had $37.50 if I'd gone along. But we were unanimous. We wanted five-day, forty-hour workweeks and more money. My job paid $75.00 in Manhattan."

The strike began on Monday, 15 April, at seven in the morning, when Guild pickets surrounded the *Press* building. Others stationed themselves outside the nearby Jamaica Armory, where the *Press*'s annual home and food show was in progress. Still another group marched in front of Benjamin Gertz's department store, then the *Press*'s largest advertising account. Only twelve *Press* reporters turned up for work that day, but with help from strikebreakers imported from Staten Island, the paper managed to publish an afternoon edition without much difficulty.

Till now, Newhouse had been intractable. With the strike, his behavior grew worse. First, he demanded that the dispute be settled by arbitration. The Guild agreed, and for ten days a panel of Jamaica clergymen listened to presentations from both sides. But on 20 April, when the arbitrators awarded the Guild nearly all of its demands, Newhouse baldly refused to accept the decision and turned instead to the police.

Three years later, an angry Fiorello La Guardia, upset over a *Press* editorial that criticized him for diverting city funds to a new airport in Queens, held an impromptu press conference on Long Island, declaring, "When [Newhouse] came to my office, he went on his knees and asked for police to beat up his reporters. . . . He said to me, 'Let us use a stick on these fellows. How can anybody make money by paying the wages they want?' "

Upon being confronted with the mayor's remarks, Newhouse brushed them off, saying they were "full of untruths." "Apparently," he continued, "the strain of dedicating the greatest airport was too much for the mayor. I cannot believe he would have made such a statement if he had enjoyed some rest. Any further comment about this matter should come not from me but from the mayor's physician." But, given his admiration for the tactics of strikebreaker Pearl Bergoff in Bayonne, Newhouse may well have demanded the police interference in the way La Guardia charged.

However he did it, the police did intercede. On the morning of Saturday, 24 April, some 150 strikers and strike sympathizers had assembled outside the *Press* building intent on establishing a human blockade to prevent the paper's mechanical employees from reporting for work. But the moment the strikers moved toward the building's main entrance, dozens of police officers — some on horseback, others on foot, but all with billy clubs drawn — descended on the demonstrators. The sudden arrival of the police had not been anticipated by the strikers, and the ensuing clash was bloody and put five guildsmen in the hospital, one with a serious skull fracture.

Pearl Bergoff himself could not have done a better job. Not only had the main entrance to the newspaper building been kept open, but the strikers had received a painfully clear message from the authorities that they had better return to the bargaining table. The following Monday, the Guild and Newhouse signed a new contract, which provided for slightly higher wages and a slightly shorter workweek, as well as for the reinstatement of all strikers and the dismissal of all strikebreakers — less than the arbitrators' recommendations but enough to make for a short-lived celebration. The *Press*'s reporters, only one or two of whom had been with the paper the last time Newhouse "settled," assembled at a summer home in nearby Amityville. "We partied all night," recalled Jackie Gebhard, "but then the next day we were on the picket line again. Newhouse had gone back on his agreement."

More precisely, he had taken advantage of some special language his attorney, Charles Goldman, had inserted at the end of the new contract, giving him "the right in good faith to dismiss employees . . . to effect economies." That morning, citing just such reasons, he ordered more than two dozen of the reinstated strikers fired.

The Guild resumed the strike, and this time, they were able to convince some of the paper's other workers to join them. Delivery-truck drivers went out first, followed by members of the International Typographical Union, and on 1 May 1937, the *Long Island Press* had to suspend publication for the first time in its 119-year history. That day, an angry Newhouse peered down from the window of his second-floor *Press* office at jeering pickets carrying signs that accused him of being "The Union-Busting Duke of Staten Island."

There was more violence — this time seventeen people required hospitalization — and finally, on 6 May, a lasting settlement was reached.

"S. I. despised the unions," explained a man who later served as publisher at one of his newspapers. "He especially disliked what they had done to him on Long Island." So it should have come as no surprise to reporters at the *Press* that as soon as the three-month grace period was over, dismissals of Guild sympathizers began again. Other forms of harassment that Newhouse had employed since 1934 were reinstated as well, with a few new twists. Maternity leave, for example, was eliminated for women who belonged to the Guild. Even subsequent pay increases were made to work against the reporters' union. "The extra money," Norman Newhouse told reporters, explaining why raises were not included in regular paychecks, "we'll put aside to see how good a management man you are."

In less than a year, the *Press*'s newsroom was back in Newhouse's pocket, this time for good.

Between 1934 and 1938, while the Guild was challenging newspaper publishers everywhere, Newhouse managed to put down four major uprisings by his reporters. As a strategist, he had acquitted himself masterfully. He had not, however, done much to enhance his reputation among his own employees, dozens of whom remained bitter for life over their treatment at his hands.

"You know," said former *Press* sportswriter George Vecsey in the fall of 1980, "it's been more than forty years since all that happened. Yet, it still makes my blood boil. I guess the reason I get so upset is that management at the *Press* was just so mean."

15 The Chief

REPORTS OF NEWHOUSE'S EXPLOITS with the Guild soon spread throughout the country. These sometimes exaggerated accounts were spread by word of mouth among newspaper executives and were carried by publications like *Editor & Publisher* and the *Guild Reporter*, both of which provided extensive coverage of the clashes at the *Press*, *Advance*, and *Ledger*. As far away as San Simeon in California, where the legendary Hearst now resided in decadent splendor, tales of Newhouse's victories over the reporters' union filtered in, mixed with accounts of the young publisher's apparent ability to work miracles with newspapers in trouble.

"The Chief," as Hearst was called, wanted to know more about this man who seemed suddenly to have taken over a major chunk of the newspaper business in the more important suburbs of New York City. So, early in the summer of 1938, he had Dick Berlin, his talent scout and head of Hearst Magazines, invite Newhouse to lunch.

Berlin wasted no time in getting around to what was on his mind. "How would you like to work for William Randolph Hearst?" he asked.

"What as?" Newhouse responded.

"As publisher of the *New York Journal*."

Newhouse was well aware that the *Journal* was Hearst's favorite newspaper, because it had served as his springboard into the big-time. During the thirties, however, it had begun to lose money — lots of it — and needed help badly. Of course he'd be interested in the job, Newhouse said. Though his other properties were already enough to keep him fully occupied, he assured Berlin that the *Journal* represented a challenge, and that he would give it whatever time was required.

Berlin's final question was a practical one. Did Newhouse mind taking the train to San Simeon to discuss the job personally with Hearst? Long trips usually made S. I. restless and uncomfortable, but he would gladly suffer that inconvenience for a meeting with the man he had admired for more than two decades.

The week before the anxiously awaited train ride, Newhouse received a call from Berlin. The trip out west would be unnecessary after all, he reported, for Hearst would be coming east that August, and Newhouse could see him then.

The meeting took place in Hearst's magnificent Manhattan apartment just before Labor Day. Sitting in one of his finest antique chairs, a little dachshund on his lap, the Chief peppered Newhouse with questions. What had he accomplished? How had he done it? And what amount of salary would be required to get him to take responsibility for the *Journal*?

Newhouse's answers proved most satisfactory, especially the one he gave to the last question. "I expect no salary," he said. "Just a share of any profit the paper makes as a result of my efforts with it."

To signal that the interview was over, Hearst reached out and patted Newhouse on the knee. The great difference in the two men's sizes made the gesture a bit awkward, but Hearst appeared genuinely pleased with their conversation. "Young man," he said, "I wish I had met you earlier."

For weeks Newhouse waited for something to come of the meeting. He had been left with the impression that the offer of a job would simply be a matter of time; yet, he heard nothing from either Berlin or Hearst. Sometime later, he came across a small notice in *Editor & Publisher* that caught his eye. Publisher W. R. Hearst, it said, had appointed a man from the Midwest to run the *New York Journal*.

Years later, another newspaper man, Paul Block, told Newhouse what had happened. Block, who had fronted for Hearst on a number of newspaper deals, fancied himself a close associate of the Chief and even boasted to acquaintances that he had been the one to introduce Hearst to Marian Davies. Thus, when he learned from Dick Berlin about the possibility that Newhouse might take over the *Journal*, he became terribly upset. Not only was Newhouse already one of his toughest competitors — Block owned the *Star-Eagle* in

Newark — but now it appeared likely that he would challenge him for his special position in Hearst's retinue. Berlin made the decision sound so imminent that Block immediately hooked his private railroad car to a train bound for California and rode directly to San Simeon, where he dissuaded Hearst from offering Newhouse the job.

Block's frantic train ride was to prove crucial to Newhouse's later success. For had Newhouse been offered the *New York Journal* job, he would surely have taken it. That, in turn, would have entailed becoming part of a huge corporate enterprise fraught with potential pitfalls for his career. Not the least of the problems would have been Richard Berlin himself, a man understood by his peers to be the most successful behind-the-scenes operator in the entire Hearst organization.

Besides, Hearst was fickle about people. Only a few of his top aides ever seemed to capture his lasting trust, and in no way did Newhouse resemble any of them. Worse still, S. I.'s limited social skills would have proved a terrible handicap among the high-powered Hollywood crowd that frequented San Simeon.

There was also the matter of the job itself. The *New York Journal* was a big-city newspaper, with problems far different and far more complex than any Newhouse had encountered before. Its home — Manhattan — was also a stronghold of New York City's newspaper unions. With the horrible reputation Newhouse had in local labor circles, a *Journal* with him as publisher might easily have become a special union target.

The most serious threat posed by the prospect of becoming publisher of the *Journal*, though, was that it would have deprived Newhouse of the control to which he had become accustomed by then. In the process, he might have lost sight — at least for a while — of his true goal of attaining a chain of newspapers of his own. Thanks to Paul Block's meddling, he could remain on his original course, at a time when new newspaper opportunities were about to come his way. One, in particular, would prove more valuable by far than any he had previously encountered.

Part IV

1939 – 1955: Opportunist

16 Syracuse

NEWHOUSE WAS ON THE SEVENTH HOLE of Long Island's Fresh Meadows Country Club when the call came in. He dashed to the clubhouse to take it, then headed straight home, where he stopped just long enough to pack a suitcase before heading off on the Staten Island ferry and up Manhattan to Grand Central Station. There he boarded the overnight train for Syracuse; in the morning he would bet $1.9 million — much of it money he didn't have — on his ability to perform yet another newspaper miracle.

He was always a fitful sleeper, and that Sunday night in the summer of 1939, as the rails clacked under his Pullman berth and shadows of the New York countryside sped past the window, he must have been particularly restless. The deal that waited at the other end of the ride was the opportunity of a lifetime. Though it involved tremendous risk, if his analysis of the situation was correct, in just a few weeks he would more than double the value and earnings of his newspaper holdings.

The seed of this dramatic transaction had been planted that spring by Smith Davis. Known for his lavish parties in Suite 40F of the Waldorf Towers, Davis made his living as a newspaper broker. Stocky, with a nice-looking but square face, he was a dynamic, aggressive salesman, whose most recent coup had been arranging Jack Knight's purchase of the *Miami Herald.* Now he planned to sell Newhouse a different *Herald.*

Owned and operated by old local stock, the *Syracuse Herald* was the most respected of the town's three daily newspapers. It sold 52,000 copies a day and had attracted nearly $1 million in advertising the previous year. However, it had fierce competition from another afternoon paper, Hearst's *Syracuse Journal,* which had a circulation of 63,000, and with the onset of a new recession in 1937, the *Herald* had begun to lose money. Despite Syracuse's reputation as a decidedly unhealthy newspaper town, the *Herald* was being offered for sale for the whopping price of a million dollars.

But Smith Davis approached Newhouse at a propitious moment. His problems with the Guild at the *Press* and the *Ledger* appeared over, his papers were doing well, he had about a million dollars in the bank, and his obsession with owning more newspapers was as strong as ever. Perhaps a way could be found to turn the situation in Syracuse to his advantage.

Newhouse immediately began investigating the town. Its economy, he learned, had remained strong during the recent recession. Located on the New York State Barge Canal midway between Albany and Buffalo, Syracuse was an important center of commerce, agriculture, and manufacturing. Steel for tools, electrical hardware, agricultural implements, furniture, chinaware, mincemeat, and soaps were key products of its diversified industries. There were six banks with a combined total of nearly $200 million in deposits, and in summer, the nearby lakes — particularly Skaneateles, Cazenovia, and Oneida — were major tourist attractions.

Then there were the newspapers themselves — the morning *Post-Standard* and the afternoon *Herald* and *Journal*. Together, they sold more than 176,000 copies a day and 269,000 on Sunday and carried nearly $3 million a year in advertising. For a city with only 250,000 residents, that struck Newhouse as tremendous. Syracuse's real problem, he concluded, was that its newspaper resources had been spread too thin.

He had dealt with a similar situation, though on a much smaller scale, only the year before on Long Island. There, both the *North Shore Journal* in Flushing and the *Star* in Long Island City had been in trouble. Though they were neighbors in northern and western Queens, they did not compete with each other or with the *Long Island Press*. Newhouse bought both in a package deal for $250,000, then merged the two into a single publication, the *Long Island Star-Journal*, serving both the North Shore and Long Island City. By eliminating one plant, he had been able to reduce his payroll by over a hundred full-time employees and to put the operation into the black almost immediately.

A similar package deal in Syracuse was likely to bring far greater rewards. It was also likely to involve greater complications. First, there was the matter of the *Journal*'s availability. Newhouse knew that Hearst's empire had fallen on hard times, and that the man he had admired for more than thirty years was selling off his unprofitable newspapers. But he didn't know until he started asking around that summer that the Hearst Corporation had already offered to sell the *Journal* for $900,000 to Jerome Barnum, the publisher of the morning *Post-Standard* and the man who had treated Newhouse and Victor Ridder so rudely in 1932. Hearst's Syracuse paper, Newhouse discovered upon further inquiry, owed some $600,000 in dividends to preferred shareholders; if they weren't paid off soon, Hearst would lose control of the *Journal* and, perhaps, his entire empire. Armed with this information, Newhouse immediately sent a feeler to the Hearst people by means of Smith Davis. For the same $900,000 that Barnum had been unwilling to pay, Davis reported back, Newhouse could have the *Journal* and do as he pleased with it.

The first piece of the puzzle had fallen into place. For a total of $1.9 million, it now appeared, Newhouse could acquire both papers. But could he reconcile their staffs and readers to a merger?

The two Syracuse papers had been fierce competitors for years and had developed strikingly different circulations. Readers of the *Journal* were treated to typical Hearst fare — big headlines, short news articles, great comics, and earthy columnists like Walter Winchell, Louella Parsons, and Damon Runyon. By comparison, the *Herald* was the epitome of respectability and catered to the city's establishment rather than to its blue-collar workers.

It would never have occurred to the papers' current owners to attempt to combine two such radically different publications, but to Newhouse they seemed made for each other. The *Journal*'s comics and syndicated features, combined with the *Herald*'s more comprehensive news coverage and stronger editorial page, would be a most attractive package. And if the merger Newhouse proposed didn't satisfy all the readers of the two papers, what choice did they have, anyway? Television had yet to be invented, commercial radio had barely been born, and the start-up costs for a new newspaper were prohibitive. Nor was the morning *Post-Standard* a true alternative, for in Syracuse, as in most of the U.S. in 1939, the afternoon newspaper was the main source of news and information. The nation's reading habits called for a paper at the end of the day, not with breakfast.

There remained but one other obstacle to Newhouse's ownership of the two papers. As he had learned from Jerome Barnum seven years before, Syracuse was a provincial, chauvinistic city, and its residents were mistrustful of downstaters, particularly big shots from New York City. To succeed with a readership that was 55 percent Catholic, he would have to keep the general public in the dark about his presence in town.

He sent a cautious response through Smith Davis to the O'Hara and Jenkins families, owners of the *Herald*: he would pay them their one million dollars, on condition that they stay on to run the combined publication and continue to give the appearance of being the paper's owners and operators. In addition, Davis reported, Newhouse would be unable to pay the entire sum in cash as the owners had hoped. After putting up $600,000 in cash for the Hearst people and promising them the remaining $300,000 in equal installments over the next three years, he had only enough cash left to cover half the *Herald*'s purchase price. But Davis soon convinced them that no one else would come anywhere near Newhouse's offer and that their continuing to run the paper, even in its new form, was a decided advantage.

The Sunday afternoon phone call to the golf course had been from Davis, announcing that Herald Company President Mary Jenkins and Publisher E. A. O'Hara had decided to accept Newhouse's terms.

Preparing the *Herald*'s plant to print double the number of papers each day was the next big task. For this, Newhouse brought in Clarence Rinne, who until that year had been general production manager of Booth Newspapers, publisher of eight dailies in Michigan. Rinne was a friend of Frederic Goudy, Chicago's famous designer of typefaces, and was himself an expert in typography, as well as all other phases of newspaper production.

Rinne had helped Newhouse before, in Long Island City and Jamaica, and by the middle of July he had whipped the *Herald* into shape for consolidated operations. At that point, Newhouse ordered the termination of 428 *Journal* employees whose services were no longer required. Eliminating their salaries was more than enough to offset the previous year's losses of $450,000 for both papers. As part of the consolidation, six Intertype machines were moved into the *Herald* building from the *Journal*'s plant, and a larger, more readable typeface, called Royal News, was instituted on the new *Herald-Journal*.

On the afternoon of 24 July 1939, the first issue of the new *Herald-Journal* hit the streets, containing a front-page "ANNOUNCEMENT!" from Mary Jenkins and E. A. O'Hara: "The *Syracuse Herald* has acquired the names of the *Syracuse Journal* and the *Syracuse Sunday American* [the Sunday edition of the *Journal*]. The *Herald* also has purchased from syndicate companies the features that heretofore have appeared in the *Journal* and *Sunday American* and which will now be published in this paper beginning with today's issue."

Though the Jenkins-O'Hara announcement carried no indication that the *Herald* itself had been sold or that anyone besides themselves had directed the merger, rumors in New York City of Newhouse's involvement in the deal were fanned by reports of his visits to Syracuse during the previous weeks. But when a reporter from *Editor & Publisher* asked if he'd been involved in the Syracuse merger, Newhouse responded by saying he had "no connection [with it] you can talk about." Had he bought the paper? "I have no announcement to make this week or any other week." Syracuse, he said, was simply "a lovely place to be."

Despite this secrecy, Newhouse wanted one group of Syracuse residents informed of his ownership of the *Herald-Journal* — the local merchants who controlled most of the paper's advertising. They, too, had heard the rumors that the *Herald-Journal* had a new owner and that he was a rough operator, who might squeeze them to death with higher rates. At Newhouse's insistence, a meeting with them was arranged.

From his earliest days walking up and down Broadway in Bayonne, Newhouse had followed two basic principles in dealing with advertisers: give them what they want, but never give anything for free. Before the merger of the *Herald* and the *Journal*, Syracuse's merchants had to pay ten cents a line to advertise in either paper; because there was so little overlap in circulation, this translated into an effective rate of twenty cents a line to reach the entire afternoon market. By combining the papers' operations, Newhouse was able to cut seven cents a line off his cost of publishing ads. The savings gave him a terrific lever to use on the merchants. He could offer the lower rates they wanted — at no cost to his newspaper — and, at the same time, obtain additional advertising.

"If you will agree to maintain your previous volume of advertising," he announced to the major advertisers, "the *Herald-Journal* will sell space to you at thirteen cents a line." The merchants could hardly believe it: instead of higher rates, they were being offered a 35-percent reduction. When Newhouse guaranteed rebates if circulation fell off from its August figure of 96,000 a day, they were sold.

The deal was, of course, even more of a bonanza for Newhouse and the *Herald-Journal*. Because newspaper circulation was lowest in August, there seemed little likelihood of his having to make good on his offer of rebates. More important, the merchants, perhaps not immediately appreciating the consequences of their bargain with Newhouse, had committed themselves to an increase of 30 percent with the paper. Newhouse was already saving more than $500,000 in salaries (by itself, enough to put the paper back in the black); now he would also pick up more than $1 million in new revenues, most of it pure profit. At that rate, he would recoup his entire investment in less than three years.

Newhouse's special understanding with the merchants of Syracuse had the effect of taking advertising away from the morning *Post-Standard* at a time when Jerome Barnum's paper could least afford it, for while Newhouse had been dickering over his acquisition of the *Herald* and the *Journal*, Barnum had begun construction of an expensive new plant for the *Post-Standard*. With the economy improving and newspaper advertising rapidly rising, the plant's formal opening in June 1940 should have been a festive occasion. But almost all the new ads were going to the *Herald-Journal*, and by the end of the next year, Barnum's paper was in so much trouble that he was reduced to offering it to Newhouse for $1.3 million — far less than the cost of its new plant. With his purchase of the *Post-Standard*, Newhouse took complete control of the city's newspapers.

On 14 January 1942, a small announcement on page one of the *Post-Standard* declared that Ernest L. Owen, formerly a newspaper publisher in Poughkeepsie, New York, had purchased the paper and was moving to town to manage it. Though Owen would serve as the *Post-Standard's* publisher, he never owned it. Yet, it was not until 1944, when Newhouse felt more secure about his presence in Syracuse, that he allowed the town's morning paper to make mention of his ownership.

Thereafter, Newhouse felt much freer to disclose his interest in both papers. One night a few years later, at a fancy local dinner party, he was introduced to the wife of a prominent Syracuse resident as the owner of the *Post-Standard.* "That's a fine paper," she gushed. "But that other terrible sheet!"

"I own that one, too," Newhouse told her gleefully.

Having caused most of the *Post-Standard's* difficulties in the first place by means of his predatory pricing practices at the *Herald-Journal*, Newhouse could now set about repairing the damage with new deals for the merchants of Syracuse. Most effective were special discounts for placing the same ad in both papers. Soon, despite severe wartime shortages and rationing, the *Post-Standard's* ad revenues were the highest in the paper's history. Not too many years later, Syracuse — once written off by newspaper people as a lousy town in which to do business — had gained so much stature in the industry that national advertising agencies began to view it as an ideal test market for their promotions.

With six newspapers now under his control — in Syracuse, Long Island City, Jamaica, Port Richmond, and Newark — Newhouse could no longer visit each of them every day, as he had when he owned just the *Advance*, *Press*, and *Ledger*. The trip to Syracuse alone consumed a full working day, but, because the city housed his most valuable property, he insisted on visiting it at least once a week. Thus, he began a routine that, with a few variations, was to last until 1977, when he was eighty-two years old.

Starting that summer, Newhouse could be found almost every Tuesday evening at Grand Central Station, boarding the overnight train for Syracuse. Once in his sleeping-car berth, he would prop his head up on three pillows and try to get a few hours' sleep before daybreak. The train would pull into Syracuse around three in the morning, but its sleeping car was gently shunted off to a siding so as not to disturb the passengers. At about six o'clock, Newhouse would emerge, an overnight bag in one hand, a small briefcase in the other. He would breakfast at the Syracuse Hotel, then walk briskly to the offices of the *Herald-Journal* at Franklin Street and Herald Place.

It was not long before both the hotel and the newspaper came to know what to expect from these visits. At the former, Newhouse quickly gained a reputation as a good tipper and seemed to go out of his way to be polite with the staff. At the latter, he was all business. He wanted a rundown, department by department, of how the last week had gone. Were there any special problems he could help with? Most of all, he wanted to know a few numbers. What had it cost per page to produce the paper during the past week? How many pages had the paper printed during that period, and how much of that had been advertising? What were the circulation figures?

Newhouse was taking the pulse of his new property. In his own mind, he had a clear idea of what the numbers should be; if there were the slightest discrepancy, he could figure out exactly what it meant. Each week, for example, the *Herald-Journal* published about twenty-five million pages. If the cost of preparing, printing, and delivering one of those pages went up by only a thousandth of a cent, or its ad revenues went down by a similar amount, there would be a loss on the order of $2,500 a week — $130,000 a year — and Newhouse would want to know what had caused it.

On each visit, he would also walk through the plant to check out its mood. However, because he did not want to be seen as meddling with the editorial product, as Hearst did, and because he was not much interested in it anyway, he scrupulously avoided the newsroom. But the other departments got the sort of attention he'd learned to give newspapers years before, when he performed some of the mechanical work himself. Just from observing a row of linotypists as he walked by, for example, he could tell whether they were working efficiently. He would also notice how many men were in the ad sales room, for he believed that shoe leather was the most important ingredient in successful advertising sales, and he was not pleased when he found the *Herald-Journal*'s salesmen in the building, even if they were talking up accounts over the telephone.

When something caught his attention, he'd pull a folded yellow sheet from his pocket. Removing the paper clip that held this makeshift pad together, he would search for an empty space and then, with the nubbin of a pencil extracted from the same pocket, jot the problem down in a scrawl that only he could decipher.

Department heads soon learned that matters that attracted Newhouse's attention would be brought up — politely, but sternly — the next week, and the week after that, and even the week after that, if need be, until they were rectified. Very little that was important to the success of the paper, it seemed to those who underwent the weekly grillings, escaped Newhouse's attention or his memory.

On these visits to the *Herald-Journal* plant, Newhouse carried a battered brown briefcase that soon became the subject of great speculation around the office, for nobody ever saw him open it. A standing joke had it that this was his money bag, and that at some point each Wednesday he would get hold of the past week's profits and stuff them into it, so as to have the pleasure of personally carrying the receipts back home. Actually, the briefcase contained material that was nearly as valuable to him as money — Louis Glickman's monthly reports on all his newspaper properties, as well as recent articles of interest from the trade press. Whenever he had a spare moment alone, he'd pull out a report or an article and study it.

After the regular round of morning meetings, Newhouse would go with one or more of his Syracuse executives for lunch at either the hotel or Walter White's restaurant, where steak was his standing order. He would then be driven to the train station, to spend the afternoon perusing the contents of his brown briefcase as the New York Central made its way back to Albany and then south along the east shore of the Hudson River to Manhattan.

Though Newhouse would remain downstate until the following Wednesday, hardly a day went by when his presence was not felt at the *Herald-Journal* in one way or another. Immediately after the merger, for example, he sent William Hofmann from the *Long Island Press* to Syracuse to keep an eye on things in his absence. Though possessing little in the way of initiative, Hofmann had long since proved his willingness to follow Newhouse's orders, and he obviously had a great deal of experience with Newhouse's management system. Clarence Rinne, who ran the production shop, also reported back regularly to him. On top of all that, the paper's new owner would often call Syracuse early in the morning from the telephone in his car — a practice that represented a major inconvenience to the *Herald-Journal*'s publisher, E. A. O'Hara.

O'Hara was a newspaper man in the traditional mold, hard-working and hard-drinking, and stories of his excesses were legion among Syracuse's newspaper reporters. Often, after a long evening at a local watering spot, he would decide he needed a taxicab, woozily telephone for one, and then order a final drink while he waited for its arrival. More often than not, this last shot for the road would lead to another, and then another, and soon the taxi would be forgotten. An hour or so later, another cab would be called, and the process might repeat itself. One night, so the story goes, O'Hara walked out of one of Syracuse's finer establishments to find fully half a dozen taxicabs lined up at the door, all waiting to give him a ride.

Years later, a friend asked how he managed to keep his drinking habits from interfering with his relationship with Newhouse. "That's easy," O'Hara replied. "Whenever I consume too much, I simply have the driver take me to the office, where I can sleep at my desk, certain not to miss the boss's call in the morning."

The Syracuse purchases meant that Newhouse was finally accorded the honor of being included with the likes of Paul Block, Frank E. and Guy Gannett, William Randolph Hearst, John S. Knight, and the Ridder brothers on *Editor & Publisher*'s annual list of "Principal Newspaper Chains of the United States." Now in his mid-forties, he had attained new heights of wealth and accomplishment. His publications, however, were far from significant. They were neither sufficiently big nor sufficiently respected to command the attention of his peers — even the notoriety he had gained from his fights with the Guild the decade before seemed to have worn off. In fact, as World War II approached, it hardly seemed possible that Newhouse would ever make a lasting imprint on the newspaper business.

17 The Good Life

FOR MITZI, S. I.'S OVERNIGHT TRIPS to Syracuse, added to the time he ordinarily put into the business, were the breaking point — she had to get away from Staten Island. When she and S. I. had first built their house there, and she'd been busy with her children, her mother, and her rock garden, she hadn't had much time to think about returning to Manhattan. In those days, the *Staten Island Advance* was everything they had.

But after her husband bought the *Long Island Press*, and then the *Newark Ledger*, the *Long Island City Star*, and the *Flushing Journal*, all that changed, and Manhattan became a powerful attraction. To Mitzi, it seemed the true center of the universe. She'd grown up there. S. I. had courted her there. And society, art, fashion — the things she most prized — all flourished there. The fact that her parents' business had failed there during the Depression only served to fuel her urge to stage a triumphant return.

S. I. must have been a little shocked, though, when he discovered exactly what his wife wanted. Even the address of the building she chose for their new home — 730 Park Avenue — was a problem. "If you came from the East Side," Henry Garfinkle later explained, "Park Avenue was a dirty word." It was simply too hoity-toity. But Mitzi was intent upon having the fourteen-room duplex apartment she had discovered on the seventh and eighth floors of a splendid building at the corner of East Seventy-first Street. Moreover, the pedigrees of the people who would be their new neighbors were made to order for her social ambitions. Composer Richard Rodgers and his wife Dorothy shared the entrance-way to the apartment Mitzi had chosen, and members of the Farkas family — then the owners of Alexander's department stores — also lived in the building. Just across Seventy-first Street to the north resided several families of Rockefellers, as well as the Marshall Fields. For her purposes, 730 Park Avenue was the ideal location.

As soon as they had purchased the apartment, Mitzi engaged John Gerald, an acquaintance of her mother's, to help with redecorating. Gerald had directed the reorganization of the Henry Ford Museum and, as he put it, had "done some large things for the Du Ponts." "In the first redecoration," he explained, "Mitzi wanted to do it in an antique French manner. Louis XVI and Louis XV. It was more or less out of the book — what all the rich people were doing then. I always kept in mind that they were small people. Luckily, despite all the hooped skirts of Marie Antoinette, there are no huge Louis XVI or Louis XV chairs."

A beautiful, spacious, wood-paneled room was designated as S. I.'s personal study; it was to serve as his main office for the rest of his life. There he maintained a filing cabinet for mementos such as the deed to the first house his family owned in Bayonne but kept few of the ordinary trappings of a huge corporate empire. There, too, he was able to introduce his boys to his business without taking them out of the house.

"A very substantial amount was involved in that first decoration," Gerald remembered. "I always talked to Sam before we went into any depth on money, and he was never tightfisted with anything Mitzi wanted."

In the spring of 1942, S. I. and Mitzi acquired a second impressive piece of property — Grace J. Maddock's eighty-acre estate in southern New Jersey. Located at Harbourton, northwest of Princeton in the foothills of the Sourland Mountains, "Greenlands" featured a fifteen-room main dwelling that dated to the American Revolution. Scattered about carefully landscaped grounds were a six-room cottage, a small pond, a swimming pool, a tennis court, a large stable, and a five-car garage. Once again, John Gerald was called in to help with the interiors and set about filling the main house with chintzes, hooked rugs, and plenty of antique pine and maple furniture. The result was a comfortable country retreat.

It was not only Mitzi's influence that led S. I. to purchase such fancy pieces of real estate and then to furnish them with so many fine things. The difficult years of his childhood had created in him an intense need to be rich, and now that he had money, he didn't hesitate to use it. So, during the early 1940s, when most of America was struggling with rationing and other unpleasant effects of World War II, Newhouse surrounded himself and his family with the kinds of luxury reserved for the very rich.

There were annual winter vacations in Florida and, as soon as the Atlantic became safe again, ocean voyages to Europe each fall. For Greenlands, he purchased a herd of Charolais cattle and joked to newspaper acquaintances that he made more on beef than he ever made with the *Newark Ledger*.

In Manhattan, there was private schooling for the boys and fine clothes for everyone in the family. Mitzi, of course, had been interested in fashion since her childhood, and now S. I. set about creating a more dapper image for himself. He bought dozens of silk ties and adopted double-breasted suits to camouflage his tendency to gain weight — the natural result of his and Mitzi's newfound penchant for dining out at New York's finer restaurants. When they had companions on such occasions, S. I. made it a point of honor to pay — which he did with $100 bills he habitually carried in his wallet.

Having that wad of cash in his pocket at all times was a source of great pride, as well as a tangible reminder that the difficult early days were over for good. Yet, aside from the security it provided, money didn't do much for Newhouse — he was just too impatient to enjoy the sorts of recreational pleasure it could buy.

"He was the itchiest fisher you'd ever see," recalled a Syracuse newspaperman who occasionally invited Newhouse on outings to the well-stocked lakes of upstate New York. Once, executives of the *Herald-Journal* even got their boss to accompany them on a fishing trip to Canada. Newhouse got in a boat, cast out his line, and caught a fish. Then, according to Steve Rogers, who was to become publisher of the Syracuse newspapers, "He put the rod down and said, 'Okay, let's go. I caught a fish.'"

On the golf course, his impatience was even more pronounced. "When he played golf around here," explained Wes Clark, dean of the School of Journalism at Syracuse University, "he used to run around the course — literally — to get the game over. He even tried using two balls once to see if it would give him more to do." Usually when he played at the Green Acres Country Club near Harbourton, he did so alone — so as not to be distracted or otherwise slowed down by partners.

But where Newhouse's impatience manifested itself most dramatically was with people. There were very few whose company he truly enjoyed, and there was nothing that seemed more wasteful to him than idle conversation. At work, he found an effective way of protecting himself from such annoyances: whenever someone entered his office, he stood up immediately to greet the visitor and then remained standing throughout the meeting. The idea was to get the intruder to state his business as quickly as possible and then be gone. "It took a great deal of determination to sit down when he was standing, and few did," explained one Newhouse publisher. And when Newhouse did relax this policy, it was usually to perch on the edge of a chair, leaving visitors with the impression that more pressing matters awaited his attention.

For the same reason, Newhouse had a horror of long business lunches and worked out various techniques to avoid being stuck in any one place for very long. At the Essex Hotel in Newark, for example, where he frequently took midday meals, he instructed the management to serve him as soon as he sat down with any non-fattening item on the menu.

In most people, such impatience would have led to frequent outbursts and moments of terrible rudeness, but Newhouse was also a man of tremendous self-discipline. "He was unfailingly polite to strangers, elevator operators, clerks, and people who worked for him," recalled publisher Dave Starr. "But the closer you were to him, the more responsible you were, the testier he could get." "He was always the soul of graciousness to his underlings," remembered Florence Glickman, widow of Newhouse's chief accountant. "My husband would say, 'When he yelled at you, you'd know you had arrived.'"

But in dealing with outsiders, politeness was always the rule. Good manners had been a trademark of Judge Lazarus, and bad manners — such as those exhibited by Jerome Barnum — had made a strong impression on Newhouse. Now that he had finally arrived, he would do his best to treat people decently, aware as well that having a good personal reputation could never hurt him in his business dealings. Mrs. Glickman recalled two incidents that put this side of his character in clear perspective. "Once," she said, "he wouldn't engage someone to do some work for him. When asked why, Mr. Newhouse explained that it was because the man was rude to waiters."

The second experience took place nearly a decade later, when Newhouse was the defendant in a lawsuit in Syracuse. "My husband went there every month for the audit," Mrs. Glickman explained. "He would have breakfast at the Cavalier Room in the Hotel Syracuse, which at that time was open only to men.

"Well, a new judge had been appointed to the case and was in the Cavalier Room for breakfast. He asked the maitre d' if he knew Newhouse and what did he think of him? The maitre d' said no finer man had been in the dining room and then told my husband about it. When the story was passed on to S. I., his response was, 'That's one time the five-dollar tip paid off.' "

Being polite, however, did little to enhance Newhouse's ability to relate to others. And, if anything, success at business had served to make him an even narrower person than he had been twenty or twenty-five years before, when he and Leo Rifkin relished their weekend adventures in the country and Sunday outings in Manhattan. Nor had Newhouse ever enjoyed reading anything but his trade journals — with the result that he remained surprisingly uninformed about subjects like politics and world affairs that so occupied the thoughts of most newspaper publishers. Most of Newhouse's acquaintances found his personality flat, almost opaque. Said a fellow newspaper publisher, who encountered him socially on several occasions but never did business with him, "You just couldn't believe this man was anything special. He never made a memorable remark."

That assessment was echoed by dozens of others. Typical was the recollection of former New York City Mayor John Lindsay: "You know, I just can't remember any of the conversations I had with him. What I do remember is that he seemed a nice man. . . . He had a twinkle in his eye."

Perhaps the most telling comment of all came from a Syracuse man who had business and social dealings with Newhouse over the course of more than three decades. "I used to tell my wife," said William Tolley, for many years chancellor of Syracuse University, " 'I think I could recite every conversation I've ever had with S. I.

Newhouse, from his opening comment to my reply, and so on.' 'Why, that would fill a book!' she said. I said, 'No, about fifteen pages.' "

Throughout Newhouse's adult life, less than a handful of men — and, save for Mitzi, no women — ever got close enough to him to discern his true personality, and those who did were mostly men much like himself — short, Jewish, born of immigrant parents, self-made. In sum, he befriended people with whom he could feel comfortable, in whose similar backgrounds he could sense an almost immediate kinship. These men happened as well to be younger than he was, and they treated him accordingly.

The man who probably got to know Newhouse best was Henry Garfinkle, the newsboy he'd put into business back in the early 1920s on Staten Island. Two decades later, Garfinkle was well on his way to attaining the goal he had set for himself as a young man. With the help of a few more interest-free loans, his Garfield News Company had expanded all over the New York metropolitan area.

After Staten Island, he went into business in Manhattan, starting on Lexington Avenue and Spring Street. Next, he expanded to Newark and La Guardia airports, then to the PATH tubes and, finally, to the Port Authority Bus Terminal. This last Garfield News location remained open 24 hours a day, 365 days a year, and was, in fact, the largest and busiest newsstand in the world.

With the profits from his business, Garfinkle was able to follow his old pal back to Manhattan, but to a building on the west side of Central Park, away from Park Avenue. He soon purchased a huge summer estate as well, in Marblehead, Massachusetts. Set on seven and a half acres of land that rolled gently down to the ocean, Garfinkle's "country place" featured a natural pool blasted out of the shoreline.

At least once every month, the two men, and sometimes their wives, got together — in Marblehead, at Greenlands, or even at the Press Box deli in Manhattan, their favorite hangout for lunch. According to Garfinkle, Newhouse simply was "not that friendly a fellow." Outside of work, his main interests seemed to be activities where he could be a spectator: sports and high-powered gossip. "Mitzi loved to rub elbows," Garfinkle recalled, "but S. I. loved to watch others."

Newhouse's other close friend during this period seemed tailor-made to accommodate those activities. He was newspaper columnist Leonard Lyons. Born Leonard Sucher on the Lower East Side in 1907, Lyons, too, was short and the child of Russian immigrants. He had worked his way through St. John's Law School, where he was first in his class, and had then practiced for five years in New York, before giving it up to write for the *New York Post*. His column, "The Lyons Den," was syndicated in dozens of newspapers all over the country.

Lyons was a gossip columnist, but he avoided the who's-sleeping-with-whom material typical of others plying his trade; instead, he reported six times a week on the doings and sayings of movie stars, political figures, artists, labor leaders, and other notables. Described as "not much of a personality, but a terrible name-dropper," he probably knew more famous people on a first-name basis than any other working journalist. According to his son Jeffrey, when S. I. and Leonard were together, which was frequently, "they just traded stories. S. I. listened a good deal more than he talked."

On occasion, S. I. and Mitzi would join Lyons for a portion of his daily rounds, which involved visiting thirteen clubs twice a day. He'd start at one in the afternoon at Sardi's and continue until around four the next morning, when he'd tie up any loose ends with a final visit to P. J. Clarke's. Then he'd return home to write his column and send it over to the *Post* by taxicab. It was understood, however, that under no circumstances would S. I. Newhouse's name appear in "The Lyons Den."

As close as they were to him, neither Lyons nor Garfinkle could supply Newhouse with the type of friendship that, by itself, could sustain him. In that regard, they were like all the money he now had — good for his sense of security but otherwise not all that meaningful. And, as S. I. once told Steve Rogers, he had more money than he could ever spend. When he got right down to thinking about it, he said, he didn't really have anything else to do but work.

18 Jersey City

IF MONEY HAD BEEN POURING in from Newhouse's newspapers before the Syracuse purchase/merger in the summer of 1939, afterwards it flowed as if from a gusher. Despite what had become a rather high style of living, by his own admission Newhouse could not find ways to spend the earnings of even the *Staten Island Advance* in a given year. Besides, his basic principle was to retain as much capital as possible within the tax laws, not to dissipate it. That, in turn, made additional purchases inevitable.

First came Paul Block's *Newark Star-Eagle*, which Newhouse got hold of that November. As a second afternoon paper, the *Star-Eagle* had been caught in a whipsaw between the still growing dominance of the *News* in central Newark and the surprising success of Newhouse's *Ledger* in surrounding areas. Finally, Block just gave up, and rather than make a deal with the Scudders, sold to Newhouse.

Following what was by then a well-established formula, Newhouse, in turn, merged the *Star-Eagle* with the *Ledger* to form the *Star-Ledger*. In the process, nearly all of the former's three hundred employees were let go. Though the combined publication remained well behind the *News* in every respect — save for its uncanny ability to print the most outrageous news stories in town — from a business standpoint, it was a healthier operation than either of its predecessors.

There followed in 1942 Newhouse's purchase of the *Syracuse Post-Standard* and in 1945 two very significant deals. The first of these was his buy-out of William Hofmann. By virtue of his share of the stock in the Long Island Daily Press Publishing Company, Hofmann owned nearly a fifth of Newhouse's entire business enterprise. The only papers he did not have pieces of were the *Staten Island*

■ 130

Advance and *Long Island Star-Journal.* By comparison, none of S. I.'s brothers or sisters had so much as a single share of common stock in any of the papers, though their contributions to the family business had been far greater than Hofmann's.

Hofmann could have continued to watch his holdings grow along with Newhouse's, but in 1945, at the age of sixty, he decided he would rather spend his remaining years fulfilling an old dream — that of owning and operating a baseball team. So he sold his 17-percent interest in the Newhouse newspapers to his boss for $2 million and then turned around and plunked down a good part of the proceeds on the Syracuse Chiefs of the International League.

At first blush, the amount Hofmann received might have seemed like an incredible windfall, but given the true value of his newspaper holdings at the time, it was just a fraction of what he deserved. In 1945, even judged by rather conservative standards, newspapers were considered to be worth at least ten times their net earnings. At the time, Newhouse's papers were making between $2 and $2.5 million a year, so Hofmann's share was actually worth between $4 and $5 million — at least twice what he got. Even at the higher price, Newhouse would have come out way ahead in the long run.

Later that year, on 15 November, Newhouse met with Walter Dear, publisher of the *Jersey Journal*, at the Lawyers Club in Manhattan. After a quick meal, they retired to the back part of the club for a private conversation, attended only by Newhouse's attorney, Charles Goldman. "Sam," said Walter, "I want to get out of the *Jersey Journal*. I want to sell my stock."

From the time of his initial employment at the *Bayonne Times*, Newhouse had coveted the *Journal* in nearby Jersey City. Published in the heart of a teeming, heavily industrialized peninsula, it was the biggest and most profitable newspaper operation in all of Hudson County, and the staff never let anyone forget it. They had pushed S. I. around mercilessly when, as a teenager, he had tried to solicit ads for the *Times*. Even when he'd succeeded, the *Journal*'s business department had made it difficult for him to get hold of the mats he needed. These and other indignities had stayed with him over the intervening years, while his appreciation of the paper's extraordinary earning potential had continued to grow.

When Newhouse first became acquainted with the *Journal* in

1912, it was in the hands of Walter Dear and his brother, Joseph A. Dear. Walter ran the business side, while Joseph oversaw editorial operations. During the succeeding years, the paper had been remarkable neither for its content nor its appearance, though once, in 1929, it did have the temerity to oppose Hudson County's powerful political boss Frank Hague, when he sought reelection as mayor of Jersey City. Hague's machine, however, forced news dealers to stop carrying the *Journal* and local merchants to curtail their advertising. After Hague had been retained by a healthy margin, the *Journal* retreated to its old neutral ways, some $50,000 poorer and sufficiently chastised that it never attempted to make big political waves again.

Not long after the Hague debacle, the elder Dear, Joseph A., brought his son Albert into the business. Albert took readily to newspapering and soon dreamed of owning the *Journal* by himself. By 1937, he was negotiating for his uncle's share of the company, and three years later, he succeeded in buying out his father. Negotiations with Uncle Walter proved both slow and fitful, but in early 1945, around the time Newhouse was buying out Hofmann, Albert believed that his uncle was ready to accept a deal that would net him $250,000 in cash and a note for an additional $150,000 in return for his half of the Evening Journal Association. He was further encouraged when Walter sent details of the proposed transaction to the U.S. Treasury Department for a ruling on its tax consequences.

Unknown to Albert, though, Walter had come to doubt his nephew's business skills, and he wanted more cash for his share of the paper's stock. Accordingly, he had secretly engaged a newspaper broker to seek a better deal outside the family. Of several potential purchasers, Newhouse was the one the broker preferred. With previous newspaper experience in Hudson County, with another paper in the state, and with plenty of available cash, he fitted Walter Dear's specifications perfectly.

"I am willing to sell now if I can get my price," Dear told Newhouse at the meeting the broker eventually arranged between them at the Lawyers Club. "I want $450,000—all cash."

"O.K., Walter, we have a deal," Newhouse said, reaching out his hand toward the older, taller man. The money was peanuts, given the larger plan he had in mind for the *Journal*. After acquiring Walter's stock, he expected to be able to get the other half from Albert. Then, he would buy the *Bayonne Times* and the *Jersey Ob-*

server in nearby Hoboken, and merge all three into a single, county-wide publication, which, he figured, would have as much earning potential as any of his other papers.

It was a plan he had thought about for months; the prospect so excited him that he discussed it with his hospital-bound father that summer. Even on his deathbed, however, Meyer could not begin to understand his oldest son. "Sammy, why?" he asked. "What do you need it for?" He died on 20 June 1945, not having received a satisfactory explanation.

One aspect of his purchase of half the *Jersey Journal* still weighed on Newhouse's mind. He could not give it the time and attention he'd been able to lavish on his other properties, and he worried that a sudden change in ownership might cause labor unrest at the paper, especially given his record of letting hundreds of workers go in each of the three mergers he'd recently engineered. So, later that month, when he met with Walter Dear to close the sale, he pleaded with him to stay on. If the sale were announced at the same time as the elder Dear's retirement, Newhouse explained, "it is going to come as a terrific shock to the employees. Their sense of security would be gone. . . . You ought to stay there and assure them of the stability of their jobs."

Newhouse persisted for the better part of an hour and finally, after assuring Walter that he would continue to receive $26,000 a year in salary, he got his way. Walter would stay at the *Journal* for an additional two years, but only on condition that his nephew approve the arrangement.

Albert still knew nothing about the sale, though. It wasn't until the next day, Thanksgiving, when Walter paid Albert and his wife, Cyrene, a visit to invite them to meet with Newhouse over lunch on Friday that Albert realized how severely his uncle had betrayed him. "There was a lot of heat generated at that luncheon," Newhouse later testified. "A lot of steam let out." From one end of the table, Cyrene Dear accused Walter of being a traitor to the family — "a modern Esau." At the other, Albert was equally enraged. Under no circumstances, he told Newhouse, would he agree to let Walter stay on at the paper. "My uncle sold out," he argued, "and now he has got to get out."

"This thing is not nearly as bad as you think it is," Newhouse assured him. "We will continue the same policies that have been pursued in the past. It is not going to make any difference to you whether I own the stock or Walter owns the stock." Newhouse topped off his appeal by suggesting that the *Journal* set up scholarships to pay for the Dears' four sons' college educations and mentioned that the oldest boy could be placed on the paper's payroll right away, just as Ed Russell had been in Newark. But Albert would have none of it. "Get somebody else," he demanded. "I don't care who you get, but Walter can't stay there."

Newhouse had his own way of dealing with people who seemed to be blocking his path. He would begin politely and reasonably, as he had with young Dear, but if he sensed that such an approach wasn't working, he would become most obstinate. "Albert," he finally said after all the sweet talk had failed to sway him, "this is just something you will have to put up with. You can't do anything about it." And then he explained why.

Unknown to Albert Dear, in 1938, the New Jersey Legislature had passed a law providing for the operation of companies whose managements were deadlocked. "If you don't approve," Newhouse said, "[Walter] will resign." That would leave the Evening Journal Association without a treasurer and thus unable to function. "If the company can't function," Newhouse concluded, "then one of us will have to go into court and ask for dissolution and have the assets sold and the proceeds divided between us. Is that what you want?"

Albert suddenly became quite agreeable. Not only would he allow his uncle to stay on for two years, he would even serve as master of ceremonies at the cocktail party at which the *Journal*'s employees would be informed of the sale and of Walter's continuing employment.

Newhouse did make one immediate change in personnel, however. The woman who had given him such a tough time picking up ad proofs three decades before was still working for the *Journal*. When Newhouse took over, she found herself out of a job. On the other hand, he took very good care of the one man in the composing room who had always helped with the proofs. Otherwise, the paper remained about the same — undistinguished in both content and appearance but highly profitable. Glickman & Company was retained to perform accounting work, of course, and Newhouse began visiting one morning a week for a couple of hours. "S. I. was very businesslike," recalled Walter Dear's daughter, Katherine, who

Sammy (*front row, center*) on graduation day in 1908:
"A tiny postage stamp taking a message out into the world."

On board the *Aquitania* in 1934: Heywood Broun's greeting party would spoil S. I. and Mitzi's return from their delayed honeymoon cruise. *Opposite:* Later, their returns were happier.

From Bayonne to Staten Island: The Tudor house that S. I. had built for Mitzi at 25 Ward Avenue was larger than the building on Avenue C—which contained both Judge Lazarus's law practice and the *Times*. Newhouse put his stamp on the interior decoration with a banister (*inset*) comprised of his first initials.

Long Island Press Resumes After Week's Suspension — Strike Settled

FOR the second time in two weeks the strike of the 62 editorial workers on the *Jamaica Long Island Daily Press* was ended Thursday with the signing of a "memorandum" to be attached to the contract signed a week ago Monday. The strikers returned to work Thursday afternoon and the paper was expected to appear Friday for the first time since the previous Saturday.

S. I. NEWHOUSE

The strike was resumed Thursday, April 29, with the newspaper guild challenging the "good faith" of the Press management in discharging 25

WILLIAM HOFMANN   PHILIP HOCHSTEIN

jured, when the picket line attempted to keep out mechanical workers.

In a half-page advertisement in the *New York Times* May 1 Mr. Hofmann stated that he was discontinuing publication "involuntarily." He said his mechanical workers had not been able to pass through the picket lines.

Police trying to push pickets away from front of *Long Island Daily Press* plant in Jamaica, L. I., April 30, when 250 American Newspaper Guild pickets protested dismissal of 25 guildsmen from the Press staff following settlement of previous three-week strike.

May 1937: *Editor & Publisher* reports on Newhouse's battle with the Guild on Long Island.

A press lord in his own right: Newhouse in his Park Avenue study in 1955—the year he "bought" Birmingham and St. Louis. *Below:* Two trusted associates. With a little help from his friend, Henry Garfinkle (*left*) became the world's biggest newsboy. The favor was returned. Harrisburg publisher Ernie Doepke (*right*) saw S. I. as "one of God's noble men."

While the Portland newspaper strike raged on, Newhouse stepped up his pursuit of new "properties." Chauffeured early each morning from his Park Avenue duplex, he finally made it to the top in 1972, when he took charge of the New Orleans newspapers. Unlike others who resisted Newhouse's advances, *Times-Picayune* vice-president Robert Gough (*right*) was glad to show the new owner around.

Time

Frank Sterrett/Oregon Historical Society

Newhouse's Louisiana purchase put him on the cover of *Time,* but it was his acquisition of Condé Nast that provided his wife entrée into society. In December of 1964 Mitzi posed for photos at home after being named one of the year's best-dressed fashion personalities. A glowing profile in *Vogue* earlier that year had affirmed her "arrival."

Wide World

Cathy Cheney

PEOPLE ARE TALKING ABOUT ...

PEOPLE ARE TALKING ABOUT ...

MRS. SAMUEL I. NEWHO

TWENTY-FIVE CENTS

JULY 27, 1962

TIME

THE WEEKLY NEWSMAGAZINE

PUBLISHER
SAM NEWHOUSE

VOL. LXXX NO. 4
(REG. U.S. PAT. OFF.)

A free press must be fortified
with greater knowledge of the world
and skill in the arts of expression

SAMUEL I. NEWHOUSE

Courtesy: Syracuse University

Dedicating the Newhouse Communications Center (*inset*) in August of 1964. The inscription in the main building's Dedication Hall was arrived at after lengthy debate. Newhouse overcame his shyness to deliver a moving speech the night before the ceremony. After the dedication, S. I. and Mitzi posed for photographs with the family, Nelson and Happy Rockefeller, and LBJ and Lady Bird.

Wide World

By 1976, the empire's creator had finally ceded control to sons Si (*left*) and Donald (*right*). Three years later, he was laid to rest alongside other family members in Baron Hirsch Cemetery on Staten Island.

Frank J. Johns

served as the newspaper's assistant treasurer at the time. "He didn't sit and relax. He was always busy. He moved rapidly and thought rapidly. One other thing I remember about him was his car. Its license plate was SIN 1. It was a big black car with a telephone in it. If there were any problems during the rest of the week, you could always get an answer from him by the telephone."

At the outset, Newhouse's weekly conferences with Walter and Albert Dear and with the paper's business manager, Rudy Lent, went well. But toward the end of 1947, when Walter's contract was about to expire, there was trouble, and Albert and S. I.'s disagreements became increasingly vehement.

Newsprint, for example, was in short supply, and Newhouse tried to convince Albert that the *Journal* should buy what it needed — some 360 tons that year — from the *Long Island Press*, which had plenty left in its stockpile. The spindles on the *Press*'s newsprint weren't quite right, so Newhouse suggested jury-rigging the *Journal*'s equipment. Albert refused and, instead, bought paper on the black market at nearly double the price Newhouse offered. Albert further antagonized his partner by hiring a series of people Newhouse found "personally obnoxious."

All along, Albert later testified, Newhouse had promised to get rid of Walter at the end of two years, but in January 1948, he apparently changed his mind. At a directors' meeting that month, he moved to renew Walter's contract, a motion Albert and Cyrene Dear voted to block. Thereafter, relations between the paper's two owners broke down entirely. Each week, the first, and usually the only, item on Newhouse's agenda during his regular visit to the *Journal* was the matter of Walter's contract. When he couldn't persuade Albert with words, he stopped signing his paychecks; soon he cut off dividends as well. The effect was pronounced. As Katherine Dear remembered, "Albert had several boys to put through school. Cutting off his salary really put the bite on him."

There was, finally, the threat of going to court to dissolve the company, and when Albert and Cyrene remained unmoved by his other efforts, Newhouse plunged ahead. The lawsuit turned out to be a long, difficult, and widely publicized affair. For the first time in his life, Newhouse was put on the stand for a healthy cross-examination. Though he would be involved in much litigation in the years to come, this was one of the few occasions he ever testified himself.

He turned out to be a formidable witness, as was evident in this exchange with Albert Dear's attorney, James Carpenter:

CARPENTER: You are the treasurer. Are you violating the bylaws when you refuse to sign a check for a salary that has been authorized by the Board of Directors? He was president of the company, wasn't he?

NEWHOUSE: Certainly, but he was not acting as president when he was doing things that were unauthorized.

CARPENTER: And those are what?

NEWHOUSE: Buying newsprint at black-market prices, paying double for it; hiring people objectionable to me, which is contrary to the bylaws.

CARPENTER: Wait a minute. Let us get into that. You say he bought newsprint at black-market prices? Didn't you refuse to authorize him to buy newsprint with the hope thereby that the *Jersey Journal* would not have paper?

NEWHOUSE: That is ridiculous. I offered him 360 tons of newsprint from my other papers, and he refused to accept it because it was inconvenient to run them on the presses, and we are running it on all our presses.

CARPENTER: As a matter of fact, he had borrowed from your Long Island paper a lot of paper, hadn't he?

NEWHOUSE: He had not borrowed a lot. He got a little, then he refused to accept the rest.

CARPENTER: Will you tell us why?

NEWHOUSE: Because it was inconvenient to run on the presses.

CARPENTER: They were rolls of paper of a size that didn't fit the *Jersey Journal*, weren't they?

NEWHOUSE: The same size that we run all our papers and every paper in the United States is running.

CARPENTER: Will you answer the question?

NEWHOUSE: What? Aren't of the size that can be run on the *Jersey Journal*?

CARPENTER: You brought over to him a spindle from one of your papers so as to enable the *Jersey Journal* to run the paper?

NEWHOUSE: That's correct. The *New York Times* uses the same spindle, too.

CARPENTER: At that time, there was a terrific shortage of newsprint?

NEWHOUSE: That's right.

CARPENTER: You say the president of the company charged with the production of that paper every day had no right to go out and buy paper to keep the paper running?

NEWHOUSE: Not at black-market prices, no, sir. He paid $100 a ton extra for it.

The case was finally decided on 12 July 1951, when New Jersey Superior Court Judge Thomas J. Stanton ruled in Newhouse's favor. As a result, a private sale of the assets of the Evening Journal Association was scheduled to be conducted the following October in the boardroom of the First National Bank in Jersey City. The auction would begin at $500,000 and would continue by means of sealed bids in minimum increments of $10,000. Dear and Newhouse were to be the only participants, each, in effect, bidding for the right to buy out the other.

Newhouse expected a quick end to the proceedings on 16 October, but by the time the bidding reached $1 million — more than twice what he'd paid for Walter's half of the company — he must have realized he was in for an ordeal. And by the time the bidding reached $2 million the paper's true value had long since been passed — the competitors' main concern now was saving face. Newhouse confided in several associates, including Phil Hochstein, that he felt that if he did not outbid Albert, people might think he'd been wrong to take the matter to court in the first place. Besides, he already had made arrangements to buy the *Jersey Observer* for $1 million, and without control of the *Journal*, he would have to back out of the *Observer* deal as well.

And so the bidding continued. Two million one. Two million two. Two million three. Finally, Albert caved in, but not before extracting a terrific price — $2,310,000 — for his half of the paper. He had been able to stay in the bidding so long because secret financial support had been arranged for him by J. I. Kislack, a Newark realtor. Kislack, in turn, had talked members of the Scudder family, whose *Newark Evening News* competed directly with Newhouse's *Star-Ledger*, into agreeing to put up as much as $3 million should Albert risk going that high.

The price Newhouse paid was sufficient to enable Albert and Cyrene Dear to buy a chain of newspapers of their own. In a few years, Dear Publications, Inc., would own papers in Lynn, Massachusetts; Gallipolis, Ohio; Sedalia, Alabama; and New Kensington,

Pennsylvania. Albert Dear, however, could not depart the *Jersey Journal* without making a few telling remarks about his nemesis's motives. "Like many other publishers," he told a reporter from *Editor & Publisher* that October, "Mr. Newhouse has a problem created by the strange tax laws that we have. Every time Mr. Newhouse buys a newspaper, he soon has money piling up to put into another newspaper." In fact, even as the *Jersey Journal* litigation was winding its way through the courts, Newhouse was buying three more newspapers — two in Harrisburg, Pennsylvania, and one in Portland, Oregon.

A few years after the bidding war for control of the *Jersey Journal*, Newhouse ran into Walter Dear again at a press association meeting. He hadn't seen his old acquaintance for some time but had been waiting to tell him something.

"Walter," he said, "I learned a lesson on my deal with you. It's not good having just 50 percent."

19 Harrisburg

MARIE RIDDER NEVER RECEIVED a satisfactory explanation of her father-in-law's strange behavior at their first meeting. "It was the last Thursday in April of 1948," she recalled. "Walter and I were going to be married on the twenty-second of May, and I was a bit apprehensive about meeting Mr. Ridder.

"We had lunch at the Park Lane Hotel in New York, but all he could talk about was S. I. Newhouse. He was so annoyed at Mr. Newhouse that he didn't even look me over. In fact, I don't think he addressed me at all. Newhouse apparently had been a great friend of my father-in-law's and had betrayed the friendship. My father-in-law was just all wrought up. He said Newhouse only looked at newspapers as businesses, and that Newhouse was tricky. That's all I ever knew. It was a very surprising encounter."

Victor Ridder had good cause to be angry. He'd known Newhouse for nearly two decades. Although their relationship sprang largely from a mutual interest in newspapers, it ran deeper than that. Victor was an ardent bridge player, and he enjoyed having Newhouse join the Saturday and Sunday afternoon games he organized at his Seventy-ninth Street brownstone. He found that his friend, though rarely very talkative, had an uncanny way of keeping track of the cards and was a terrific partner.

The 1932 deal for the *Long Island Press* had also drawn the two young newspaper publishers closer. Thanks to it, the Ridder brothers had been able to avoid financial embarrassment, and Newhouse had acquired his first big money-maker. For more than fourteen years after this important transaction, Victor and S. I. had remained on what seemed to others to be good terms. Then, in June 1946, in the capital of Pennsylvania, a state in which neither man had ever shown much interest, a newspaper publisher died. With his death were sown the seeds of Victor Ridder's betrayal.

Vance McCormick had for years been one of Harrisburg's leading citizens. A cousin of the Chicago McCormicks (who ran the International Reaper Company), he first made a name for himself at Yale, where he was a football star, leading the team's "Flying V" formation. In Harrisburg, he was an unstinting civic activist whose good works were legion. In addition to serving as mayor in the early 1900s and being a key supporter of Woodrow Wilson's presidential campaigns, he led the drive to reclaim Harrisburg's frontage along the Susquehanna River. His sense of civic duty was such that he financed local street improvements out of his own pocket.

McCormick's greatest contribution to local affairs, though, came from the newspapers he ran in Harrisburg. He acquired the morning *Patriot* in 1902 and founded the *Evening News* in 1917. In stark contrast to the city's third daily paper (the Stackpole family's staunchly conservative evening *Telegraph*), both McCormick publications were actively liberal. Both were also highly profitable; by the time of McCormick's death, they sold more than 83,000 copies a day in Harrisburg (61,000 *Evening News*'s and 22,000 *Patriots*) and earned more than half a million dollars a year.

At his demise, McCormick left a large estate, and with it a $2-million federal tax obligation. His executors determined that the simplest way to satisfy this huge debt would be to sell the Patriot Company, which published the newspapers. They would be picky about choosing a buyer, though, because Mrs. McCormick wanted to ensure that her husband's most prized possession did not end up in the wrong hands. The Stackpoles, for example, were out; Vance abhorred their politics and would have heartily opposed a newspaper monopoly in Harrisburg. Out-of-towners and chain operators would also be discouraged. Finally, Annie McCormick had a consideration of her own. She wanted the new owner of the *Patriot* and *Evening News* to be someone from society's upper crust — a person whose good family and high social standing would by itself bring distinction to the newspapers.

In June 1947, the Patriot Company was put up for sale, and Mrs. McCormick retired for the summer to Bar Harbor, Maine, leaving executives at the local Dauphin Deposit Bank to sort through suitors. The bank figured the Patriot Company was worth at least $2.3

million — an amount a group of local businessmen appeared willing to offer. However, bank officials grew uneasy when it appeared that the Harrisburg group would have trouble making good on its bid. Worse, the other interested parties — including Frank Gannett, John Knight, the Ridder brothers, and Newhouse — were all chain operators, and all were from out of town.

While negotiations for the Patriot Company continued, Annie McCormick held a lavish reception after one of Bar Harbor's big summer weddings. Among the guests was Newhouse's old ally Edwin Russell. Lacking his father's unpredictable nature, Edwin had inherited L. T. Russell's extraordinary good looks and gregariousness. In 1940, having worked for Newhouse for five years as Associate Publisher of the *Newark Ledger,* he enlisted in the British Royal Navy. After Pearl Harbor, he transferred to the United States Navy and served with distinction in Africa and Europe, and later in the Pacific.

Between tours of duty, Ed Russell became party to a most propitious union. On 15 May 1943, he was married to Lady Sarah Spencer-Churchill, daughter of the Duke of Marlborough, granddaughter of Consuelo Vanderbilt, and, most significant, first cousin of Winston Churchill. It was Lady Sarah's family and social connections, in fact, that five years later brought the couple to Bar Harbor and to Mrs. McCormick's party.

By this time, Ed Russell, now in his early thirties, had obviously become very much a social creature. He was, as one long-time acquaintance described him, "slim, narrow-faced, a jodhpur type. You could mistake him for a Britisher, and he certainly was not out of place on a Du Pont estate at a social occasion." He was also just the sort of person to whom Annie McCormick would be attracted.

As the two became better acquainted at the reception, their conversation turned to what Edwin did for a living, and he told her about his naval exploits and his position at the *Ledger* in Newark. The more she listened to this strikingly handsome war hero and Churchill relative, the more Annie McCormick felt he was the right man for her husband's newspapers. She told him about the situation at the Patriot Company and the trouble the bank was having finding a satisfactory buyer. Would Russell and his wife and two young children be interested in moving to Harrisburg and taking over the *Patriot* and the *Evening News?*

In no time at all, Russell was on the phone, placing a long-distance call to Newhouse, whom he knew to be greatly interested in the Patriot Company. Because of Mrs. McCormick's and the bank's bias against out-of-towners and chain operators, Newhouse had sensed that there was little chance he would be allowed to buy the papers, no matter how much he was willing to pay for them. And even if those considerable barriers could be overcome somehow, he suspected that his being Jewish would disqualify him from a serious shot at Harrisburg. Now, with Ed Russell's phone call, he suddenly had a tremendous advantage over the other bidders, for Russell could provide him with the social standing and the promise of local ownership that he needed. Just as William Randolph Hearst had used Paul Block as a front to buy newspapers in cities where Hearst himself was unacceptable to the sellers, so Newhouse would now use Ed Russell.

Before leaving Bar Harbor that weekend, Russell had agreed to serve as a straw man for Newhouse and, in addition, had obtained a commitment to sell from Mrs. McCormick. He then headed off to Harrisburg to pass muster before the Dauphin Deposit Bank and Trust Company. Only a few days previously, word had leaked out in newspaper circles that the bank was seriously considering giving the deal to the Ridder brothers, despite their obvious failure to meet Mrs. McCormick's qualifications. Russell's war record, his connection with the Churchills, and his recommendation from Mrs. McCormick, combined with the fact that he suddenly had $2.3 million on deposit at Manufacturers Hanover Trust in New York, dashed the Ridder brothers' chances and broke the logjam over the sale of the Patriot Company.

On 25 August 1947, the documents were signed in Harrisburg, and the next day the *Patriot* and *Evening News* ran front-page stories informing their readers of the sale. "Edwin F. Russell, Formerly of Newark, Is Publisher," headlined the *Patriot*. "Served in Navy in Recent War; Married Churchill's Cousin." Lengthy profiles of the new owner appeared in both papers, as well as the texts of formal statements by Russell and Mrs. McCormick.

"These papers," said McCormick's widow, "have been not only publishers of news but have consistently advocated civic and municipal improvement and advancement, and protested against destructive and anti-social forces. . . . Mr. McCormick was strongly of this opinion, and I believe that this can best be assured by ownership of the papers by an individual of the highest integrity and character . . . who will give the papers his personal attention."

In short order, the Russells purchased a house in Harrisburg, at 115 North Street, and moved to town. No mention was made anywhere in the newspaper stories or in Russell's conversations with the bank or even with Mrs. McCormick that the true buyer was S. I. Newhouse, the very sort of chain operator Vance McCormick had detested and the sort of person whose social credentials his widow would have found utterly unacceptable. "Certainly, none of us knew of the connection between Newhouse and Russell," W. D. Lewis, then a vice-president at Dauphin Deposit and subsequently chairman of the bank's board, explained. "We would have preferred to have the purchaser of the paper not be a chain operator and that the purchaser live here. Those people who cared were fooled, including the bank."

It wasn't until several years later that Lewis got the true story from Russell. "We were in a general discussion," he recalled. "He said he was an agent for Newhouse." Another person to whom Russell fessed up was Ernie Doepke, then advertising manager for the Patriot Company and, later, Russell's successor as publisher. "Ed Russell and I were very good friends," Doepke explained. "Ed told me the whole story. He bought the paper with S. I.'s money, in Bar Harbor, Maine. I am sure the understanding was from the beginning."

The ruse went beyond mere silence about the Russell-Newhouse connection. For one thing, Newhouse submitted a bid of his own for the Patriot Company, offering $50,000 more than Russell. He would thus appear a loser in the selection process, and suspicions about his involvement could be blunted.

For his part, Russell suggested publicly that he and Newhouse had had a falling-out. "The deciding factor in my decision to break away from the Newhouse organization was almost a complete difference between us on the editorial policies and responsibilities," he told *Editor & Publisher* at the time. In the same interview, he emphasized that he had quit his job with Newhouse in Newark and that he was not about to "surrender the independence I have gained in the acquisition of [the *Patriot* and the *Evening News*]." More than three decades later, Russell continued to insist that he had not acted as a front man. "There was no borrowing from Newhouse," he maintained. "I have no idea how Newhouse got to Harrisburg."

Despite such protestations, Russell apparently remained Newhouse's loyal undercover agent throughout his first years in Harrisburg. His next assignment was to arrange for his principal to take over the only remaining competition, the *Harrisburg Telegraph*, which meant getting to the Stackpole family. The running of the *Telegraph* had been entrusted to a brother, A. H., but ownership was divided between him, another brother, and two sisters.

"Eddie Russell wined and dined A. H. in New York," recalled Meade Detwiler, a Stackpole in-law in Harrisburg. Very soon, a deal was reached whereby the *Telegraph* would be sold — for a mere $400,000. "E. J. [the other Stackpole brother] was very disturbed about the sale," Detwiler continued. "He didn't know to whom they were selling. Nor did his sisters. Newhouse's ownership came as a surprise to us."

On 19 January 1948, Newhouse announced that he had bought the *Harrisburg Telegraph*; Brigadier General Albert H. Stackpole, he said, would stay on as editor and publisher. In a little over two months, though, the *Telegraph* was out of business, and Stackpole was installed in a new sinecure, as Executive Editor of the Patriot News Company, which had just purchased the *Telegraph*'s features, subscription lists, and comics as part of what was becoming a Newhouse trademark — a newspaper merger. As far as the residents of Harrisburg were concerned, however, Ed Russell remained in charge of the new operation and, ostensibly, was majority owner of the expanded *Patriot* and *News*. Explained a man who was with the *Patriot* at the time, "There was a period when there was a smoke screen still maintained."

In fact, it wasn't until 29 September 1949, that a small weekly publication called the *Harrisburg Home Star* made the ownership question a public issue. "Is Russell really the owner, as he claims to be?" the *Home Star* asked that week. "Or is he merely a figurehead representing the Newhouse interests?"

When he added the *Telegraph*'s nameplate to that of the *Evening News*, Newhouse took an additional step to ensure continued dominance of Harrisburg's newspaper business. From the time of the sale of the *Telegraph*, there had been talk in town that some of the same local businessmen who had tried to buy the Patriot Company the previous year were now interested in starting a newspaper of their own. The suspension and merger of the *Telegraph* might provide them, at a relatively low cost, the machinery they needed to get their new publication off the ground. Without equipment, though, there could be no new paper, and the very day the merger was announced — 27 March 1948 (Good Friday) Newhouse ordered all the *Telegraph*'s presses and linotypes broken down and carted out of the plant.

Just as suddenly, during the next few weeks, a full complement of Newhouse people arrived in Harrisburg to supervise the enlarged operations of the Patriot Company. Phil Hochstein became a frequent visitor in town; another loyal Newhouse man, Eugene Farrell, came from the *Long Island Star-Journal* to serve as managing editor of both the *Patriot* and the *News-Telegraph*; one of S. I.'s cousins, Pat Newhouse, came down from Syracuse to run the circulation department; Glickman & Company started overseeing the books; legal matters had to be cleared with Charles Goldman or one of his associates; and S. I. himself began slipping into Harrisburg every Friday morning.

All along, Victor Ridder had suspected that Newhouse was behind Ed Russell, but whenever he confronted Newhouse about the matter, S. I. denied that he had played any part in Russell's obtaining the Patriot Company. It wasn't until that last Thursday in April, when he was about to meet his future daughter-in-law, that Ridder learned of the massive infusion of Newhouse personnel into the Harrisburg papers. At that point, it was apparent to him that Russell had been fronting for Newhouse all along. What most infuriated Victor about this revelation was that the Ridder brothers had practically given Newhouse the *Long Island Press*; now, it appeared, the ingrate had stolen the Harrisburg papers from them and had also lied about his role in the transaction.

Victor Ridder wasn't the only one angered by the Harrisburg merger. Especially hurt were some two hundred local people who were put out of work. One of them, Paul Walker, an engaging columnist who had been with the *Telegraph* for years, went to Newhouse personally to ask that his column be taken on by the *Evening News*. The response he got was anything but conciliatory. Said

Newhouse, "We can get schoolboys to put names in the paper out of the telephone book."

Newhouse could care less who wrote the local gossip columns. In Harrisburg, as elsewhere, his concern was to build up the business side of his newspapers, and there was much to be done. As Pennsylvania's capital city, Harrisburg boasted a large state government payroll — nearly one in every four local workers. There were also busy steel mills that hired from "the hill" — the row upon row of slums in the poor section behind town — and a large dairy industry that supplied the nearby Hershey factory. Overall, it was a healthy community, whose retail sales per capita far exceeded those of the rest of the state, as well as the national average.

Despite its vigorous economy, Harrisburg had no Sunday newspaper. In this Pennsylvania Dutch community, there were still blue laws and, it was generally believed, strong sentiment against any commerce on Sunday. To Newhouse, Sunday had an altogether different meaning — it was the best advertising day of the week. He also knew that Sunday papers from Philadelphia, 105 miles to the east, sold briskly in Harrisburg. When the citizens of Dauphin County (which included Harrisburg) voted to rescind a ban on Sunday movies, he knew it was time to break with tradition.

The key to the success of a Sunday edition lay at least as much with the merchants of Harrisburg as with the town's newspaper readers. "We had to get Monday night open in the business community," explained Ernie Doepke, who at the time was in charge of ad sales. "So we had a meeting of 300 to 400 business people at the Penn-Harris Hotel. We had dummy papers we'd printed, and we put on a good dinner and show for the merchants. We told them they'd make it rich if they followed our plan.

"This was all S. I.'s decision. At first we sold ads at a big discount. There were lots of contests, too. The paper took hold — 60,000 the first year (September 1949 to September 1950). In five years, the Sunday circulation was 150,000. Yet, the town only had 22–24,000 homes! Next to Philly, we were the paper in the state."

During its early years, the Sunday *Patriot-News* was anything but a glorified handbill. Not only was it chock-full of popular features — the usual array of comics, columns, and social notes, supplemented by a rotogravure magazine — but it also offered extensive coverage of national and local news and sports in three large front sections. Each Sunday the paper carried the text of a complete novel.

After merging the *Evening News* with the *Telegraph* and bringing the Sunday edition of the *Patriot-News* on the scene, Newhouse had yet another plan for Harrisburg. As a matter of principle, Vance McCormick had steadfastly refused to publish in the *Patriot* or the *Evening News* advertisements for alcoholic beverages or patent medicines and related nostrums. "There was $1 million of advertising laying around to pick up at practically no expense, and S. I. knew about the situation before he bought the papers," said Ernie Doepke. In March 1951, when the papers changed their policy with regard to such ads, only one person objected: Vance McCormick's widow, who demanded that they be stopped immediately or that her husband's name be removed from the papers' masthead. His name was removed.

Owning the papers in Harrisburg added a new stop on Newhouse's newspaper route. He'd arrive early Friday morning to inspect the new plant he had built soon after acquiring all three papers. Operating out of Ed Russell's office, he would go through his usual routine on each visit, speaking with department heads, getting the numbers, and seeing to it that the *Patriot* and *Evening News* were adhering to strict guidelines about the ratio of advertising to news in their pages.

He usually took lunch at a little bit of a place near the Penn-Harris Hotel and then, at two o'clock, hopped aboard the train for Trenton, where his chauffeur waited to drive him to Greenlands for the weekend or back to Manhattan. Like clockwork, the next round of newspaper visits would begin promptly at eight the following Monday morning with a stop at the *Long Island Star-Journal*.

To Ernie Doepke, who was first ad manager, then general manager, and finally publisher of the Patriot Company, Newhouse "was one of God's noble men." Born within a month of each other, they were bonded together by Doepke's unabashed admiration for Newhouse — an admiration Doepke said he felt the first time he met his new boss, in September 1947 at a private meeting at the Penn-Harris Hotel. "I was privileged just to be one of his fair-haired boys," he explained. "He was shrewd — a great analyzer of the community — and he had a good sense of people, though he was almost shy."

"He was not at all a socializer," Doepke continued, "except in his own home. When my wife and I visited his New York apartment, there was never a word about business. He wouldn't drink anything but Pinch bottled Scotch, and he always kept it flowing freely.

"I remember one story that shows what kind of man S. I. was. He used to have the Russells, the Doepkes, Ted, his boys, and sometimes Norman over to his apartment before the annual convention of ANPA [the American Newspaper Publishers Association, which met each spring in New York City]. It got to be kind of a sting in the other publishers' minds, and I told him he shouldn't do this. His hair almost stood up. 'Don't you tell me who my friends are!' he said. But the next year he hired a suite at the Waldorf and had all the publishers present."

As he came to be better acquainted with his boss, though, Doepke began to sense in him a strong strain of loneliness. The Harrisburg train station, for example, was only a block away from the new Patriot Building in downtown Harrisburg. Yet, S. I., who never cared much for protocol or VIP treatment, always asked to be met there when he came to town. And when it was time to return to Trenton later in the day, he would invariably ask Ernie to ride with him in the club car.

"He couldn't stand being alone like that," Doepke recalled. "We'd get in the club car and go to work on his famous Pinch bottle. He drank a lot, but he could hold it pretty well." And thus the two of them would ride to Trenton most Friday afternoons, talking about business and digging deeper into the Scotch. Around four o'clock, Ernie would be left to make the return trip to Harrisburg by himself.

20 Portland

A. J. LIEBLING, the rotund journalist/gastronome considered by many to have been the inventor of modern press criticism, coined a special phrase to describe Newhouse. He called him a "journalist chiffonnier," *chiffonnier* being the French word for "rag man" or "rag picker." By this, Liebling meant that Newhouse seemed to spend his time digging in the garbage can of American newspapers, picking around for castoffs to claim as his own. There was also the clear implication that no paper accumulated this way could have much journalistic merit.

In terms of Newhouse's holdings at mid-century, such an assessment was accurate. Virtually all of the papers he had acquired were throwaways, and none had developed a reputation for high-quality reporting or writing. But in late 1950, Newhouse made a deal that, for the first time in his life, put him in charge of a publication of real stature.

At the time, the Portland *Oregonian* was widely regarded as the finest American newspaper west of the Rockies and north of San Francisco. For its size — it had a daily circulation of around 200,000 — the *Oregonian* had the best crew of editors and reporters to be found anywhere in the United States. Looked at as a business, however, the Portland paper was more typical. For some time, it had been in the hands of its founders' second- and third-generation descendants. Some were well along in years and in failing health; none had risen above the others to give the paper the clear financial guidance it so desperately needed.

At the close of World War II, the heirs of Harvey Scott and Henry Pittock made the mistake that was to prove their undoing. Despite rising costs and declining cash flows, they decided to construct a new headquarters for their newspaper in downtown Portland. To make matters worse, they engaged the city's only world-renowned architect, Pietro Belluschi, who set about designing on a grandiose scale. The result was a building that cost nearly twice the amount budgeted for it.

Midway through construction, the *Oregonian*'s board selected a new president, a local banker by the name of E. B. MacNaughton. He saw immediately that the only way the Pittocks and Scotts could keep their newspaper alive — and their inheritances intact — would be to sell. Thus, in the summer of 1950, the year of the *Oregonian*'s one-hundredth anniversary, MacNaughton went shopping for a buyer. From his experience as head of Portland's largest bank, he knew that no one in town would come up with the cash he thought the paper was worth, so he sent feelers to banking friends back east. At the same time, he was greatly worried by the prospect that he might have to hand the *Oregonian* over to a publisher whose editorial policies would not be in tune with conservative, staid, inbred Portland.

That July, MacNaughton was given Newhouse's name. He had not heard of him before but became most interested when Newhouse was described to him as a new kind of newspaper operator — someone whose interests were purely financial and who believed in preserving a newspaper's existing, locally established editorial content. MacNaughton did a little checking, primarily of the Syracuse newspapers, and was encouraged by what he heard: the editors of the *Herald-Journal* and *Post-Standard* were, indeed, left alone. In an era still smarting from abuse at the hands of chains — most notably Hearst's — when editorial policies that often turned out to be misguided were dictated from central headquarters, the possibility of selling to an outsider and still maintaining the *Oregonian*'s honor loomed at least as large in MacNaughton's mind as Newhouse's ability to pay. That, too, he verified, with a call to the Chemical Bank of New York.

The idea of buying a newspaper on the other side of the country had never occurred to Newhouse. All along, as his holdings and financial resources grew, he had planned to continue picking up new properties in his part of the country — basically in the territory that was within easy striking distance of his home in New York City. However, a major problem had developed with this approach, in that, by 1950, he had pretty much exhausted the local supply. He had no interest in buying "funerals," as he called papers that were in no position to turn a profit, and now that the postwar economy was taking off, good buys within a reasonable distance of Manhattan — like the Harrisburg papers — simply would not come along very often.

Moreover, as the economy picked up, so, too, did his own newspapers' profits. Newhouse was awash in huge cash reserves; unless he made a big purchase soon, he would be forced to forfeit a large chunk of his earnings to the federal government under the IRS's surplus profits rule, which had been reinstated in 1939.

Since conducting the Syracuse sale, newspaper broker Smith Davis had taken on a young new associate, Vincent Manno, and both of them were searching for a deal for Newhouse. That fall, Davis caught up with MacNaughton in Washington, D.C., and learned from him directly that rumors that the *Oregonian* was for sale were well founded. Davis also ascertained that Newhouse would be an acceptable buyer, but he was shocked by the price tag. At the time, it was generally accepted in the industry that a newspaper was worth some multiple — usually ten — of its net earnings. Though strapped by the costs associated with its new building, the *Oregonian* still managed to turn a profit of $250,000 a year. Thus, according to the formula, it was worth in the vicinity of $2.5 million. But MacNaughton said he wanted $5.6 million — all of it in cash. It was the largest amount of money anyone had ever dared ask for a newspaper.

Newhouse, however, not only had the cash on hand but had also developed a unique method of assessing a newspaper's worth that made the deal seem quite attractive to him. Because most of the papers he had purchased were losing money when he first got hold of them, he put relatively little stock in the present earnings figures that served as the basis for other potential buyers' calculations. What was important to him was something else — what he called "the potentialities" — and these were discerned by looking first at a paper's market. Did it have a sound, diversified economic base? Was it growing? Then, he would examine the newspaper's relationship to that market. He had not always been in a position to insist that a prospect hold a monopoly in the area, but he always inquired. And if the answer were no, he required that it at least be the dominant publication in town. Only after he had obtained satisfactory answers to those questions would he concern himself with the numbers on recent profit-and-loss statements. It was an eminently reasonable approach to take, but one which had escaped the rest of the industry.

What Newhouse read about Portland in his market guides was encouraging. The city's population had grown rapidly from 305,394 in the 1940 census to 363,141 by mid-decade, and it showed no signs of slowing down. Moreover, N. W. Ayer's Advertising Directory described that part of Oregon as an "important trading center and port of entry," with a diversified industrial base, which ran the gamut from shipbuilding to lumber and canned goods.

As far as the other criterion — market position — was concerned, Portland did have a second newspaper, the afternoon *Oregon Journal*. It was not for sale in 1950, but Newhouse believed the *Oregonian*'s inherent advantages were such that it would be only a matter of time before the *Journal* would be forced to sell, much as the *Herald-Journal* had pushed the *Post-Standard* into his hands in Syracuse. (At least one person close to the negotiations over the *Oregonian* believed Newhouse also secured a promise from the owners of the *Oregon Journal* that they would sell to him when the proper time came. "There was a handshake," claimed Jerome Walker, who covered Newhouse's purchase of the *Oregonian* for *Editor & Publisher*. "S. I. had an agreement that the *Journal* would be his." Today, there is no one alive who can prove or disprove the existence of such an agreement. Subsequent events at the *Oregonian* and the *Oregon Journal*, however, were to demonstrate an unusually cooperative relationship between management at the two papers.)

Having reached favorable conclusions as to his prerequisites, Newhouse still had to set an exact dollar figure for the *Oregonian*. His approach to this kind of problem was ingenious. Aided by his accountant, he would make a conservative estimate of what he could make a property pay over the next decade; that figure would then represent its worth to him. Given his basic faith in the business and his ability to avoid taxes by reinvesting earnings, he could quite realistically come up with values many times those set by the then accepted industry standard. The *Oregonian* proved no exception. Newhouse figured he could earn at least $8 million with it by 1960. Thus, when Smith Davis announced that MacNaughton wanted $5.6 million, he was quick to accept.

Coming up with the money was the easy part. Far more difficult was the sixteen-hour plane ride to Portland to make a final inspection. Newhouse always found long trips difficult, but airplanes posed a special problem, for he tended to be airsick in the slightest turbulence. Traveling to and from Portland, unless he was to spend a whole week on board a train, required flying.

The day he went, a major storm covered the Pacific Northwest and forced his plane back to Boise, Idaho. "This storm is terrible," Newhouse told MacNaughton from a phone booth at the airport. "I've had enough. I'm taking the next plane east." MacNaughton, worried that the deal might be becoming unraveled, reminded him that doing so would only mean bouncing around in more bad weather. Besides, Newhouse had traveled most of the way already. Why not continue on to Portland, through the clear skies that were forecast for Idaho and Oregon the next day? He relented.

Upon his arrival, he was given a tour, first of the downtown business district, which met all his expectations, and then of the *Oregonian*'s new plant. The circumstances of the latter tour, however, struck MacNaughton as quite odd. He recalled Newhouse saying that because of his reputation with organized labor, he was worried that he might be recognized there, and insisting that they postpone the inspection until around eight o'clock that evening when the building would be relatively empty. Newhouse also proposed to MacNaughton that they sneak in through a side door. When he had seen the place at last, all he could say was, "It's three times too big."

The next day's long flight back to New York was another bother, and as soon as he got home, S. I. asked brother Ted if he would make a trip to Oregon. Ted, who had none of S. I.'s aversion to flying, left on Thanksgiving Day, arriving in Portland the next morning, in time for the city's annual Fairy Tale parade. He, too, was given a walking tour of downtown and a brisk run through the *Oregonian* building before returning to New York. Back home, he assured his brother that he would be glad to fly to Portland once a month to report on how things were going out on the West Coast. With that final obstacle cleared, Newhouse could go ahead with the purchase.

In the meantime, it was agreed that he would delay announcing his latest acquisition until after 4 December, when the *Oregonian* planned to print a special edition commemorating its one-hundredth anniversary. The deal was kept so quiet that on the day the paper celebrated its pioneer roots with a host of articles about what it called "The *Oregonian* Century," only publisher Mike Frey among the regular staff knew that in less than a week an obscure New York publisher would remove the *Oregonian* from local hands for good.

Buying the *Oregonian* made Newhouse a national figure almost overnight. No longer would reports of his newspapers' exploits be confined to the back pages of trade journals like *Editor & Publisher* and *Advertising Age*. On Sunday, 10 December 1950, his purchase of the *Oregonian* was reported by Walter Winchell on his immensely popular radio program. The following day, he was mentioned prominently in newspapers all over the country, including the *New York Times*, and later in the week, both *Time* and *Newsweek* covered the deal. Everywhere it was noted that S. I. Newhouse had just consummated the largest single transaction in American newspaper history.

For Newhouse, there was much more to the purchase of the *Oregonian* than the enormity of the price — it represented a major shift in his overall approach to newspapers. In one bold move, he had broadened his newspaper horizons to include the entire U.S., not just the northeast corridor that ran from Syracuse to Manhattan to Harrisburg. Furthermore, by delegating responsibility to one of his brothers, he had dramatically expanded the number of newspapers he could handle at one time.

Perhaps most satisfying of all to Newhouse was his sense that he no longer could properly be called a ragpicker. The paper he had just purchased enjoyed an excellent reputation. Besides, once it paid off its new building and tightened up its business practices, it would be as profitable as any he owned. Thus, it was little wonder that he was excited on the night of his second visit to Portland. After a few

Scotches in his room at the Benson Hotel, he placed a call to Ernie Doepke in Harrisburg. It was about one o'clock in the morning on the east coast when the call came in, but Doepke remembered Newhouse's first words exactly: "Ernie? It's S. I. I'm in Portland, Oregon. I just bought the *Oregonian*. It's the biggest, best buy I ever made in my life."

21 Meeting the Press

BEFORE HE PURCHASED the *Oregonian*, Newhouse had granted only one lengthy interview, and that had been to one of his own reporters at the *Staten Island Advance*, on the occasion of the newspaper's fiftieth anniversary. Not surprisingly, the article that appeared on that date, 21 March 1936, was filled with praise for its subject. "A shrewd young lawyer from Bayonne walked into the *Staten Island Advance* the blustery afternoon of October 19, 1922 and bought out the business for more money than its owners had ever hoped to get for it," the piece began.

> But the price seemed fair to S. I. Newhouse — for that was the buyer's name — because, at 27, he was an old hand at the publishing game, and he had always looked upon The Advance as a real opportunity begging for a taker. . . .

> Success! Here, indeed, was success to dim the lucid fantasies of Horatio Alger — and the secret of it all?
> "Oh, it's the break you get; it's all in the breaks," the publisher told one of his reporters the other day in the first interview of his career. "Lady luck has smiled on me."
> . . . His modesty does him an injustice. . . . Resolute, methodical, staid in business, he is affable, droll in his lighter moods, with a rollicking boylike laugh.
> He is a man of small stature, broad shoulders, trim, sturdy figure, quiet dress, and agile walk. . . .

"S. I." has few friends, no confidantes. . . . He never smoked until he was 25 and now — at 41 — he has quit tobacco because it gives him no pleasure. He drinks occasionally and moderately for sociability's sake. . . .

Golf and bridge are his hobbies, and he plays the latter so well that he is constrained to say so himself. Singularly shy about serious attainments, he is a positive braggart with a fistful of cards and a good partner at bridge.

"If you must know," he boasts, "I think I am a damn good contract player — 'Bill' Braybrooks to the contrary notwithstanding." . . .

Wise, temperate, tolerant — S. I. Newhouse is wide awake today at the stewardship of civic responsibility his own success foisted unto him.

Newhouse's second major encounter with the press occurred in the late 1940s, when he agreed to participate in informal discussions each spring with the owner of *Editor & Publisher*, James Wright Brown, and one of the magazine's reporters, Jerome Walker. The meetings took place over lunch at the Union League Club in Manhattan. "They were enjoyable," recalled Walker. "He was terribly honest in telling what he did. He even admitted to the surreptitious ways he bought some of his properties." It was clearly understood, however, that the discussions were for background information only, and Walker never mentioned anything they discussed in the articles he wrote.

Otherwise, there were no requests for interviews, and Newhouse was allowed to continue to add to his properties without much attention from the media. After 10 December 1950, however, all that changed. Suddenly, everyone wanted a chance to talk to the man who had just made newspaper history. For a while, all the attention made for a heady experience, and Newhouse even hired a New York City public relations expert, Ray Josephs, to handle the press for him. In addition to convincing Walter Winchell to give big play to the announcement of the record-shattering purchase, Josephs cranked out an appropriately laudatory profile of Newhouse for insertion in the *Oregonian* the following day, 11 December 1950, when the paper finally notified its readers of the change that had taken place. Though much of the text of the Josephs release had been lifted word for word from the profile that had appeared in the *Advance* in March 1936, it was dutifully sent out over the Associated Press wire and served as the basis for profiles of Newhouse that appeared soon afterward in other newspapers and in *Time* and *Newsweek*.

But soon Newhouse's attitude toward the press changed dramatically. He was by nature a shy, private person who preferred doing things to talking about them. Moreover, he quickly became sensitized to the dangers of too much personal publicity. He had seen how Hearst had been transformed by the media from working man's hero to public enemy in a matter of years. He was also sensitive about events in his own recent past. He knew, for example, that his vicious treatment of the Guild on Long Island and in Newark would not bear close scrutiny. Nor would his persistence in hounding L. T. Russell out of Newark and into a mental institution. Nor, for that matter, would the underhanded manner in which he had gotten hold of Vance McCormick's newspapers in Harrisburg.

There were still other concerns that argued against opening himself up to full press coverage. For one thing, he was painfully aware of how much anti-Semitic feeling existed in American newspapering. Should his Jewish heritage be played up, he could be prevented from buying papers he might otherwise be able to get his hands on.

Finally, there was the matter of the competition. Newhouse, obviously, was not the only person looking to buy newspapers. There were a host of others, not the least of whom were Frank Gannett, John Knight, and the Ridder brothers, and he had certain trade secrets — like the amount of money his papers earned and the way he assessed a newspaper's cash value — that he didn't want anyone to know about.

The upshot of all of this was a genuine, abiding mistrust of the press. "He came to despise publicity," explained his long-time chief editor, Phil Hochstein. "The rest of his family shared his fixation about this." As a result, an unwritten rule was developed within the Newhouse organization. It dictated that, as a general matter, interviews with S. I. himself were to be granted only to reporters with whom his people were already acquainted and with whom they felt comfortable. Only on special occasions would others obtain access to the boss — usually when a major purchase had just been announced. Even then, the courtesy would be extended only to representatives of major publications — such as *Business Week, Time,* or the *New York Times* — and to trade magazines like *Editor & Publisher* and *Advertising Age.*

With such an arrangement, it was not surprising that Newhouse enjoyed a highly favorable press. Typical was the lead in the article Jerry Walker wrote about his purchase of the *Oregonian*: "Samuel I. Newhouse, who bought his first newspaper on a self-earned shoe-string 30 years ago, laced up seven-league boots, strode across the continent, and sealed up the biggest deal of his fabulous career this week."

Outside of Walker and Josephs, the first representative of the press to get to Newhouse during this period was Collie Small of *Collier's* magazine. Small was given not only direct access but also the special privilege of being allowed to tag along for a day as Newhouse made his newspaper rounds in the New York City area. It was no coincidence that Small's editor, Louis Ruppell, had recently been on a Newhouse retainer, nor was it much of a surprise that the article *Collier's* printed was filled with hearty praise for its subject. "At fifty-six," Small wrote, "Sam Newhouse is one of the most remarkable men in the newspaper business.

> For a man who stands only five feet three, he casts an extraordinarily long shadow. . . . The adjective "fabulous" has recently been applied to Newhouse by seasoned observers of the newspaper scene. . . . He is a brave bull among timid bears. . . .
>
> Newhouse looks at least 10 years younger [than his age] . . . feels that he has been blessed with the right combination of luck and common sense, plus an ability to work hard.

• • •

Nevertheless, Newhouse's emphasis on luck appears to be exaggerated. His success in building an empire has bordered on the phenomenal, and he has not done it either by sleeping late or by carrying four-leaf clovers.

Reporters who did not enjoy Walker's and Small's advantages and who had not been cleared ahead of time by Hochstein or Josephs were invariably treated quite differently. Right after New-house bought the *Oregonian*, for example, a reporter from the *Oregon Journal* happened to be in New York. From Portland, he received instructions to interview the competition's new owner. But when he arrived at the *Long Island Press* building, the reporter was met with a total brush-off.

"There was a big limousine in front of the building," he recalled. "Newhouse's office was at the top of some stairs. He was sitting at a roll-top desk. He was so small his feet didn't touch the floor, and he seemed ill at ease. He kept telling me he didn't give interviews, and I kept telling him I was there because my editor had told me to get one.

"After about fifteen minutes, he pushed a button or something, because a big chauffeur — over six feet tall — with black gloves on entered. The chauffeur was rubbing his knuckles with his hands. So I left."

Those who didn't abide by the Newhouse organization's rules or who wrote something that upset them, were dealt with more harshly. Even the slightest suggestion of criticism in *Editor & Publisher*, for example, would meet with swift retribution. Recalled Jerome Walker: "Ted would simply lower the boom. They ran a pretty fat schedule of ads with us, and he pulled them whenever he read something he didn't like."

Perhaps John Lent, a graduate student in journalism at Syracuse University in the early 1960s, met with the greatest opposition. In the fall of 1963, by which time Newhouse had become one of Syracuse's main benefactors, Lent prepared a term paper about him. It was so well received that several professors suggested he turn it into a book. Subsequently, the School of Journalism's dean, Wes Clark, arranged expense money for Lent and even managed to get him an interview with Hochstein — all in the hope that the book might prove a fitting tribute to its subject.

Lent, however, directed most of his additional research to Newhouse's troubles with the Guild during the thirties and eventually produced a rather fragmented, but clearly disapproving, account of his career. Because of the negative view it presented, Syracuse would have nothing more to do with the book. Ultimately, Lent had to borrow money from his parents and contract with a vanity press on Long Island to bring the book out. Edward Uhlan, the self-proclaimed "rogue of publishers' row," was the man he chose for the job.

"John Lent showed me it was all authentic, and I agreed to publish his book," Uhlan recalled. "I had it set in type, and I had the manuscript copy edited, and then I called the Newhouse newspaper here, the *Long Island Press*. I got his brother Ted, who said, 'My brother is a big and busy man. Anything you'd say to him, you can say to me.'

"So I offered the book to Ted Newhouse to make sure there'd be no litigation. I wanted Ted's reaction to it. He said, 'Sure.' Three days later he called. 'I don't need no blankety-blank book about my brother!' he said. When I told him I would still publish, he said, 'I'm going to sue you for every dime you've got!' He wouldn't even return the manuscript."

One week later Uhlan received a summons to appear at the local district attorney's office. According to Uhlan, the manuscript he had sent to Ted Newhouse was on the desk, and an assistant district attorney — "a nice Italian guy" — told him, "I understand you're about to commit criminal libel."

"He said he was just making a friendly suggestion," Uhlan recalled. " 'Can I give you a piece of advice?' he said. 'Frankly, the Newhouses can get pretty rough.' I went ahead and published the book."

Newhouse, Newspapers, Nuisances was not reviewed in a single Newhouse newspaper and, Uhlan explained, "went nowhere. We sold about a thousand copies between me and the author." The threatened criminal prosecution, however, did not materialize.

Even when Newhouse did cooperate with the press, he tended to be uncomfortable and to simplify the events of his life drastically. At one point, the *New Yorker* planned to make him the subject of one of its famous profiles. After some preliminary interviews, it gave up. "They said he just wasn't a person," recalled Phil Hochstein, who served as liaison for the project.

"The old man just wasn't the anecdotal type," recalled Mort Reichek, who did a profile of him for *Business Week* in 1976. "He was a colorless man in many respects. He was cordial but not forthcoming. It was frustrating — he gave simplistic answers."

Newhouse's prosaic responses to interviewers' questions were not simply evidence of a reductionist mind at work, however; Newhouse wanted to be recognized as possessing what one magazine writer called "flamboyant casualness." So while he actually put a great deal of thought and careful preparation into almost all his acquisitions, he went out of his way to give interviewers the opposite impression. Of the 1939 *Herald-Journal* purchase/merger, for example, he told *Esquire*'s Ann Chamberlin, "I never saw Syracuse before. The newspaper broker said: 'Do you want to buy Syracuse?' and I said 'Sure.'"

Newhouse made the *Oregonian* deal seem even more offhand. According to the version he gave *Collier's* Collie Small, he didn't even know the *Oregonian* was for sale when newspaper broker Smith Davis called. Their conversation supposedly went like this:

> "Sam," Davis said, "I can get the *Oregonian* for you."
> "How much?" Newhouse asked.
> "I think I can get it for around five and a half million."
> "Go ahead," Newhouse said.
> "Wait a minute," Davis protested. "Don't you want me to tell you about it?"
> "No," Newhouse said and hung up.

Altering the record this way was one thing, but when it came to earlier incidents in his life, Newhouse was even less reliable. For many years, for example, he told reporters — inaccurately — that he had won his first court case, and that the candidate he'd backed for party leader on Staten Island had won. He also maintained to the end that his father had not actually failed in business; rather, his partner had made off with the proceeds. In fact, John Dreimuller, the partner, remained in Greenville, New Jersey, for years after the failure of Meier Newhouse & Co.

Newhouse also used to tell reporters that he had learned the newspaper business by attending myriad night courses at New York University. A check of the records shows that he enrolled in just two classes at NYU and completed only one of them. Finally, Newhouse steadfastly kept the true details of his experiences in Fitchburg to himself, telling interviewers that he had purchased the *News* solely for its underpriced newsprint contract.

* * *

Newhouse's relations with the press were, at best, paradoxical. His growing reticence with regard to personal publicity — and his remarkable success at manipulating the media — meant that, despite his importance to the growth and development of modern newspapering, during his lifetime he was never more than a shadowy figure on the horizon of public opinion.

22 Local Autonomy

THE SIMPLE FACT that Newhouse would part with $5.6 million for a medium-sized paper like the *Oregonian* was the catalyst for one of the most significant changes in American publishing. Not since the booming pre-Depression era had anyone even considered paying that much for a paper.

In the intervening two decades, the newspaper business had languished. Prices for newsprint, lead, and ink had risen continually, along with wages, especially after World War II. There was also strong competition from radio, which was in its heyday, and television, which promised to be an even more effective communications medium.

As if those problems weren't enough, the industry was beset by a far more troubling ailment. More than most businesses of their size and influence, newspapers were predominantly family-run affairs and, as such, seemed to have productive lives of about three generations. By 1950, the typical American paper was very similar to the *Oregonian* — around a century old and in the hands of the third generation.

Of course, for those newspaper family members who were actually in charge, there were still decided benefits inherent in such operations. Not least of these were enhanced social stature and political clout in their communities. But for most newspaper people, these once-prized family jewels had become tarnished possessions indeed.

The failure of newspapers to command big purchase prices in recent decades had only added to the overwhelming sense of disconsolation that had infected the field. And then, from out of nowhere, came Newhouse's prodigious bid for the *Oregonian*. As a result of

■ 164

it — and of the other similarly high bids it engendered — other newspaper families — especially in the Northeast and Southeast, where papers typically were older — suddenly began to think the unthinkable. If the price and the other terms were right, they might sell, too.

For Newhouse, whose own horizons had been so broadly expanded by the *Oregonian* deal, the most pressing aspect of this new development was determining how best to benefit from it. The most promising possibilities, he realized, were in the South, where labor costs were lowest, and profits, accordingly, were high. Yet, he was a northerner and, worse, a Jew. In fact, he was the only major chain operator in the country with such a background. If he wanted a share of the new business, he would have to develop a new strategy that would make him more attractive to genteel families in the South.

In that regard, Portland banker E. B. MacNaughton had taught him a valuable lesson. In many ways, the men and women who owned the *Oregonian* were as patrician as any Southerners. And when, during the course of the protracted negotiations, MacNaughton emphasized repeatedly that Newhouse's policy was not to interfere with his newspapers' editorial affairs, and that turned out to be the key ingredient in the historic deal, he readily took the hint. "A newspaper is more than a press and rolls of [news]print," Newhouse declared on the occasion of his purchase of the *Oregonian*. "It must have continuity of tradition. Such continuity is best achieved by retaining and aiding the men and women who gave the newspaper its character."

There was, of course, very little in Newhouse's prior newspaper experience to support such a statement. In one way or another, he had remade practically every publication he had gotten his hands on; and at most he had replaced many of the men and women who were in charge. But given how little was generally known about him and his prior journalistic practices, this conflict never surfaced. Besides, the *Oregonian* was unlike any of his previous acquisitions in that it already produced a sound editorial product. Those changes that Newhouse wanted to make in its operation involved improving promotion of circulation and advertising and paying closer attention to financial details — the very areas where improvements would be difficult, if not impossible, for readers to detect.

On his first visit to Portland after buying the *Oregonian*, he went out of his way to build upon his new philosophy. "It would be silly," he told the paper's editor, Robert Notson, "sitting in New York and trying to tell you how to edit this newspaper. As managing editor, you must determine what will go into it."

For publishers like Hearst and Pulitzer, the approach Newhouse began to promote during the early 1950s would have been unthinkable. Such publishers installed loyal subordinates at most of their papers and regularly teletyped instructions to them about everything under the sun, including how to slant the news on particular issues. But Newhouse rarely read any of his papers — he preferred the *New York Times* — and did not care what they printed as long as advertising and circulation continued to climb. Thus, an arrangement that called for local and independent editorial control — but with regular consultation on business matters — was perfect for him.

Soon Newhouse and his advisors came up with a special expression to describe their approach. "Local autonomy," they called it. The idea was by no means a new one. As far back as 1928, Frank Gannett had used the same term to describe the guiding principle behind the direction of his chain of newspapers. In Gannett's hands, however, "local autonomy" was largely a public relations gimmick. He continued to refuse to allow his papers to accept liquor advertising and issued all sorts of other rules from his base in Rochester — including one that forbade any of his employees to use the word "chain" to describe his newspaper holdings.

"Local autonomy" was to become the most significant development in modern chain newspaper ownership. Though Newhouse did not invent the notion, he was the first major newspaper owner actually to put it into practice. In turn, his apparent dedication to the principle raised two important questions. Would local autonomy work to bring new properties — especially those located in the South — into his hands? More important, what would be the effects of local autonomy on the papers' editorial content? The former question met with a resoundingly affirmative response in 1955, when the owners of three Southern newspapers practically begged Newhouse to buy them out.

The first was the 103-year-old *St. Louis Globe-Democrat*, owned by seventy-year-old, staunch conservative E. Lansing Ray. "I wanted the *Globe-Democrat* to carry on the policies established by my family over three-quarters of a century ago," he said that March, when he sold to Newhouse for $6.5 million. "To me, the vital feature of his operation is that each of his newspapers is complete master of its own destiny." (Ray, who was retained as publisher, died later the same year, making Newhouse the unwitting beneficiary of a $1-million life insurance policy. That windfall was the first of a series of lucky breaks that helped to net him approximately $15 million during his first six years of ownership of the *Globe-Democrat*.)

Later that year, Newhouse was approached by representatives of the Hanson family, who wanted to sell him the *News* in Birmingham, Alabama, and the *Times* in nearby Huntsville. "The decisive reason for selling to Mr. Newhouse was his established reputation for insisting that his newspapers be operated locally and independently," explained Clarence B. Hanson, Jr. As part of the deal, Newhouse stipulated that Hanson would remain as publisher and president of the *News,* at least until 1973. He also agreed to a sales price of $18.7 million — another record.

At the time, the *News* was netting nearly $2 million a year. That alone met Newhouse's criterion of having new acquisitions pay for themselves within ten years. But there was also the Huntsville paper, then a rather unimportant publication in a sleepy little town near Alabama's northern border. In a few years, the U.S. military would decide to locate its Redstone arsenal nearby, and the *Times* would become a gold mine in its own right.

Having been instrumental in netting Newhouse major newspapers in Portland, St. Louis, and Birmingham — as well as the surprise in Huntsville — local autonomy clearly had proved its utility. There remained, however, the larger issue of the influence of the principle on journalism. Would it serve to strengthen his newspapers, enabling them to serve their readers and communities more effectively?

The experience of the *Oregonian* during the first five years of Newhouse's ownership suggested that the new practice was indeed a healthy departure. During the late 1940s, the paper's declining profits had taken a heavy toll in the newsroom. There was still a superb staff of reporters, editors, and photographers, but overtime pay and travel allowances, once taken for granted, were discouraged, as were investigative projects. The announcement that a cost-conscious New York chain operator had purchased the paper only fueled anxieties in the editorial department. However, after a few weeks of Newhouse's ownership, the staff realized that, in the words of one reporter, "our fears of what was going to happen were not going to materialize." "All of a sudden," said another, "there was plenty of financial support for news gathering. There was even money for air fares!" "The *Oregonian*," said a third, "just got better and better."

"I remember one incident that was typical," recalled Wallace Turner, who had been with the paper since 1943. "There was a car dealer on the East Side of Portland. It was bought by people who used phony sales techniques. All this was brand-new to Portland. Taking keys to cars for appraisal and not giving them back for hours. That sort of thing. These people were also very big advertisers in the *Oregonian*. Well, their license came up, and we wrote a story that tore their ass off. *And management supported us!* This wouldn't have happened pre-Newhouse."

Encouraged by such support, Turner and fellow reporter Bill Lambert soon took on a group of gamblers from Seattle, Washington, who were planning to get Portland racketeers, teamsters, and law-enforcement officials to join them in opening the city to gambling and prostitution. "Every one of us knew this was going to be cataclysmic," said Turner. "We knew we were going to have a lot of trouble. It cost hundreds of thousands of dollars [in expenses and legal fees], yet the Newhouse people never complained." The *Oregonian*'s two-year investigation not only helped keep Portland relatively free of such influences but won the newspaper the Pulitzer Prize as well. Ever true to his new policy, Newhouse subsequently admitted that he "didn't even know they were doing it."

Throughout this honeymoon period at the *Oregonian*, Newhouse understood that the attention of the newspaper industry would be directed to Portland, to see if the big spender would make good on his high-sounding promises for the paper. Because he had so much to prove and so much ultimately to gain by succeeding, he infused the operation with cash, loans of newsprint, and whatever else it needed. And for those first five years, the *Oregonian* stood as a powerful testament to the virtues of Newhouse's practice of local autonomy.

What happened at the *Oregonian*, however, was the exception rather than the rule. Most of Newhouse's other papers — by then, there were nearly a dozen — suffered dreadfully from a lack of editorial vision and seemed all too willing to pander to the lowest common denominator. Upon closer inspection, it was evident that local autonomy had done nothing to improve their lot.

The experience of the *Newark Star-Ledger* was typical. That paper was, in the words of a man who worked there from 1946 until 1956, "a pretty wild operation." "We pulled a lot of screwy stunts," explained John McDowell. "I remember one time when the New York papers broke the story that all the racketeers were going to Jersey due to an investigation by the district attorney. So I spent a day with binoculars patrolling the Hudson River, so we could run a big page-one spoof of the New York papers."

A good number of the *Ledger*'s pranks involved a pig farmer and perennial candidate for public office by the name of Henry Krajewski. "One time," McDowell recalled, "the *Newark News* wanted another horse-trotting track in Monmouth County. Well, if the *News* was for it, we were against it. I dreamed up the stunt that pig trotting was the sport of ancient Irish kings. We got a lawyer to draw up a formal application for a trotting track, and we got Henry Krajewski to agree to file in Trenton with the State Racing Commission.

"On the way, though, we stopped at some bars and got inspired. We went to the state hospital farm and stole a pig — Henry chased it down and put it in a gunnysack. Then we went to Trenton. We went by a men's clothing store and got a bright tie to put on the pig, and then we dropped the pig off at the State Racing Commission. The secretary was screaming, and we took pictures."

The *Ledger* at this time relied also on heavy doses of cheesecake to aid newsstand sales. Hardly a day went by when the paper did not publish in its first few pages a photograph of a scantily clad, bosomy woman. Nearly any excuse would do, including the "Guess My Husband" contest and the unveiling of new spring and summer fashions. Page three of the 10 March 1954 *Ledger* was typical, carrying a two-column-wide, seven-inch-high photograph of actress Sheree North in a strapless bathing suit. Below that was another large, provocative photograph bearing the caption "Lili St. Cyr strips to Debussy on harp."

Not all the *Ledger*'s activities during this period were quite so lighthearted. Particularly noteworthy was the paper's constant and unflinching support of Wisconsin Senator Joe McCarthy. From the time of his 1950 Lincoln Day address to the Women's Republican Club in Wheeling, West Virginia, McCarthy was front-page material in the *Ledger*. At first, the paper's treatment of him mirrored that of most other American newspapers. It gave prominent play to his charges, never questioned them, and rarely offered those whom he'd attacked the opportunity to rebut his accusations.

Within a year or two, however, many papers around the country, including the *Newark News*, had begun to catch on to McCarthy. But while they printed their doubts about his charges of Communist infiltration of the government and their concerns about his methods of investigation, the *Ledger*'s support for him reached a fevered pitch. McCarthy's reelection in the fall of 1952 was reported in a huge, front-page banner headline, accompanied by an editorial that asserted, "His opponents and critics now say that his victory by such a staggering proportion is 'appalling.' We think it was to have been expected and that it is . . . a fortunate event. . . . [We] do not believe 'McCarthyism' to be an important issue."

When McCarthy brought his dog-and-pony show to nearby Fort Monmouth a year later, the *Ledger* covered his inquiry into an alleged spy ring at the Fort's radar installation as heavily and as sensationally as it could. The paper's headlines grew larger as the senator's charges grew wilder. Never once during this period, though, did the *Ledger* bother to look into any of the senator's charges, and when certain of its syndicated columnists, Drew Pearson among them, began to attack McCarthy, the *Ledger* refused to print the revelations.

Finally, in the spring of 1954, McCarthy's Army hearings were televised, allowing Americans to see for themselves the danger he represented. Still the *Ledger* stuck by him, calling the televised hearings "a public disservice," and that fall, when the Senate voted to censure him, the *Ledger* refused to budge: "McCarthy," the paper editorialized on 3 December, "was slapped around in a manner that creates what may prove a troublesome precedent in the future."

Other American newspapers remained equally misguided about

Joe McCarthy and McCarthyism, but none conducted itself in public as the *Newark Star-Ledger* did. "One time," recalled McDowell, "we talked the Army-Navy Union into making McCarthy 'Man of the Year.' This was during the Army hearings. We rented an LST landing boat and took it across the Hudson River. We picked up McCarthy on Manhattan and ferried him back to New Jersey. He walked ashore like MacArthur at Corregidor."

Reporting favorably on McCarthy was one thing. Organizing parades in his honor was another. Still worse was the stifling of his critics. But most reprehensible of all was the paper's practice of allowing itself to be used as a conduit for charges McCarthy himself didn't dare make in public. "We'd get documents all the time from McCarthy," recalled a *Ledger* reporter. "Many of our stories were based on this information." One person who suffered from this practice was New Jersey Senator Clifford Case. On a tip from McCarthy's office, the *Ledger* tracked down Case's sister in upstate New York and determined, to its satisfaction, that she was a Communist. The clear implication was that Case, who was involved in a difficult election campaign, was one too.

Though the *Ledger*'s coverage of Joe McCarthy was especially reprehensible, it also demonstrated the depth of Newhouse's commitment to the principles of local autonomy. For, during the time that the *Ledger* supported him so unabashedly, McCarthy made a special point of attacking Newhouse's pet property, the *Oregonian*, as "left-wing" and even sued the *Syracuse Post-Standard* for libel. That lawsuit, the only legal action the Wisconsin senator ever filed against a newspaper, ended up costing Newhouse $16,500 and a public apology. Still, he neither said nor did anything to suggest that his Newark newspaper should change its ways.

If McCarthy and McCarthyism dominated American life during the first half of the 1950s, the latter part of the decade was preoccupied with the struggle for civil rights. No newspaper could have been closer to the heart of this struggle than Newhouse's *Birmingham News*. Even the timing of his purchase of the paper, on 2 December 1955, coincided with a watershed event — the arrest of Mrs. Rosa Parks in Montgomery for refusing a driver's orders that she take a seat in the rear of the bus.

At the time, Birmingham was a steel town, a rough, tough, redneck city, whose leading newspaper reflected the sentiments of the white majority that dominated the community's affairs. The *News* was, as one Southern journalist described it, "hard seg." It was that way when Newhouse bought it, and, encouraged by his policy of editorial noninterference, it published opinions that seemed only to grow stronger and less enlightened during the half-decade that followed. In its news stories, as well as its editorial columns, the *News* consistently argued for segregation, against federal involvement in voter registration drives, against sit-ins, against the Congress for Racial Equality (CORE), and for the continuation of apartheid in the Union of South Africa. Though conditions for black people in Birmingham were atrocious, the *News* steadfastly refused to report on any of the multitude of racially motivated incidents that led local church leaders to describe the city as "an American Johannesburg."

It was not until the spring of 1960 that the situation there came to the nation's attention. A *New York Times* reporter, Harrison Salisbury, had traveled south to investigate race relations in three cities — Nashville, Baton Rouge, and Birmingham. It was readily apparent that the last stop on his tour was a place of unparalleled hatred and violence. "I quickly compiled a list of horrors," Salisbury explained later. "Beatings, police raids, floggings, cross burnings, assaults, bombings (dynamite seemed to be as common as six-packs), attacks on synagogues, terror, wire tappings, mail interception, [and] suspicion of even worse."

On Tuesday, 12 April, the *Times* printed his dispatch from Birmingham in a remarkable page-one article entitled "Fear and Hatred Grip Birmingham." "[M]ore than a few citizens, both white and negro," Salisbury wrote, "harbor growing fear that the hour will strike when the smoke of civil strife will mingle with that of the hearths and forges. . . . No New Yorker can readily measure the climate of Birmingham today."

Newhouse's *Birmingham News* reprinted Salisbury's piece word for word but with a different headline. "*N.Y. Times* slanders our city — can this be Birmingham? . . ." The following day, the *News*'s editorial writer described Salisbury's article as "an amazing recital of untruths and semitruths, employed to justify conclusions obviously implanted in the writer's mind before he ever crossed the Mason-Dixon line [that] has provided the nation with a picture of

Birmingham maliciously bigoted, noxiously false, viciously distorted."

There was more. In addition to its continuing criticism of Salisbury, the *News* sent a reporter to New York City to report on crime there. A couple of weeks later, when the *Times* mistakenly transposed the names of Alabama and Mississippi on a map of the South, the *News* continued its attack: "Here's some news 'fitten' to print — Alabama in Mississippi, *Times* of N.Y. 'decrees'!"

Salisbury's report on Birmingham raised an additional issue — that of press freedom in the city whose leading newspaper Newhouse owned. On 6 May 1960, less than a month after Salisbury's articles had appeared in the *Times*, Birmingham's three city commissioners — including Theophilus Eugene "Bull" Connor — sued Salisbury and his paper for libel, asking $1.5 million in damages. As part of their suit, lawyers were allowed to subpoena telephone records of the Tutweiler Hotel, where Salisbury had stayed while in Birmingham. Suddenly, the whole city knew the names of most of the sources for his article. "Blacks," he recalled, "got threats of arrest. Educators encountered difficulty with their trustees, clergy with their vestrymen." The *News*, though, was almost gleeful in its accounts of these revelations and ignored the clear breach of confidentiality that had occurred.

On 6 September a county grand jury indicted Salisbury on forty-two counts of criminal libel. Again, the *News* sounded a victorious note, for its editors knew that the legal actions could not help but keep a hostile press out of Alabama. "We have no hesitation," editorialized the *Chicago Tribune*, "in saying that these [cases against Salisbury and the *Times*] are the most serious challenges to freedom of information to have arisen in many years."

Still Newhouse stuck by the principles of local autonomy. "Since [1956], S. I. Newhouse has taken no steps to interfere with or influence the editorial policy or local management of the *News*, and he has not suggested any editorial position on a local, state, or national matter," declared publisher Clarence Hanson in a sworn affidavit dated 2 May 1973. "Conversations between Mr. Newhouse and members of his family on the one hand and me and others in *News*' management on the other have been exclusively about business and financial matters."

* * *

Over a decade and a half after Salisbury's visit to Birmingham, local archivists came across a huge stash of materials in an old firehouse that was about to be demolished. There were tape recordings, notes, photographs — all the property of Bull Connor. The discovery proved once and for all what many in the civil rights movement in Birmingham had believed all along — that the city's police commissioner had established his own private intelligence network in Birmingham. Connor had thus obtained surveillance over practically every outsider who came to town during those troubled days of the early 1960s.

Of course, such a system necessitated a large number of informants and spies at the bus depot, in various hotels, and at the post office — and the tipsters included reporters working for Newhouse's *Birmingham News*.

Though Newhouse rarely read his own newspapers, he could not have remained ignorant of the *Ledger*'s coverage of McCarthy or of the *Birmingham News*'s closed mind on civil rights. Nor did he necessarily agree with what those papers were publishing. As far as he was concerned, that was beside the point; what was important was that he had become the third largest newspaper owner in the United States, behind Scripps-Howard and Hearst, and that his assets were worth at least $200 million. "I'm not out to save the world," he declared at the time. "I buy papers because they're there. I like to make them go."

"Notwithstanding his business acumen," wrote Robert Shaplen in the *Saturday Review*, "[Newhouse] can properly be called the 'organization man' of journalism, embracing as he does the contemporary concept of economic gain ahead of meaningful influence in the marketplace of ideas."

But Shaplen's was a lonely voice. "You have to remember," explained Newhouse's publicist, Ray Josephs, "this was a time when press criticism was practically unheard of. Mr. Newhouse was aware that some people were critical. But he took a very Olympian view of it."

Part V

1955 – 1962: Empire Builder

The Oregonian Oregon Journal

Vol. XCXX — No. 30,000   WEDNESDAY, NOV. 11, 1959   24 PAGES   PRICE FIVE CENTS   Vol. LVII, No. 212

Stereotypers Strike 2 City Dailies

News in Brief—

FARM SUPPORT CHANGES (AP) — President Eisenhower and Secretary of Agriculture Ezra T. Benson agreed Tuesday on a new farm program including legislation to base price supports of stored commodities, particularly wheat, on market prices rather than the parity formula.

U. S. STEEL ELECTS HEAD — Leslie B. Worthington, Tuesday was elected president of United States Steel corp. Worthington succeeds Walter Munford, who died in September after accidentally wounding himself with a kitchen paring knife. Worthington had served as president of Columbia-Geneva division with headquarters in San Francisco.

NEW SUB ADDITION — The Atomic-powered Triton, the mightiest submarine known, joined Uncle Sam's Navy Tuesday. It will operate as the eyes and ears of the fleet. The giant sub was commissioned at Groton, Conn., with an expression "Congratulations and Good Luck" from President Eisenhower. She is the latest addition to the Navy's Ever-increasing nuclear undersea force.

TV QUIZ FIXING — The Federal Communications Commission Tuesday announced it will try to find out if it can take action under existing law against those responsible for TV quiz show fixing and other rigging in broadcasting. Otherwise, it will consider whether to recommend that Congress put some new laws on the books.

FIRE PROBE REVEALING — Investigators said they now possess what they call "startling facts" about the fire that destroyed the tanker Amoco Virginia Sunday at Huston, Texas with a loss of eight lives. Coast Guard Cmdr. Charles F. Kaminski, heading the Houston portion of the probe would not elaborate pending a formal hearing later.

REDS EXCHANGE MOVIES — The first U.S. film exchange was launched Tuesday with a gala premiere of the Russian film "The Cranes are Flying" and official hopes that it will lead to better understanding. Only a few hours earlier in Moscow the U.S. film "Marty" was shown to a Soviet audience. The premieres, thousands of miles apart, were cited as a milestone in cultural exchanges.

CUBANS CONTINUE INSULTS — Cuba's foreign ministry officials indicated Tuesday the distribution of an anti-American pamphlet will continue despite an official protest.

NURSE ALICE THOMPSON checks heart beat of William Falagen, 43, at Hahn hospital in Philadelphia. Flanagan was found semi-conscious in gutter. When his heart stopped during examination, doctors flushed his chest cavity with 20 gallons of warm water, brought heart back to normal rhythm.

'Frozen' Heart Revived

PHILADELPHIA, Nov. 10 — (UPI) — Doctors saved the life of a man with a "frozen" heart by pouring 20 gallons of warm water from an ordinary faucet into his chest cavity.

The 43-year-old laborer's heart had not functioned normally for more than three hours when the doctors took what was believed to be an unprecedented move to return his heart to normal operation.

The patient, William Flanagan, was found semi-conscious from exposure to the cold Saturday in a North Philadelphia gutter. His case was made known Monday night.

Flanagan was taken to the hospital by police but his heart stopped beating while an intern, Dr. Edward Brunner, was examining him.

The physicians made sure the heart was beating normally before closing the opening in the chest and inserting a tube in Flanagan's throat to help his breathing.

Finally, with all hope almost gone, the team of four specialists attempted to warm the healthy pouring six quarts of sterile saline solution into ...

Specialists at Hahnemann Heart Clinic slashed open the chest cavity and massaged Flanagan's heart. They administered artificial respiration through a tube in his mouth.

Patient Remains Blue

Although the blood was kept in circulation by massaging the heart, breathing was kept up artificially, the patient remained critical, the patient remained critical.

Physicians first tried a defibrillator which usually restores normal heart action with electric shocks. But it did not work. Four types of heart stimulants were injected into Flanagan's body without effect. Hot water bottles and heated blankets also failed.

... linked a hose to a nearby hot water tap. Then trey turned the hose directly into the chest cavity and flushed the heart with about 20 gallons of water.

Rhythm Returns

The normal rhythm returned gradually as the blood passed of the case. Circuit Judge Paul R. Harris granted the dismissal.

Within minutes, his body temperature rose from the low 80's to 92 degrees.

Flanagan began moving his arms and legs. Although the chest cavity still was open, ...

Berry Men Deny Peril

WASHINGTON (AP) — Growers heatedly denied Tuesday that cranberries with a cancer-producing content are on the market. But a AP Stores headquarters in New York announced withdrawal of the berries and their products from sale in all of its 4,000 odd nationwide food chain.

One big group of farmers de ...

Ike's Brother Put on Board

WASHINGTON (AP) — Edgar Eisenhower, brother of President Eisenhower, has been named to the board of trustees of Americans for Constitutional action, it was announced Tuesday.

The organization was founded a year ago with the declared aims of opposing inflationary government policies and helping elect conservative candidates.

Eisenhower, a Tacoma, Wash., lawyer, will serve without pay. Other trustees are retired Adm. Ben Morrell, chairman of the board, Charles ...

Readers Will be Served

This issue of The Oregonian and the Oregon Journal has been produced under different ...

The Portland Stereotypers Union called its members out on strike at 1 a.m. Tuesday and the Oregonian and the Oregon Journal, faced with a newspaper-less day, combined resources, having the company to hire a stopgap-half employes for the replacement.

Mother Freed By Court After She Changes Story

A confused 19-year-old mother, Mrs. Ruth Kilgore, who was held in jail following her confession she killed her baby by smothering it, walked from the Multnomah County courthouse Tuesday with her husband and mother a free woman.

An autopsy performed by Dr. W. L. Lehman indicating that the baby had not been smothered, and a change in her story led Dist. Att. Charles Raymond to ask the court for dismissal.

Quake-Hit Road Drops 18 Feet

WASHINGTON (AP) — The government said Tuesday it has found a four-mile stretch of highway near Yellowstone Park that sank more than 18 feet as a result of the earthquake there last August.

The Coast and Geodetic Survey said this was the greatest ...

Newspapers Join Efforts To Publish

Initial Issues To Serve Most Area Subscribers

The Oregonian and the Oregon Journal, Oregon's only metropolitan newspapers which serve the vast area of the entire state of Oregon, southern Washington counties, western Idaho and northern California, were struck Tuesday at 1 a.m. by the Portland Stereotypers Union.

The striking union, which numbers 28 employees of The Oregonian and 26 on the Journal, performs one of the vital functions in production of newspapers, their casting of metal cylinders which, locked into place on the presses, print the news, editorial, pictorial and advertising contents of the newspaper.

Snow Downs 3 Jet Planes

GREAT FALLS, Mont. (AP) — A blinding snow blizzard ...

23 In Vogue

IN A LAND whose image of press lords had been shaped so dramatically by *Citizen Kane*'s portrayal of William Randolph Hearst, Newhouse was an enigma. He had no yacht and no castles. He did not carry on with movie stars. He did not try to affect the outcome of elections or tell presidents how to run the country. He did not even seem to care what his newspapers printed.

That Newhouse avoided making a public spectacle of himself, however, did not mean that he lacked Hearst's ambition. "Beginning in 1950," explained Ernie Doepke, "there was only one thing on his mind — to build an empire."

At the time he first expressed this desire, he already had, in addition to the newspapers, a national news service in Washington, D.C., and radio stations in Syracuse and Portland. Other broadcast properties would come his way as he acquired additional newspapers. What was missing were magazines, and he soon began to search in earnest for publications to match Hearst's immensely successful trio: *Cosmopolitan*, *Good Housekeeping*, and *Harper's Bazaar*. A $20-million offer to Curtis Publications (which produced the *Saturday Evening Post*) fell through, but then, in 1959, Newhouse got on the trail of what he liked to call "a hot one."

That spring, he learned from a Wall Street acquaintance that Iva S. V. Patcevitch, president, chairman of the board, and chief editorial executive of Condé Nast Publications, was shopping around an option on his company. It took Newhouse less than two weeks to track down the debonair, silver-haired "Mr. Pat" and to arrange through him to buy control of the most glamorous magazine house in the world. For though Condé Nast himself had been dead for more than twenty years, his successors — the Berry family in

England and Patcevitch — had perpetuated his interests. Posthumously dubbed "The Man Who Was Vogue," Nast had helped to invent café society and, for several decades after the turn of the century, had attempted to set standards of taste on both sides of the Atlantic.

On the surface at least, the $5-million purchase represented a quantum leap for Newhouse. It appeared to take him from the grey world of newspapers, whose cheap black ink smudged easily and whose interest usually lasted only until the next day's edition, to the glittery, trendy, fashion-conscious domain of *Vogue*, *Glamour*, *House & Garden*, and *Young Bride's*. Such niceties notwithstanding, he viewed magazine publishing the same way that he regarded newspapering. Success required attracting the readers that advertisers wanted and keeping costs down, and in 1958, Condé Nast had not done a successful job of either. On gross revenues of $30 million, it was losing over $500,000 a year.

Newhouse had always been impressed by the fact that women's magazines carried vast amounts of advertising and had tremendous potential for growth. Their only real problem seemed to be an overabundance of competition, but by the time he bought Condé Nast, he already had a solution in mind. Street & Smith, the oldest magazine firm in America, was also up for sale, and it published a group of women's books strikingly similar to Condé Nast's — *Charm*, *Mademoiselle*, and *Living for Young Homemakers*. *Charm* was a direct competitor of *Glamour*, just as *Living for Young Homemakers* duplicated much of the coverage of *House & Garden*. If he merged the two firms, he could achieve the same sorts of savings he'd managed with newspapers in Long Island City, Syracuse, Newark, and Harrisburg. Moreover, *Charm* and *Glamour* combined would be the first fashion magazine in the country selling more than a million copies.

The Street & Smith acquisition went through in August, and Condé Nast was on its way back to profitability. After all, what advertiser could resist a package that included *Mademoiselle* for the fashion-conscious teen or young adult, *Glamour* (incorporating *Charm*) for women eighteen to thirty-five, and *Vogue* for women "for whom fashion is a way of life"?

Things got even better for Condé Nast the following year when Newhouse had it lease its unprofitable sewing pattern operations to the Butterick Company. Less than twelve months later, *Living for*

Young Homemakers was incorporated in *House & Garden.* And in 1963, Newhouse ordered Condé Nast to shut down its printing press in Greenwich, Connecticut. For years the Condé Nast Press had been a mainstay of Greenwich's economy, publishing not only its own magazines but also major outside publications like the *New Yorker* and *Scientific American.* Altogether, it provided regular employment for some one thousand people. But by shutting it down and having his magazines published by midwestern printers on a contract basis, Newhouse figured he could save at least $800,000 a year.

Newhouse's ownership also brought to Condé Nast the devotion and friendship of Henry Garfinkle. By 1959, Garfinkle's Garfield News Company had become one of several subsidiaries of another company he controlled — American News, later called Ancorp National Services. Through it, he ran the Union News Company, which, with outlets coast to coast, was the largest retailer of newspapers and magazines in the country. Garfinkle also operated Greater Boston Distributors and Manhattan News, which dominated the wholesaling of magazines in the Northeast Corridor.

In the words of his adopted son, Henry Garfinkle was "a tough, streetfighting man." That is, he would not hesitate to use his position of dominance within the newspaper and magazine distribution business to his own advantage. According to an account in the *Wall Street Journal,* Garfinkle received an annual fee of $30,000 a year from the *New York Times* just to agree to carry the paper on his Manhattan newsstands. From the *Daily News,* he allegedly exacted $26,000 a year. Other publications — like *Time, Fortune, Newsweek,* and *Reader's Digest* — which refused to pay the tribute occasionally were delayed for months, sometimes years, at airports, railroad stations, and bus terminals throughout the United States.

"His business personality," reported the *Journal,* "is gracious and charming and improves with the importance of his guest. His real personality is ruthless." The article went on to recount Garfinkle's connections to the Joseph Bonnano organized crime family and to convicted income tax evader, William Molasky. Henry Garfinkle, the *Wall Street Journal* concluded, was "a rough dealer."

But as far as Garfinkle was concerned, Newhouse was a special case. The two men's personal and business ties made them virtually inseparable. After providing Henry with the interest-free loans he needed to get started in the newsstand business, S. I. had signed his surety bonds. He had also arranged for cafeteria concessions at certain of his newspapers to be awarded to a company Garfinkle controlled. Socially, too, S. I. and Henry were close. With their wives, they traveled together to Acapulco and Florida during the winter. In New York, they attended the opera together. And, according to Garfinkle, "Whenever there was a big dinner or a family gathering, I was there with him. I used to visit his mother and father when they were ill. I even named my son Myron after his father."

"Let's face it," Garfinkle later explained at his Hampshire House suite, "we were best friends. Anything I could have done to help the man, I'd do." Such help was significant — by the time Newhouse merged Street & Smith into Condé Nast, his pal controlled about 50 percent of all newsstand magazine sales in America. Thus, in addition to providing immunity from the Retail Display Allowance, Garfinkle's friendship eliminated any concerns Newhouse might have had about delays affecting his magazines or of the placement they would receive on the country's newsstands. "Let's be honest with each other," Garfinkle allowed. "If you put one newspaper or magazine at the front of the stand, you know what happens."

Henry's son supported this assessment. "My father was a great fan and rooter for S. I.," he explained. "He'd help him any way he could. For example, if they brought out quarterly magazines or one-shot publications, they wouldn't have to do an acid test like a newcomer would have to. The Newhouses never had to do anything."

On those rare occasions when he discussed his business affairs with members of the press, Newhouse invariably fell back on a stock reply to explain his success. Great careers, he would observe, are "built on accidents, fate, and timing." But with Condé Nast, as with most of his ventures, he left little to chance. Thanks to his own skills and to Henry Garfinkle's friendship, Condé Nast managed a remarkable recovery from the moment he took charge. Within nine months, its losses of $500,000 in 1957 and 1958 had been transformed into net profits of $1,627,252.

24 Coming Out

THOUGH NEWHOUSE LOOKED on the acquisition of Condé Nast as little more than one in a long series of important business deals, he was quite aware of what it would mean to his wife. Mitzi had spent the better part of the last three and a half decades tending to family matters — supervising the operation of their homes, encouraging her husband, and rearing their two boys. Though hers was far from a dreary existence — money and servants eased the household chores considerably — it had not been entirely satisfactory. Now, with her husband gone most of the time and Si and Donald grown, married, and out of the house, she was once more lonely, as she had been when she and S. I. first moved to Staten Island in the twenties. Worse, while her husband was busy setting the newspaper world on fire, she had received precious little attention.

Settling gracefully into the role of doting grandmother would never be enough for the ambitious Mitzi, who wanted nothing less than to be accepted by the worlds of high society and high fashion. It was not lost on her husband that there could be no surer way to gain entrée to these circles than through the purchase of a magazine house that included *Vogue*. The name alone had come to be considered as synonymous with haute couture, while its contents had come to serve as a sort of international fashion diary for the upper crust.

Even the timing of the Condé Nast purchase coincided with an important date for the Newhouses. That spring, they were to celebrate their thirty-fifth wedding anniversary. S. I. had hoped to keep the deal secret until 24 May, but a leak to the press forced him to announce his "present" a few weeks ahead of schedule. Thereafter, in all the publicity that surrounded the transaction, he emphasized his wife's role as one of the purchasers. And he began telling business associates a delightfully apocryphal version of how he had come across Condé Nast in the first place. One Sunday morning as he was leaving their apartment for a stroll along Park Avenue, he explained, he happened to ask Mitzi if she wanted anything. "She asked for a fashion magazine," he would say with a straight face. "So I went out and got her *Vogue!*"

Newhouse's purchase of the magazines came at a time when old-line New York society was giving way to a new set, the so-called "beautiful people." Traditionally, social standing had been determined by family history — what a person's father or grandfather had done or how much money he or she had inherited — but in the late 1950s, it came to be as much a result of publicity as anything else. Thus, though Mitzi had none of the conventional qualifications, her status was assured the moment she assumed a seat on Condé Nast's board of directors.

She received instantaneous attention. "The fashion industry heaved a sigh of relief yesterday," wrote influential New York newspaper columnist Eugenia Sheppard ("Inside Fashion"). "Mrs. S. I. (Mitzi) Newhouse, who with her husband now owns a controlling interest in Condé Nast, is keen on high style from every angle." A week later, Sheppard noted that Mitzi "has been deluged with cables and invitations from the Paris Couture since the news broke that she and her husband have acquired a controlling interest in *Vogue*. . . . Lunching with Jessica Davies, *Vogue*'s editor in chief, at the Colony [Club] yesterday, Mrs. Newhouse wore a sky-blue suit, belted in black."

Soon, anyone who paid attention to such things knew that Mitzi was extremely petite (standing at most five feet tall and weighing less than eighty pounds), wore French dresses (mostly originals designed by Givenchy and the House of Dior), chose jewels created by David Webb, and sported a hairdo fashioned by the Parisian stylist Carita. When not too busy with plays, art exhibitions, or the opera, it was reported, she liked to collect fine French furniture and to play canasta.

Mitzi, of course, pushed her new position to the hilt. As one acquaintance put it, "After the Condé Nast purchase, Mrs. Newhouse began to take herself very seriously." "It was obvious," said another, "that she was a terrible climber." Increasingly, she began to hold formal dinner parties in her French dining room and to hang out with the crowd that frequented the Pavillon and Colony Clubs. On special occasions, she would rent entire restaurants and fill them with carefully selected guests. One night, S. I. and Mitzi took over the Côte Basque, then considered among the world's finest eating establishments. Their guest of honor was Estée Lauder, who arrived in a pale pink crepe dress with matching pale pink makeup. Other invitees included Sophie and Adam Gimbel, Diana and Reed Vreeland, Martha and Cleveland Amory, and C. Z. and Winston Guest. A few years later, after Truman Capote held his famous black-and-white masked ball, Mitzi decided to have her own "in" party — to be limited to persons five feet tall and under. In organizing these soirées, she relied heavily on William Raidy, an independently wealthy man who wrote theater reviews for the Newhouse newspapers.

Mitzi's rapid ascent in society received a strong helping hand from *Vogue*, which reported frequently on her activities. The magazine poured out its most lavish praise in a June 1964 feature entitled "PEOPLE ARE TALKING ABOUT ... Mrs. Samuel I. Newhouse." Accompanying a dramatic, full-page, Cecil Beaton photograph that showed her neatly coiffed, bedecked with jewelry, and arrayed in a dress that appeared to have been woven out of strands of gold was a brief article that described Mitzi as "pastel, fragile, with the look of Belleek porcelain." The magazine continued:

> Like clasped hands, the interests of Manhattan and those of Mrs. Newhouse fit together, for she has long had a major delight in music, particularly in opera. A woman of astonishing energies, she takes special pleasure in fashion, French furniture, American abstract paintings, Dixieland jazz, opening nights at the theater, and her six grandchildren. . . . Easy, organized, amused, with a feeling for the amenities of life, Mrs. Newhouse has 'an open pleasantry,' to use a phrase by Jane Austen.

The article concluded by describing "her gaiety of spirit, her furious curiosity, her talent for listening, and her root capacity for fundamentals." Curiously, there was no mention anywhere in the magazine — not even on the masthead — that Mitzi and her husband owned the publication.

Soon thereafter, the former Parsons Design School dropout achieved her ultimate goal. Mitzi Newhouse was placed at the top of the list of the year's best-dressed fashion personalities — a list that included such notables as Mollie Parnis, Mary Quant, Helena Rubenstein, Gerry Stutz, and even her neighbor, Dorothy Rodgers.

Aside from fashion-related events and dinner parties, the place at which Mitzi was most visible was Sardi's on Broadway opening nights. There, the elite of the theatergoing crowd would gather, in black tie and evening dress, to await first the arrival of members of the cast and then the early reviews. S. I. loved the spectacle of shows like *South Pacific, My Fair Lady, Barefoot in the Park, Hello, Dolly!, Fiddler on the Roof,* and *Man of La Mancha.* But he enjoyed even more the suspense of those first nights, for that was when a play's fate would be determined.

For Mitzi, the impetus to become a first-nighter was far different — with entrée provided by one of her husband's friends, she would be seen. According to Vincent Sardi, proprietor of the famous after-theater hangout, "S. I. and Mitzi were introduced to me by Leonard Lyons. They started coming here in 1947 or 1948, after opening nights, to meet Leonard." Later, when the Newhouses' status entitled them to reserve a table of their own — number 50, near the front door — Lyons would join them.

As might have been expected, Mitzi's society-consciousness encouraged her frivolousness. Each fall, she insisted on making the rounds of the fashion houses of Europe, spending tremendous amounts of money on new clothing and jewelry. And though she couldn't stand being outside in the sun, she liked to spend part of each winter in Acapulco, because that was where the jet set went. Her greatest extravagances, however, were reserved for Apartment 7B at 730 Park Avenue.

Just after Mitzi and her husband acquired Condé Nast, she had the apartment redone in a gold-and-beige decor that visitors described as "nouveau awesome." "Mitzi loves decorating," explained John Gerald, "and when she'd get bored, she'd bring in a decorator and say, 'It's a mess. You know what I want. Fix it.' A lot of people think Mitzi's very difficult. She's tried out all the decorators in New York."

There was, sadly, a side to Mitzi's social climbing that went beyond mere shallowness. On those first nights at Sardi's, for example, she would greet dozens of men and women from her carefully chosen table near the front. With those whose status was unquestioned, she was the epitome of graciousness. But with those she considered to be of lesser social rank, her demeanor could be like ice.

Typical, too, was the slap a sister-in-law suffered in the early 1970s. In 1973, a repertory theater group of which Mrs. Norman Newhouse was president filed for bankruptcy in New Orleans, listing debts that amounted to less than $100,000. There was no help from the Samuel I. Newhouse Foundation, of which Mitzi was a director. Yet, that May, Mitzi used her influence to have the foundation give Joseph Papp $1 million to make the New York Shakespeare Festival a regular part of Lincoln Center. Though the gift represented the largest sum ever donated to an operating theater, it must also have been a tremendous embarrassment to Norman's wife when it was reported in New Orleans. Said Mitzi in New York: "I know I'm going to get a great big bang out of this little contribution I'm giving today."

What was most interesting about Mitzi's behavior was her husband's response to it. In others, there was nothing S. I. deplored more than social pretense and wasteful spending, but Mitzi was a special case. As Henry Garfinkle explained, "She was different than he was — very different. But he adored her." "Anything that satisfied Mitzi satisfied him," recalled interior designer Gerald. There was nothing S. I. would not do for the woman he referred to as "my little package of dynamite," including arranging jobs for her two brothers. Hugo Evans (né Epstein) became an associate in Charley Goldman's law firm, and Walter, circulation manager for the newspapers in Syracuse and, later, for the *Globe-Democrat* in St. Louis.

"She could do no wrong," recalled one long-time family friend. "She could tell him off. She could abuse him. She could dominate him. And he never talked back. But she also deserves a lot of credit for bringing him out."

"In the early 1950s," the man explained, "I would have dinner with them in New York when she would do all the talking. You'd hardly get four or five syllables out of him. But then, one night in the late 1950s at the Drake Hotel, Harold Hirsch, an investment banker, had invited a small group of people. After dinner in the drawing room, Sam Newhouse got to talking about politics, and my jaw almost dropped open. He was talking about the international situation as well as the domestic and was making shrewd observations about the direction in which the country was going. I said to myself, 'My God, how Sam has grown!' He'd met so many people and had been able to take their measure. I remember walking out in the corridor with one of the other guests. 'You know,' he said, 'I've never seen that side of Mr. Newhouse.' "

For most of the other men assembled at the Drake Hotel that evening, the ability to talk effectively and sensibly about world affairs was practically second nature. But for Newhouse, it was the product of years of effort and coaxing, largely by Mitzi, and for that, S. I.'s closest associates were grateful. It would not have done, they thought, for the man who wanted to become the owner and operator of the largest publishing empire in America to be perceived by his peers as having no interests outside the newspaper business.

25 The Solid-Gold Pyramid

WHERE WAS NEWHOUSE'S MONEY coming from? That question had been asked by newspaper people from the moment he announced the price he paid for the *Oregonian*. Thereafter, as his acquisitions piled up, so, too, did curiosity about his finances.

By the time of the Condé Nast deal, newspaper analysts were so suspicious of the source of Newhouse's funds that they discussed openly the possibility that he was laundering money. Some went so far as to suggest that his newspaper operations had been used as a front for the notorious Reinfeld mob, a group of booze-peddling hoodlums whose boss had made millions during prohibition. Newhouse's penchant for secrecy, his Jewish heritage, and his taste for Haig & Haig Pinch — part of Reinfeld's stock-in-trade — all served to fuel the speculation.

Actually, Newhouse had paid for the acquisitions himself and, in most instances, had done so legitimately. That others remained skeptical simply indicated the extent of his mastery of the business. Certain elements of his success should have been apparent — his skill at identifying good markets, for example, and his regular attention to key financial indices at each of his properties. But there were other aspects that went unrecognized throughout the 1950s. Two, in particular, made it possible for him to surpass the competition so spectacularly.

The first was his way with taxes. "They played every tax game there was," recalled one man who once served as publisher for several Newhouse newspapers. That meant that every cost that could conceivably be written off as a business deduction was, that assets were depreciated as rapidly as possible, and that new acquisitions were "written up" as high as the law allowed. Such techniques were rather standard, though. Where Newhouse developed a special advantage was in the way he avoided paying taxes on the profits that remained to him after the payment of corporate taxes.

Following revision of the federal tax code in 1939, all corporate surpluses deemed unnecessary by the IRS were to be treated as dividends, even if they were never distributed. For someone in Newhouse's position, the consequences could have been disastrous. "He told me about his problem with accumulated earnings," recalled a business acquaintance. "He knew the exact percentage of taxes he would have to pay to the Federal Treasury, to New York State, and to New York City. He said he would have sixteen cents left on the dollar!"

Thanks to an ingenious device created by his accountant, Louis Glickman, and implemented by his attorney, Charles Goldman, Newhouse was able to avoid paying taxes on accumulated earnings and, thus, to multiply the value of his earnings several times. Doing so involved the creation of a special corporate structure for the various newspapers. At the top was a central holding company known as Advance Publications, Inc. (API), whose 1,000 shares of common stock — 10 voting and 990 nonvoting — were all held by Newhouse.

API, in turn, served two basic functions. It published the *Staten Island Advance*, and it was the conduit through which Newhouse owned the rest of his newspapers. As such, API owned all of the stock in the Long Island Daily Press Publishing Company. Then, on a fifty-fifty basis, it shared with its subsidiary ownership of the Herald Company in Syracuse, the Morning Ledger Company in Newark, the Patriot News Company in Harrisburg, and the Evening Journal Association in Jersey City. In turn, the Patriot News Company owned Condé Nast, the Herald Company owned the *Syracuse Post-Standard*, and so on, so that the overall arrangement took the form of a pyramid.

These intercorporate relationships, however, existed only on paper. Officials at the *Harrisburg Patriot* and the *Harrisburg Evening News,* for example, had nothing whatsoever to do with the operations of *Vogue, Glamour,* and *Mademoiselle*, although, according to the various legal documents drawn up by Goldman and Glickman, they were responsible for the affairs of the company that published the magazines. For, in practice, the pyramid was completely collapsible, with each block accountable only to the man at the top.

Because the Goldman-Glickman construct kept the various enterprises separate — for tax purposes at least — each could claim the right to its own surplus. Taken together, the accumulation that resulted was many times what the IRS would have allowed had Newhouse simply treated all of his operations as a single corporation.

The second key to Newhouse's financial success was his aversion to borrowing from banks. Ever since childhood, when he watched his mother struggle to come up with fifty cents or a dollar each week to repay small loans she had obtained from a special account established by the synagogue in Bayonne, he had been leery of borrowing. His anxieties were only heightened when he saw what happened first to the *Bayonne Times* and later to the *Long Island Press* and *Syracuse Journal* when their owners fell behind on bank notes.

Each of these experiences ultimately redounded to Newhouse's great benefit, having made a powerful impression on him. "Banks," he explained to an acquaintance, "can make you sell." Thus, in 1955, when he realized he would need help with the purchase of the *Birmingham News*, he became unusually anxious. The prospect of borrowing from the Chemical Bank so troubled him that he rounded up every available penny to keep the borrowing to a minimum. This included cleaning out the account of the Samuel I. Newhouse Foundation, a charity his lawyer and accountant had created as an additional tax dodge years before. The foundation's stated purposes were purely philanthropic, but the temporary use of its assets allowed Newhouse to limit his borrowing from the Chemical Bank to around $10 million of the $18-million-plus purchase price.

For a man of Newhouse's resources — at the time, he was worth somewhere in the vicinity of $200 million — such a loan should have been insignificant. Nonetheless, that winter, he told Ernie Doepke how much it bothered him. "You know," he confided to the Harrisburg publisher, "I had to borrow to buy Birmingham. And you know how I hate to borrow." He was beginning to realize that by paying huge prices for papers like the *Oregonian* and the *Globe-Democrat*, he had inadvertently raised the price tag on every other newspaper in America. No matter how adept Glickman and Goldman were at helping him avoid taxes, he was going to need higher profits if he was to be able to finance an empire without getting deeper into debt.

26 Striking It Rich

THE FIRST NEWSPAPERS to feel the financial squeeze from New-house's drive to create an empire were those in Harrisburg. There, for more than five years, editorial budgets had been lavish, at least by the owner's standards. "Those first few years," recalled one of the *Patriot*'s editors, "he had something to prove here, just as he had something to prove when he bought Portland." But in late 1955, as a direct consequence of the Chemical Bank loan, all that ended. Cuts were made everywhere in the newspapers' operations, with the result that the lifeblood simply drained out of the editorial department.

"I have a personal feeling that the paper just wasn't so good after the mid-1950s," explained a local public relations executive who followed the *Patriot* closely over the years. "I can't put my finger on anything in particular. They just lost their aggressiveness."

Another man, who put in a long stint with the Harrisburg newspapers, was less charitable: "It was a damned shame. As the state capital, this town was — and is — a gold mine for news. But the local papers just stopped covering it. After a while, they didn't even have separate newsrooms. They just recycled the same stories all day long. God, it was awful."

Soon, other Newhouse newspapers were feeling the effects of the owner's new lust for cash. At two, the *Globe-Democrat* in St. Louis and the *Oregonian* in Portland, the consequences were especially damaging.

For many people in St. Louis, Newhouse's involvement in 1955 meant immediate improvement in their morning newspaper. From the moment he bought the *Globe-Democrat*, he set about infusing its operations with some of his other newspapers' most talented advertising, production, and circulation managers. Most noticeable were the efforts of Richard Hiller Amberg, who took over as publisher in the fall of 1955, when E. Lansing Ray died. A big, energetic man who had previously served as publisher of the *Syracuse Post-Standard*, Amberg was a great crusader as well as a great promoter, and under his leadership the *Globe-Democrat* came to life. He cleaned up its appearance, focused on suburban and local coverage, and launched a spate of campaigns for civic improvement. Oddly enough, Amberg's most lasting contribution was his emphasis on the women's pages. By turning them into a major attraction and touting them with lavish fashion shows and other bold promotions, he attracted thousands of new female readers, as well as millions of lines of new advertising.

Just beneath the surface, however, the introduction of so many Newhouse people created serious problems at the *Globe-Democrat*. All the new managers wanted, it seemed to those who worked under them, was higher profits. During their first three years at the paper, the new managers were responsible for dramatic improvements in revenues, yet salaries hardly budged, and demands for greater productivity were incessant.

"For us, 1955 to 1959 was a most difficult period," recalled Rollin Everett, who then headed the Guild unit at the *Globe-Democrat*. "The difficulty was the tightening-up of personnel policies. The people they brought in really made life tough for us. At times, we felt we were being deliberately provoked."

The Guild's greatest concern was the failure of the *Globe-Democrat* to invest in a formal pension plan. Although the system established by the Pulitzers' *St. Louis Post-Dispatch* was recognized as a national model, Newhouse had no intention of allowing his St. Louis profits to be tied up that way. He would not even discuss the matter with his employees' bargaining representatives.

At the same time, however, he was willing to enter into a different set of talks. The *Post-Dispatch*, in need of a replacement for its rickety printing plant, had approached him about buying the *Globe-Democrat*'s facilities on Franklin Avenue in downtown St. Louis. Where the *Post-Dispatch*'s equipment could barely publish one paper a day, the *Globe-Democrat*'s was capable of handling twice that every day except Sunday, when larger papers would make the feat impossible. Discussions between Newhouse and the Pulitzers were still going on in late February of 1959, when the *Globe-Democrat*'s 332 Guild members went out on strike over management's refusal to negotiate a pension plan.

It was the ideal moment to conclude the arrangements necessary to transfer the *Globe-Democrat*'s building and equipment. Barely one week after the strike had begun, Newhouse made the announcement. His St. Louis paper would move its editorial, advertising, and circulation departments to a building nearby and would discontinue its Sunday edition. As a result, the *Globe-Democrat*'s entire production crew, whose support had been essential for the Guild's strike to shut the paper down, would be put out of work. In return, Newhouse was promised a cheap rate on printing and was handed several million dollars in cash — more, certainly, than the market value of the Franklin Avenue plant.

"The sale of the building was a total shock," recalled one of the strikers. "It just knocked the stuffing out of us. It made us feel like we'd been set up. If it was a trap, we walked right into it." When the Guild returned to work some ninety-nine days later, its members' retirement benefits were less secure than before. The strike had been quashed, but to hear Newhouse explain things, the sale of the building was all the Guild's fault. "We had no choice," he told *Time* magazine. "They had a gun at our heads."

For the most part, the residents of St. Louis seemed to accept his explanation. Had they been aware of certain other aspects of Newhouse's treatment of their morning newspaper, however, they might have been less charitable. For one thing, when E. Lansing Ray died in late 1955, his estate included the proceeds of a life insurance policy worth $1 million. Its sole beneficiary was the *St. Louis Globe-Democrat*. Rather than use the money to benefit the paper, though, Newhouse appropriated it to help pay off the loan he had taken out to buy the *Birmingham News*.

In addition, as part of the deal by which he originally purchased the *Globe-Democrat*, Newhouse agreed never to sell the paper to its rival, the *Post-Dispatch*. Should he go back on his word, the agreement provided that Newhouse transfer half of the proceeds of the sale to the estate of E. Lansing Ray. Yet, none of Ray's heirs ever received anything from the sale of the newspaper's building and printing presses.

Two years later, Newhouse cut a second deal with the Pulitzers. Effective 1 January 1961, the two papers would share their profits. Thirty percent of the net proceeds of their combined operations would go to Newhouse; the remaining 70 percent, to the Pulitzers. The 1959 printing contract, one of Newhouse's attorneys explained later, "proved to be extremely expensive and burdensome to Pulitzer, resulting in substantial losses to Pulitzer."

The existence of this new arrangement, however, was kept a tightly guarded secret in St. Louis for many years. Not only did it come dangerously close to violating the antitrust laws — U.S. Justice Department officials say it did — but it also meant the end of serious newspaper competition in a city that had come to enjoy and respect the rivalry that existed between its two dailies.

For Newhouse, the new setup represented the icing on the cake. On an initial investment of $6.5 million, he had already been able to take more than $15 million in cash out of St. Louis. Now he was assured a third of all future profits of both local newspapers as well. Considering that the *Post-Dispatch* still held the lead in circulation and maintained a two-to-one advantage in advertising lineage, that in itself was remarkable. But Newhouse's shrewd bargaining also served to accomplish an unintended result. By seriously undermining the *Post-Dispatch*'s financial position, he virtually assured that that once great publication would never regain its former glory.

For years, the *Oregonian* had been the most loosely managed of Newhouse's papers. It was, thus, the one most susceptible to budget cutting.

"The reins were first tightened around 1958," recalled a man who was then in the paper's management. "They brought in a new, efficiency-minded composing room superintendent from California, and Don Newhouse began to assert himself more."

This Newhouse was S. I.'s younger first cousin. After starting as an office boy at the *Long Island Press* and graduating from the Massachusetts Institute of Technology with a degree in engineering, Don was sent to Portland in 1951. At first, he did little more than watch what went on in the back shop and was conspicuous more for his bashfulness and badly crossed eyes than for any technical expertise. Over the next five years, however, he became a force to be reckoned with.

The savings Don Newhouse and the new efficiency expert effected in production did not go unnoticed in the newsroom. Solely to cut costs, for example, the *Oregonian*'s design was simplified, and fewer banner headlines were used. Late sports scores were held for subsequent editions, and last-minute changes on breaking news stories were discouraged.

These changes were minor annoyances, however, compared to management's sudden stinginess about pay raises. By the mid-1950s, it was clear to everybody at the paper that the *Oregonian*'s financial position had improved markedly, yet none of the benefits seemed to be accruing to the employees. Pulitzer Prize-winning reporter Wallace Turner, who left the newsroom in 1956 to begin his rackets investigation and then received a fellowship at Harvard, was perhaps in the best position to observe the results of management's newfound tightfistedness. He recalled that, when he left, the *Oregonian*'s newsroom was a happy, upbeat, hardworking place. "But when I came back [a year later], I suddenly realized animosities I couldn't imagine." Money, Turner explained, was the central grievance: "There were antimanagement feelings everywhere, because there were limits on everybody."

In 1959, when the stereotypers' cushy contract came up for renegotiations, publisher Mike Frey, after consulting with Newhouse in New York, ordered the *Oregonian*'s key labor negotiator, Bill Morrish, to fight on every issue that pertained to salary or productivity. Toward the end of the unusually harsh negotiations, Morrish pulled out a surprise much like the one Newhouse had employed in St. Louis. This time, it was a new piece of equipment, known as the M.A.N. machine. Not yet installed at any other American newspaper, it would eliminate three out of every four stereotypers' jobs at the *Oregonian*. With this one masterful stroke, the paper's least productive union was backed into a corner. The stereotypers could either accede to the gutting of their department or strike. Their international union, fearing the installation of the M.A.N. machine at other papers, ordered a strike.

Had the extreme belt-tightening measures begun in 1956 not antagonized nearly every union employee at the newspaper, the stereotypers' walkout would have been a short-lived affair, for theirs was not a well-respected union. But so much hostility had developed toward management that a general strike over the issue of the stereotypers' contract was conceivable, and Frey's uncompromising attitude only exacerbated the situation.

Moreover, encouraged by his success at union busting in St. Louis, Newhouse had even higher hopes for Portland. He wanted to be in a position to make newspaper history by continuing to publish the *Oregonian* even if all of its unions walked out.

Preparations began at around the same time that he started the economy drive at the *Oregonian*. First, he arranged to have his brother Theodore and Mike Frey appointed to the American Newspaper Publishers Association's Newspaper Publishing Premium Fund Committee. Previously, Newhouse had taken little interest in the ANPA's activities, but this committee got special attention, because it was in the process of establishing strike insurance for America's newspapers. In return for annual premiums of $12,262.50, the *Oregonian* would be entitled to recover as much as $10,000 per day in the event of a strike. Equally important, Newhouse and Frey secured from their Portland competitor, the *Oregon Journal*, assurances that it, too, would stand by the *Oregonian* in the event of a strike. (This curious promise could well have been an outgrowth of the "handshake" deal Jerome Walker believed Newhouse had cut with the *Journal*'s owners back in 1950.)

The heart of their plan was even more extraordinary. Starting in mid-1959, Newhouse had Frey direct the *Oregonian*'s most trusted nonunion personnel — mostly supervisors in the advertising and circulation departments — to report for extra duty. Late at night, after the city edition had been put to bed and the regular production crew had gone home, Frey's men would sneak into the back shop, where Don Newhouse and others trained them to operate the equipment.

The strike didn't begin until 10 November 1959. The day before, Leo McCoy, who specialized in such newspaper problems, received a call by prearrangement at his office in Oklahoma City, Oklahoma. "Get as many people to Portland as fast as you can," he was told. Within hours, three planes carrying fifty-nine well-seasoned strikebreakers, many toting rifles and shotguns, were on their way.

Early the next morning, a picket line was established outside the *Oregonian* building, and at nine o'clock the *Oregon Journal*'s top people arrived to hand over the paper's masthead and its other typographical furniture. For the rest of the day and into the afternoon, a makeshift crew led by Don Newhouse struggled to put together a twenty-four-page newspaper. "It was a pretty poor typographical product," recalled Bob Notson, then the paper's editor and later its publisher, "and the printing was uneven. It looked strange with two flags on it. But it was a paper."

Late that afternoon, when the *Oregonian–Oregon Journal* rolled off the presses, Newhouse achieved his goal. In the process, he had helped create the worst labor battle in Portland's history.

The wait for the end of the Portland strike turned out to be longer and more violent than anyone had expected. As far away as Oklahoma and Florida, strikebreakers' homes were attacked, and in Portland delivery trucks were dynamited, with all sorts of lesser sabotage being perpetrated inside the newspaper plant. Nearly a year after the strike started, on the evening of Sunday, 16 October 1960, an unidentified gunman severely injured Don Newhouse with a shotgun blast through the basement window of his house in the Portland hills.

All the while, Newhouse continued to dicker for the *Oregon Journal*, which ceased to be a legitimate competitor the moment it agreed to cooperate with the *Oregonian*. On Friday, 4 August 1961, its owners and their representatives agreed to sell for $8 million. Within the month, the Sunday edition of the *Journal* was gone, and the paper's remaining operations moved to the *Oregonian*'s plant on Southwest Broadway. The strike continued, however.

Toward the end, Portland's mayor, Terry Schrunk, paid Newhouse a secret visit in New York. The unions, he said, were ready to go back to work. Newhouse immediately flew to Portland for a meeting at which he planned to help Frey arrange to accept the strikers' capitulation. But Frey wouldn't go along. He'd rather quit, he informed his boss, than let the unions back into his paper. So be it, said Newhouse, and returned to New York as quietly as he'd arrived.

The Portland newspaper strike officially lasted for five years, four months, and twenty-five days. It cost hundreds of employees their jobs and wrecked countless other lives. It also cost the city the independence of its afternoon paper. But nowhere was the strike's toll greater than at the *Oregonian* itself.

"The paper had a magnificent staff before the strike," recalled Wally Turner. "All across the board were top-drawer people, people who owned the town. Then, afterwards, the paper sank clear out of sight. It kept only those [reporters] who couldn't move on."

The list of *Oregonian* strike losses was stunning. Turner, for example, landed at the *New York Times*, which later made him chief of its West Coast Bureau. His sidekick, Bill Lambert, went to the *Philadelphia Bulletin*, where he was awarded a second Pulitzer Prize. Sportswriter Jack Rosenthal went on to become an editor of the *Times*'s editorial page, and in 1982, he, too, won a Pulitzer. Ed Jones became executive editor of the *Wall Street Journal*; Jack Bolter, news editor at CBS; John Dierdorff, a vice-president with McGraw-Hill; and Phil Hager, Supreme Court correspondent for the *Los Angeles Times*. Many of the others landed at the *Portland Reporter*, one of the few decent strike newspapers ever published in America. It folded a few years later.

No paper could sustain such losses without serious harm to its editorial content, but once the strike ended, the *Oregonian* made little effort to find qualified replacements. Instead, it assured those reporters who crossed the picket lines during the strike that their jobs were secure.

Many residents of Portland and St. Louis came to believe that Newhouse had planned the newspaper strikes in their cities in advance, as part of a cold, calculated drive to smash the unions. Such a view gave him too much credit and, perhaps, not enough blame.

The strikes, especially the one in Portland, were horrible tragedies that no individual could have orchestrated. Their avoidance, however, was well within Newhouse's power. Instead, he helped his people prepare for the worst, thus assuring trouble; and when it occurred, he chose to let events run their course, knowing that, ultimately, he would be the beneficiary.

27 On Top

IN THE LATE 1950s, Newhouse's drive to create an empire acquired a renewed sense of urgency. He was fast approaching sixty-five and was all too aware that neither his mother nor his father lived much beyond that. Already, sister Ada and brother Louis had passed away, as had Louis and Theodore's wives. The effects were profound. According to one of his cousins, "S. I. began to worry that he did not have that many years left. He still looked and acted like a much younger man, but he was very aware of his own mortality."

Before he was done, though, Newhouse wanted to own more newspapers than any other publisher in America. "They are my passion, my delight," he said, and during the late 1950s and early 1960s, his desire to own more became so intense that he got involved in dozens of potential deals, many involving a broker by the name of Allen Kander. Through him, Newhouse made firm offers for the *Charlottesville Observer* ($10 million) and the *Baltimore Sun* ($40 million), as well as serious bids for papers in Wichita, Nashville, Buffalo, and Detroit. Their progress was monitored by Charles Goldman, who filed regular reports in memoranda that rarely ran to more than two paragraphs. Typical was a note delivered on 5 January 1961:

> TO: SIN
> FROM: CG
> Kander telephoned me yesterday, and I talked to him with reference to Detroit. Again, the usual double talk, with some indication that he is to have a meeting with Blake McDowell early next week — but I have my doubts.
>
> CG

In addition to working his finders constantly, Newhouse began to engage in extra reconnaissance on his own. Between 1957 and 1962, he got together regularly with LeRoy Keller, a tall, pleasant man who then represented United Press International. Through the news service, Keller was privy to a great deal of newspaper gossip. "We would meet at six o'clock in the evening at the Mayfair Hotel, across from his apartment," he recalled. "Later, it was the King Cole Room at the St. Regis Hotel. After two Scotches, he would depart and go home."

Like most men, Keller found Newhouse "very difficult to talk to. I never could really get to him. He talked in generalities, and he was impenetrable as a personality. But he sure liked to know what was going on in the newspaper business. He was so intent upon building an empire that he had no other interests. He never talked about his family or his friends. He wanted to buy any newspaper anywhere if he felt he could get it for a reasonable price."

After adding the *Oregon Journal* to his holdings in mid-1961, Newhouse suddenly found himself needing just two more newspapers to attain his goal. He had seventeen to Scripps-Howard's eighteen, and his pace quickened still further. How frenzied his search became was indicated by a tactic he adopted that year — walking into the headquarters of publications he wanted and asking the publisher "How much will it take to buy your paper?" On one occasion, an owner jokingly named a figure he thought at least three times too high. Newhouse had his checkbook out and had begun to write down the amount before the other man could tell him he was kidding.

During this hectic sprint to the top, no rumored sale was too insignificant to pursue. In the spring of 1962, for example, he traveled all the way to Beaumont, Texas, on the off chance that the papers there might be for sale. They were not, but the next day, as he was attempting to fly to Florida to meet Mitzi, he missed connections in Houston, a city he had not visited previously. It took only a quick look around that booming town before he was on the phone to Allen Kander in New York. "This place is incredible!" he declared. "Can you come down here and try to buy the *Houston Post*? I'm willing to start at $40 million."

Kander did as requested but found the *Post*'s owner, Oveta Culp

Hobby, unwilling to sell at any price. However, while still in Texas, the broker got wind of an interesting bit of gossip. The voting trust that controlled the two New Orleans newspapers, the morning *Times-Picayune* (circulation 175,151) and the afternoon *States-Item* (circulation 163,650) was on the verge of falling apart. He relayed this information to Newhouse in Florida and was instructed to pursue it.

With the help of a New Orleans broker whose partner was a member of one of the families that controlled the Times-Picayune Publishing Company, Kander orchestrated the attack. On Friday 1 June, final arrangements were made, and the stage was set for Newhouse to buy New Orleans. The total price was to be $42 million — another American newspaper record, as well as a good deal more than the U.S. had paid for the entire Louisiana Purchase in 1803.

Newhouse's policy of local autonomy, it turned out, was the essential ingredient in the deal. "The New Orleans people knew how we worked in Birmingham," he later explained. "I believe that some owners would rather deal with us because of this fact." What he did not say was that the New Orleans papers, though tremendously profitable, were journalistic disasters and so ardently segregationist that even the want ads and obituaries included racial distinctions.

Late the following Tuesday, a muggy day interrupted frequently by rain showers, Newhouse arrived by plane and took a suite in the Royal Orleans Hotel. In the morning, he would tour the plant before closing the deal. First, though, he was intent upon celebrating. "Mr. Newhouse was generally shy and quiet," reported Dan McCoy, a photographer assigned by *Business Week* to cover the historic purchase. But that night in New Orleans, "He was really high."

Newhouse had good reason to revel, for he had finally grasped the Golden Bough of American newspapering. As of Wednesday, he would own nineteen newspapers — one more than Scripps-Howard and eight more than Hearst — and would be responsible for a total daily circulation in excess of three million.

The following day, after his personal triumph had become official, the Ray Josephs Public Relations Agency in New York released a carefully drafted statement. "I am not a chain publisher," it quoted Newhouse as saying. "I want to be remembered as a creative custodian of newspaper tradition and newspaper effectiveness."

Though the remarks were characteristically oblique and self-deprecatory, they could not mask the true meaning of his achievement. Far from being a caretaker, Newhouse was a pioneer, and, by his success, he had come suddenly to symbolize a dramatic change in American newspapering. It was a development that would affect the public's perception of the press as much as it would alter the nature of the press itself.

Previously, a thick, lustrous veneer of romance and public-spiritedness had enveloped American journalism. In a land that practically enshrined the values expressed by the First Amendment, printing the news was considered a high calling. Newhouse's rise to the top of the newspaper heap signified something else again. It demonstrated that newspapering was a business — nothing more and nothing less — and that he was its boldest and most successful practitioner.

That summer, after the purchase of the New Orleans papers, *Business Week* and *Time* magazines prepared cover stories, which served as the first major public recognition of Newhouse's role in reshaping modern journalism.

Reported *Business Week*:

Samuel I. Newhouse is a unique "press lord," totally unlike the strong men of the press for whom the term was created years ago. For a century, the tradition has been that the owner should be a strong personality in the affairs of his community and country. . . . In Newhouse's view [that] type of "press lord" is an anachronism today. . . . Newhouse considers himself a "specialist" in newspaper ownership.

Time was even blunter. "Sam Newhouse never pretended to be a public benefactor," the magazine quoted Phil Hochstein as saying. "He doesn't claim to be with the people. He's a capitalist."

The magazine continued:

Among the country's newspaper giants, Sam Newhouse seems to know best how to make daily newspapering pay. This solid-gold pyramid was erected by a man who knows nothing about the editorial end of journalism and cares even less. To him, newspapers are "properties," usually identified by locale. . . . When he is moved to talk about the printed matter in his papers, Newhouse sounds like an atheist discussing the relative merits of Christianity and Buddhism.

28 Disgruntled Heritors

"HEARST TRIED TO TAKE CITIES by storm, but the new men prefer a rendezvous at the back gate," wrote the *New Yorker*'s A. J. Liebling. "Mr. Samuel I. Newhouse, the archetype, specializes in disgruntling heritors, or profiting by their disgruntlement."

Family problems seemed especially ripe grist for Newhouse's mill. In the late forties and early fifties in Jersey City, for example, he was able to acquire the Evening Journal Association by exploiting the rivalry between Walter and Albert Dear. Around the same time, in Portland, problems within the Pittock, Scott, and Jackson families netted him the *Oregonian* and the *Oregon Journal*. And in New Orleans, a multifamily struggle provided the lever he and his brokers needed to acquire the *Times-Picayune* and the *States-Item*.

Others were less eager to exploit such feuds, and with good reason. Not only were they bound to be unpleasant, but they also involved substantial risks. That is, invading the realm of a troubled newspaper family carried with it the possibility that the interloper would be sucked into the fray. Nonetheless, in the space of just nine days in the summer of 1960, during his final rush to the top, Newhouse twice ran such risks. Each was to plague him for years.

"You've seen a vaudeville show, haven't you?" Harry Tammen asked his first city editor at the *Denver Post*. "It's got every sort of act — laughs, tears, wonder, thrill, melodrama, tragedy, comedy, love, and hate. That's what I want you to give the readers."

An ex-bartender, Tammen had purchased the paper in 1895 in partnership with Frederick Bonfils, an unprincipled lottery promoter who had previously been run out of Kansas City. Over the years, the two shrewd operators made millions on their $12,500 investment. Little did they realize, however, that one day the *Post* itself would become entangled in a struggle that met all the requirements of their outrageous editorial formula.

Tammen and his wife, who were childless, left their half of the *Post* to two trusts — one to benefit Denver Children's Hospital, the other to a grandniece named Helen Crabbs Rippey. Bonfils and his wife, Belle, on the other hand, produced two headstrong daughters who were to spend disproportionate parts of their lives vying for their father's attentions. At first, May, the elder, was the unquestioned apple of Frederick's eye. But his demands on her proved too much, and in 1904, having just turned twenty-one, she eloped to Golden, Colorado, with a piano salesman. This so upset her father that he refused, despite many requests, to send May her belongings. He also changed his will. Unless she were to obtain a divorce, he would cut her inheritance in half.

In the meantime, the younger Bonfils girl, Helen, quickly replaced May in the eyes of both of her parents. After Belle and Frederick died, there ensued a bitter lawsuit between Helen and May. In the end, May settled for 15.67 percent of the stock in the Denver Post Company, while Helen received control of the remainder of her parents' estate, including 34.33 percent of the paper. At the time, dividends from the *Post* were tremendous — May's shares, for example, earned her an average of $212,000 a year for the first decade after the settlement. No amount of money, however, could still the fierce animosity that had developed between the two sisters.

May, who invested her dividends wisely, retreated to an 800-acre estate just outside of town, where she surrounded herself in material opulence, including a collection of jewelry that became world famous. Helen, on the other hand, moved to New York, where she attempted an acting career, and where she and her husband, George Somnes, produced plays and musicals on Broadway. At the same time, she remained fiercely loyal to her dead father who, while living, had dominated her so totally that she remained blind to the sometimes extortionate methods he and Tammen had employed at the *Denver Post.* "They weren't yellow journalists," explained a local lawyer. "They were blackmailers."

At the end of World War II, Helen determined to make the *Post* a shrine to her father's memory. In the process of building a new plant for the paper and hiring a new editor, she spared no expense, one result being that dividends were cut drastically. After 1948, May's annual dividend check dropped to $80,000, about a third of what it had been.

As far as Helen was concerned, no proper monument to her father would mention his defiant daughter. Hence, she gave the *Post*'s new editor, E. Palmer ("Ep") Hoyt — whom, interestingly, she had lured away from the *Oregonian* in 1946 — careful instructions on the subject. May's name was not to appear in the newspaper, unless it was in a story that cast her in an unfavorable light.

For years May suffered quietly the indignities inflicted on her by Helen. But in 1959, when she was in her mid-seventies, two events pushed her over the brink. That spring, certain of her livestock won prizes in an important show, but the *Post* failed to cover the event. She was outraged and, for the first time in the thirteen years Ep Hoyt had been editor, called to complain. The gist of her angry call was that she was about to do something that would make him — and by implication, her sister — sorry.

Then, that 30 July, May's first husband, Clyde Berryman, whom she had divorced more than a decade before, died. The obituary that the *Post* printed the following day contained several references to Berryman's marriage to May, still a sore subject, and prompted her to place a second call to Hoyt. "This is the last straw," she shouted to him over the telephone. "You are going to regret this."

May's idea of revenge was to find a buyer for her stock — a buyer who would not only pay handsomely, but who would also make life difficult for her sister and for Ep Hoyt. May inquired of friends of her father in Wichita and Oklahoma City and was informed that S. I. Newhouse was the man she should talk to. Once he got hold of a piece of a newspaper, they told her, he would never let go. Moreover, he was known as a bear on expenses. If May wanted to put the squeeze on Ep Hoyt, selling to Newhouse was as sure a way as any of getting the job done.

Though May's central motive in selling to Newhouse was revenge, her second husband, Ed Stanton, recalled that when the two of them finally met, in mid-1960, "Mr. Newhouse simply charmed her." In both stature and demeanor, he reminded May of her New York jeweler, Harry Winston. Furthermore, Newhouse told her that he would be glad to accede to two conditions she wanted included in the contract of sale: that he would never sell May's stock to Helen, and that, should he gain control of the Denver Post Company, he would appoint May honorary chairman of the board.

Had May known of Newhouse's previous dealings with her sister and with Hoyt, she might have been even more excited at the prospect of selling to him. For Newhouse had become acquainted with Ep Hoyt at ANPA meetings during the early 1940s, and the two had quickly developed a healthy disregard for each other. Relations between them were sufficiently adversarial that upon his purchase of the *Oregonian* in late 1950, Newhouse had asked newspaper broker Smith Davis to deliver a message for him in Denver on his way back to New York. "You tell Ep Hoyt," Newhouse instructed Davis, "that he made the *Oregonian*. And I stole it from him!"

Nine years later, around the time May Bonfils Stanton first determined to sell her stock in the *Post*, Newhouse met privately with Helen to see if he could interest her in selling him her share of the paper. "Without having access to any figures," he told her at the River House in New York, "I would pay you at least twenty million [dollars] for the paper, and if you will show me some figures, I might be willing to pay you considerably more." Helen, however, had no intention of giving up her father's paper — no matter what the offer.

On 27 May 1960, Newhouse flew to Denver to work out the details of his agreement to purchase May's stock. Though he subsequently claimed that he could not recall whether he stopped long enough in Denver to spend the night — "A three-and-a-half-million-dollar purchase," he explained, "was not a very significant one" — it was clear at the time that he expected to be able to take control of more than just May's interest in the paper.

His plan of attack revolved around the obligations of the Children's Hospital and Rippey trustees to obtain a reasonable rate of return on their holdings. "Under the laws as I understand them," he explained in a deposition taken nearly a decade later in New York, "a charitable trust must get the most income it can from its assets . . . and because of the nature of the [Rippey and Children's Hospital] trusts, I had the feeling that if a satisfactory offer were made, they would be willing to sell." What he meant was that dividends on the *Denver Post* stock had fallen in recent years, providing an annual return of about 4 percent. Even that figure, though, was arrived at by fixing the stock's value at $120 per share. By paying May twice that for her stock, Newhouse had simultaneously depressed the trusts' return to around 2 percent — half what a savings account would pay and certainly not enough to satisfy the trustees' fiduciary responsibilities.

He had another reason to feel optimistic about his chances of parlaying May's feud with her younger sister into control of the *Post*. Helen's first husband had died in 1956, and just the year before, at the age of sixty-nine, she had shocked even her closest friends by marrying her forty-year-old chauffeur, Edward Michael ("Tiger Mike") Davis. Davis was an uneducated, gruff Texan who was described by acquaintances as "the foulest-mouthed man alive." No one in Denver could understand how a pillar of local society could marry such a man. Newhouse, however, was thrilled by this development, for it suggested to him that Helen Bonfils had lost control of her senses and, thus, might be willing to change her mind regarding the sale of her stock.

Had such a chance to make quick work of the *Denver Post* existed during the late spring of 1960, it disappeared on 3 June, when May Bonfils Stanton formally announced the sale of her stock. In a statement that she had not cleared with her buyer but that was clearly crafted to antagonize her sister, May insisted publicly that she, and not Helen, had always been her father's favorite.

Newhouse was astonished by May's graceless behavior, but Helen's determination and resourcefulness proved even more surprising. She possessed a kind of pride reserved only for the very vain and the very rich and, being both, she was willing to spend the rest of her life defending the monument to her father.

Within a month, Helen had arranged for the *Post* to buy the Children's Hospital trust stock without Newhouse so much as having a chance to bid on it. Soon thereafter, she had the Denver Post Company's articles of incorporation amended to prevent minority shareholders like him from obtaining positions on the paper's board of directors. Finally, several years later, she arranged to round up the Rippey trust stock as well.

The struggle for control of the *Denver Post* persisted for years, until Newhouse decided to bring it to a head with an ultimatum issued on Valentine's Day of 1968. He would sell his stock to the company and get out of the picture once and for all if the *Post* would pay him $450 a share for his stock. The amount was nearly twice what he had paid and was four times what the company thought it was worth. But if the *Post* wouldn't meet his terms, he was prepared to file a massive lawsuit against Helen Bonfils and the newspaper's managers for conspiring improperly to prevent him from acquiring control. After several counteroffers, none of which proved acceptable, Newhouse filed his suit.

The *Post* responded by hauling out some heavy artillery of its own, in the form of lawyer Arthur Goldberg, formerly Secretary of Labor, Justice of the Supreme Court, and U.S. Ambassador to the United Nations. Before agreeing to take the case, however, Goldberg thought he ought to pay Newhouse a visit.

"I didn't know the man," Goldberg recalled of their meeting, which was held late that summer in Newhouse's Park Avenue duplex. "Yet he stalked around like a little Napoleon. I'll always remember that. He was very cocky. He said, 'I'm going to buy that newspaper, and I'm prepared to pay $600 a share.' Well, that was out of this world."

"I asked him a simple question," Goldberg continued. " 'Why do you want the *Denver Post*? It isn't making a lot of money.' And he said, 'The name is a great name. It will be a jewel in my crown.' I remember those words, because you don't buy and sell newspapers to be a jewel on someone's crown."

At the same time, though, Goldberg worried that the *Denver Post* people wanted him merely for his name and hesitated about taking the case. He was to make up his mind a few weeks later, at a luncheon reception he was hosting in New York. "A fellow by the name of Garfinkle," he recalled, "comes up to me and has the presumption to say to me, 'My friend S. I. Newhouse is very disappointed in you.' I said, 'Disappointed in me for what?' He says, 'You're considering taking a case against him.' "

"Well," Goldberg continued, "that reflected a colossal egotism — that I should be afraid of taking a case against Sam Newhouse! What kind of a statement is that to make to an ex-Supreme Court Justice! So the next day I told the office, 'We'll take that case.' "

The trial, which was handled by one of Goldberg's associates in early 1970, saw Newhouse largely victorious. It was not until two years later that the former Supreme Court Justice would become actively involved, making an impassioned plea before the Tenth Circuit Court of Appeals. Goldberg's central point was crystal clear. "The *Denver Post*," he said, "is a great newspaper." If it were to fall into Newhouse's hands, it would almost certainly lose that distinction. Though it was not based on especially sound legal grounds, Goldberg's argument carried the day. In a unanimous opinion, handed down on Friday, 29 December 1972, the Court of Appeals declared:

> A corporation publishing a newspaper such as the *Denver Post* certainly has other obligations besides the making of profit.... A corporation publishing a great newspaper such as the *Denver Post* is, in effect, a quasi-public institution.... Such a newspaper corporation also has an obligation to those people who make its daily publication possible.... The facts show [the *Denver Post* management's] motive ... was to benefit the public, the corporation, and the employees....

With this decision, Newhouse's thirteen-year battle for control of the Denver Post Company was at an end. But the damage he had inflicted on the newspaper had only begun to show. The *Post*'s legal fees alone exceeded $1 million. Far more harmful was the effect the lawsuit had on morale and leadership at the paper. From the date of its filing in 1968 until its resolution five years later, every major proposal to modernize or otherwise improve the *Post*'s operations was put on a back burner. As a business, the paper became so stagnant that, in 1974, the first full year of operations after the lawsuit, it netted only $523,000 on gross revenues of $60,143,000 — a rate of return of less than 1 percent. And though Helen Bonfils had defeated first her sister May and then her sister's surrogate, S. I. Newhouse, the *Denver Post* would not long be able to maintain its independence. On 22 October 1980, the paper was sold to the Times Mirror Company of Los Angeles, a conglomerate that owned the *Los Angeles Times*, *Newsday*, the *Dallas Times-Herald*, and the *Hartford Courant*.

Where Newhouse's experiences in Denver read like scenes from a Gothic novel, his role in Springfield, Massachusetts, was more picaresque. On Friday, 17 June 1960, he paid $4.5 million for outright purchase of 42 percent of the stock in the old New England company that published the morning *Union* (circulation 81,000), the afternoon *Daily News* (100,000), and the Sunday *Republican* (112,000). As part of the transaction, he was granted the option of buying an additional 45 percent of the company in 1967. Thus, to obtain absolute control of the three papers, all that was required was that he be willing to wait seven years. In his haste to build an empire, however, Newhouse proved incapable of such self-restraint.

The first of the Springfield papers had been founded in 1824 by Samuel T. Bowles II as the *Weekly Republican.* Under succeeding generations, the *Republican* prospered and became one of the great dailies of the nineteenth century. Control of the company, which eventually came to publish the *Union* and the *News* as well, passed from Bowles II to Bowles III to Bowles IV, and in the early 1930s to Sherman Hoar Bowles, the great-grandson of Samuel T. Bowles II.

Sherman Bowles was as eccentric as he was raw-boned, and his management of the company infuriated his cousins, who also had inherited stock in the family business. Perhaps most irritating to them and to Bowles's wife and children (from whom he was estranged) was his practice of placing most of the newspapers' earnings in a trust for employees' pensions. Bowles then used the fund as his own plaything, buying a skyscraper at 120 Wall Street in New York City, restaurants, a hotel, and healthy positions in a series of blue-chip corporations. The investments were remarkably successful, with the result that the employees' trust fund became one of the few overfunded pension plans in America, as well as one of the most generous.

When he died in 1952, Sherman Bowles left no will. After a brief legal struggle, his stock was placed in a trust to be managed for fifteen years by the papers' pension fund for the benefit of his wife and children. At that point, it would become their property outright. The fund's trustees, however, were led by Sidney R. Cook, the papers' treasurer, a short, round man who now attempted to style himself after his former boss. Soon after the pension fund took control of Sherman Bowles's stock, it obtained another twenty-three shares from one of the cousins, assuring Cook control of the paper at least until 1967.

The cousins and the direct descendants of Sherman Bowles chafed angrily under such an arrangement, for while the papers' profits poured into the pension fund, they received limited dividends and were given next to no say in the company's operations. Finally, in January 1960, one of the cousins, a New York City public relations man named William H. Baldwin, decided to try to find a way out of the situation. Though he owned just six shares — less than 4 percent of the total — Baldwin was quite familiar with Newhouse's reputation for paying large sums for newspapers. He arranged a meeting at the Park Avenue duplex to see if Newhouse would be interested in buying the cousins' stock.

Newhouse said he was not — unless some way could be arranged whereby he could also obtain the Sherman Bowles family's 45 percent, and with it, majority control of the newspaper. So that spring Baldwin and Bowles's son Francis set about making the necessary arrangements with Mrs. Bowles and her other children.

Newhouse was amazed by the financial details the Bowles relative revealed to him. Not only was there nearly $20 million in the pension fund — some of which he was certain he could get his hands on — but the newspapers were earning, after taxes, more than $1 million a year. They also owned, free and clear, batches of valuable real estate, including the Sherman Bowles Airport in nearby Agawam. The airport alone was worth more than the $4 million he had agreed to pay the various factions of the Bowles family.

The day the deal was consummated, Newhouse asked for a meeting with treasurer Sid Cook. Cook's family had lived in the Springfield area since 1930, and he had forty years' worth of work invested in the *Union*, *Republican*, and *News*. To say the least, Cook was not pleased by the sale. The meeting with Newhouse that afternoon at the Hotel Taft in New Haven did little to comfort him. From the outset, Newhouse behaved as though he already owned the papers and started giving Cook orders. "When you go back to Springfield," he said, "I want you to put your name on the masthead as publisher. I pay my men $60,000 a year. And I know that you are getting $19,000."

Cook, however, was not for sale, and the next day, he vented his feelings about Newhouse to the papers' other managers. The new owner was impolite, aggressive, demanding, and defiant, Cook reported, and he expected that they would be hearing more from him soon. At his urging, the group drafted an editorial for the front page of the Sunday paper:

The announcement of the sale came as a shock. The work and pride of four generations is at an inglorious end. Inroads by outsiders into New England business are attaining galloping proportions. . . . Principle, integrity, and courage are giving way to the lure of easy money. . . .

. . . Samuel I. Newhouse of New York is a stranger to this area. He is reported to purchase newspapers as one would "collect objects of art." He typifies absentee chain ownership. . . . This represents his first invasion of New England. It is not good for the community.

Newhouse called Cook first thing Monday morning to complain about the editorial and to demand an invitation to visit the newspapers, as he put it, "to let people see I have no horns." Cook responded that he felt it would be unwise. Newhouse's purchase had created serious employee unrest; a visit would only make things worse. Instead, the two men set a meeting for four o'clock the next afternoon at Newhouse's Manhattan apartment.

At that meeting, Cook barely had a chance to sit down before his host gave him a piece of his mind. "If you are down here thinking you can take over this deal," he said, "you're crazy. I'll never do anything of this kind. I never sell anything — I only buy." He reminded Cook that he knew the trust agreement that bound the Bowles family stock "backwards and forwards. You needn't think I'm going to wait seven years to get in there. And that pension fund of yours — that's not invulnerable either."

Sid Cook was not the sort of man to be cowed by such threats, nor was Newhouse one to make them idly. That August and again in October, Newhouse had the Boston law firm of Hale & Dorr file lawsuits in state and federal court against the Springfield newspapers, their directors, and officers, and the managers of their trust funds. The gravamen of the complaints was that "at all times, it has been the policy of the defendants . . . to subordinate the interests of the company and its stockholders to the interest of the pension funds."

Faced with this barrage of litigation, the newspapers' managers hired a high-powered Boston lawyer of their own, Robert Meserve of Nutter, McClennen, & Fish. They also began to make good use of their most potent resource — the newspapers themselves. First there were angry editorials charging that Newhouse was "determined to control, for personal ambitions, power, and profit, every means of communication he can acquire on the American scene." Soon, the papers were reprinting from other sources stories critical of Newhouse.

But where Cook's propagandizing was most remarkable was when it came to covering the courtroom testimony in the various lawsuits filed against him and the other managers. Each day, a factually accurate, but biased, account would appear first in the afternoon *Springfield News* and then the next morning in the *Springfield Union*. The headlines usually cast Newhouse in a bad light — "Plans Raid on Employee's Funds" or "Attacks Added Widows' Benefits" — while the stories recounted pertinent testimony.

Publishing these articles was just the beginning. Each week, newspaper employees put in hours of overtime to mail tear sheets to more than a thousand carefully selected recipients — including the editors of trade magazines, the head of the Anti-Trust Division at the U.S. Department of Justice, the District Director of the IRS, and hundreds of newspaper publishers.

The hearings dragged on longer than any in the history of the Commonwealth. In fact, it was not until 1966, the year before Newhouse would have taken control anyway, that they were finally settled. "All this could have been avoided," Sid Cook explained years later, "if Mr. Newhouse had been more reserved. But he wanted to come in early."

He also wanted to get his hands on some of the assets held by the newspapers' pension plan. On 1 January 1968, he terminated the old fund and purchased a one-premium, $16-million annuity from the Aetna Life Insurance Company. He also distributed an additional $1.5 million to the employees of the Springfield newspaper, leaving them with the impression that the trust was exhausted. Actually, there remained millions more, which were returned to the company, and thus to Newhouse.

29 The Living Monument

NEWHOUSE FIRST MET William Pearson Tolley one night in 1945 at a large dinner given by motion-picture-theater magnate J. Myer Schine at New York's Waldorf-Astoria Hotel. At the end of the first course, a tall, handsome, friendly-looking man approached him at his table. "Chancellor Tolley," the man said, "I'm Sam Newhouse, and I'm a newspaper man. I've always wanted to meet a university chancellor." Newhouse did a quick double-take, while the stranger pointed at the place card in front of him. It read, "William P. Tolley."

"I'm sitting in your seat," Tolley explained, "because you're sitting in mine. Stay right where you are." The two men shared a laugh, and Tolley walked back to the table where Newhouse's place card lay. This was Newhouse's introduction to the man who, during the following three decades, would do more than anyone else to bring respectability and honor to his name.

Trained in the Methodist ministry, Tolley happened upon a life of academic administration, first at Drew University, then as president of Allegheny College, and, beginning in 1942, as chancellor of Syracuse University, his alma mater. His accomplishments at Syracuse were many, ranging from strengthening the faculty to eliminating segregation in the women's dormitories and at the medical school. But Tolley's most visible and most lasting contribution to the university stemmed from the fact that he was, in academic fund-raising parlance, a builder. During his tenure on the campus, he raised more than $100 million — money that enabled Syracuse to embark upon a capital improvement program unmatched in its history. Tolley was always on the prowl for new donors, and that night at the Waldorf-Astoria, when he saw that the owner of both of

Syracuse's daily newspapers had inadvertently taken his seat, he realized that he had been handed a marvelous opportunity to introduce himself.

It was not until four years later, in May 1949, that Tolley decided to ask Newhouse for a gift to his university. The approach he used was rather curious, but the reception he received was completely in keeping with Newhouse's character.

"When I went in to see him," the chancellor recalled, "I said, 'Mr. Newhouse, I couldn't sleep very well last night, because I couldn't make up my mind how much to ask you for. I knew that what I ought to ask for is $1 million, but my common sense told me you don't know me well enough and I don't know you well enough for you to give me $1 million. The time will come when you will, but I don't think it's here now.' "

" 'Then I thought,' " Tolley continued, " 'well, why don't I ask for a quarter of a million? But again, you don't know me well enough or the university well enough that it would be right to ask for that kind of gift at our initial meeting.

" 'Finally, the answer came to me about three o'clock this morning. So I say to you today, "I want you to give me $100,000 toward the campaign." '

"All he said was, 'I'll let you know tomorrow morning,' and that was the end of the conversation." The next day, Newhouse sent word that he would pledge the amount requested and would donate it in increments spread over the following ten years.

Tolley determined that he should not go back to Newhouse with additional requests until the initial pledge had been paid off, with the result that the two had little to do with each other for the next few years. In 1955, however, their relationship underwent a dramatic change, the catalyst being Newhouse's purchase of the *St. Louis Globe-Democrat*.

Officials at Syracuse — in particular, those affiliated with the journalism department — were well aware of the University of Missouri School of Journalism's aggressive courtship of potential donors. Now, they quickly initiated a campaign to get Newhouse cemented to their school. The first step was the awarding of an honorary degree, which took place at commencement exercises that June.

Tolley soon found that the surest way to lose Newhouse's interest was to discuss university affairs with him. "You could have talked to him until doomsday about the importance of scientific research or the humanities," the chancellor explained, "and he wouldn't have heard you." In fact, the only aspect of school life that did seem to catch his fancy was sports, especially football, and in that regard the late 1950s and early 1960s were ideal for Tolley. Under the legendary Ben Schwartzwalder, the Big Orange had become a perennial college football powerhouse, and Newhouse thoroughly enjoyed watching the games and being introduced to the great coach. Soon he was arranging for his newspapers to provide jobs for some of the players.

The fall weather in Syracuse was not always cooperative, but whenever it drove Newhouse from the chancellor's box at midfield, he could retreat to the second floor of an old gymnasium nearby. There were plenty of windows that offered excellent views of Archbold Field, and it just so happened that the second floor of the old building was also the home of the university's journalism department. Tolley took advantage of these occasions to begin to plant in Newhouse the notion that a former women's gymnasium was not the proper place for one of Syracuse's most important departments.

Dean Wes Clark added a few not-so-subtle touches of his own to the campaign. First, he wrote a paper about the university's need for a new School of Journalism and had it printed up and sent around to various newspapers, including Newhouse's. Then, he arranged for an architecture student to make a fancy model of a new journalism building. Clark gave the model prominent display on the second floor and made a point of being in his office on Saturdays when the weather was bad and the football team was playing at home. "S. I. was much too smart to ask me about it," he recalled. "But Mitzi said, 'What is that?' and I was glad to explain."

Around the same time, Newhouse's younger son, Donald, who had attended the university, married a local girl, Suzie Marley. Suzie's parents were big, round-faced, pleasant people who were quickly accepted into the family, and Newhouse came to feel special kinship for Harry Marley, an uneducated man like himself who had begun as a junk dealer and ended up a millionaire. The Marleys were big boosters of Syracuse.

Newhouse developed still more ties to the university when Leonard and Sylvia Lyons's sons decided to go there. By the late 1950s, it had become almost a regular event for the Lyonses, Marleys, and Newhouses to attend football games together in Syracuse and to visit with Chancellor Tolley afterwards.

In 1959, when Newhouse had paid off his first pledge, Tolley asked for a bigger gift — $1 million — for the new School of Journalism that he and others had been hinting at for years. "I don't think I talked to him for more than five minutes," the chancellor remembered. "He just said, 'I'll do it.' " That October, Syracuse made Newhouse a trustee, and before long, his financial commitment to the new School of Journalism had been raised to cover unanticipated construction costs and a ten-year endowment for operations.

In view of how easy it had been to get Newhouse to pledge the money for a new School of Journalism, Tolley devised an even bolder scheme — an entire new quadrangle on the university campus. As he envisioned it, the site would house a complete School of Communications, emphasizing radio, TV, magazines, and audiovisual skills — in addition to teaching the basics of news gathering.

On 9 May 1962, during one of Newhouse's midweek visits to Syracuse, Tolley sprang the idea on him. "Sam," he said, "I know you don't give to Israel, and the people in the Jewish community don't like you too well for that reason. But it's time for you to move up to the big leagues. You ought to make a major gift." Tolley then described his proposal, focusing on a special point: it would constitute a "living monument." Most people, he explained, even the richest and most powerful, had to die before memorials were constructed in their honor. But Syracuse would be able to dedicate the world's most up-to-date center for the study of communications in Newhouse's name in less than two years, when the first building, for which he had already committed $2 million, was completed.

"I'll leave it up to you on the timetable," Tolley said, "but I want $15 million."

Mitzi was flabbergasted when her husband told her of Tolley's proposal. She felt that such a gift was totally out of line. "Outrageous" was the word she used to describe it. But though Mitzi was able to dominate her husband on most matters about which they disagreed, he was firm about wanting to go ahead with the gift of a communications center. Although he had not originated the idea, he realized that the school would provide the final touch that his empire needed — a way to legitimize his massive communications holdings in the eyes of the rest of the world.

The announcement of the gift — the largest ever made to the university by a living donor — was set for the following 1 November. In the meantime, Newhouse took measures he hoped would add to the celebration. On 1 October, in a secret meeting in room 523 at the Sheraton-Fontenelle Hotel in Omaha, Nebraska, he and his two sons made a formal offer of $40 million for the *Omaha World-Herald* (circulation 251,966). Two weeks later, he returned to Nebraska to talk to the paper's board of directors. At that meeting, the *World-Herald*'s owners agreed that on 31 October, the day before the announcement in Syracuse, they would formally ratify the sale. Newhouse was so proud of what he had done that he leaked the information to a reporter from a New York paper, which, on 31 October, printed the story under the heading "NEWHOUSE BUYS PAPER IN OMAHA."

In the interim, however, the people in Omaha had experienced grave misgivings over the deal. Without telling Newhouse, they had gone out and found another buyer during the week before the sale was to be announced. He was Peter Kiewit, a wealthy Nebraska contractor, who not only wanted to keep the *World-Herald* in local hands but was capable of matching Newhouse's offer with more than $40 million of his own.

It wasn't until Wednesday, 31 October, that Newhouse, already in Syracuse, learned what had happened. He refused to comment publicly on the matter, but Charley Goldman most likely echoed his sentiments when he told an acquaintance, "This is a day of infamy in the annals of journalism." W. Dale Clark, the Omaha banker who conducted both sets of negotiations, sent Newhouse the following communication later that day:

Dear Mr. Sam —
I'm sorry about the turn of events. Babe Ruth held the home run and strikeout records — simultaneously and concurrently. Your performance thru the years has been much, *much* better. This has turned into a believe-it-or-not experience. It could not happen — but it did. A local man with the pride, ability, money, willingness, and desire — all in a mix — result, spontaneous combustion.

Notwithstanding this great disappointment, Newhouse went ahead with the announcement of his gift to Syracuse. His publicist, Ray Josephs, had been briefed well in advance by university officials and produced a release that was carried prominently in Newhouse's newspapers.

While the release emphasized the size of Newhouse's donation and the broad range of activities proposed for the center, it said nothing of the questionable manner in which a sizable portion of the gift was to be funded. Starting in 1960, Newhouse and his accountants arranged a system whereby seven of the newspapers were to be billed a total of $30,000 a year for a period of ten years "for certain services." On paper at least, the services were to involve newspaper research; yet, little, if any, such assistance was actually rendered. By means of this arrangement, Newhouse could claim business deductions for money that actually had been used for the building. Soon thereafter, a similar arrangement — worth another $50,000 a year — was entered into by Newhouse on behalf of the Portland *Oregonian*, the *Harrisburg Patriot* and *Evening News*, and three broadcast properties. Overall, nearly 10 percent of his gift to Syracuse was supplied by this phony "research program."

That Newhouse knew about the arrangement is clear. For one thing, Dean Clark remembers complaining to him about it. Clark's gripe was that he wasn't allowed to spend the money for the purposes for which it was designated. For another, Newhouse regularly sent Tolley letters regarding the status of his pledge to the university. Each letter credited the so-called research payments toward the pledge. Their final communication on the subject occurred in early 1969, the year of Tolley's retirement. Along with $5,932,500 that was properly donated to the university by the S. I. Newhouse Foundation, the letter listed some $268,750 in "payments made by various companies during the years 1960 to 1968 inclusive, under the 'initial' research program," as well as "payments of $338,750 made by various companies during the years 1962 to 1968, inclusive, under the 'supplemental' research program."

Beyond the questionable nature of this funding arrangement lay the matter of its implications for Newhouse's attitude toward the other communities — besides Syracuse — in which he owned and operated newspapers so profitably. For they received very little in the way of charitable contributions in return for the millions they poured into Newhouse's bank accounts each year. (An inspection of the tax returns of the S. I. Newhouse Foundation nearly two decades later showed, for example, that in 1977 all charities in the vicinity of Portland, Oregon — one of his most profitable cities and a key participant in Syracuse University's "supplemental" research program — received from it the munificent sum of $9,000. A total of $2.1 million was given out that year, with the largest single contribution — nearly a quarter of the total — going to a repertory theater in Manhattan.)

In January 1964, Tolley and Newhouse began making final preparations for the 5 August dedication of the first building in the Newhouse center. First, they had to decide on a quotation that was to be displayed on the building in a place reserved for it by the architect. It wasn't until that May, after lengthy discussion among Phil Hochstein (who usually prepared drafts of Newhouse's public statements), Tolley, and various university officials, that Newhouse agreed to the following:

"A free press must be fortified with greater knowledge of the world and skill in the arts of expression."

There were, of course, other, far weightier matters to deal with. For one thing, Newhouse wanted to find someone to perform the dedication of the building, someone who would give it the stature he felt it deserved. At Tolley's urging, Newhouse decided to start at the top with President Lyndon Baines Johnson, who had been in office only a few months since the November 1963 assassination of John F. Kennedy, and who would be beginning his own election campaign that Labor Day. Through the *New Orleans Times-Picayune*'s Washington, D.C., correspondent, Allen Poe, Newhouse arranged to meet with Louisiana Congressman Hale Boggs. Boggs, in turn, provided an entrée to the President. The two men were to meet at the White House in March to discuss the matter over lunch.

When he arrived, Newhouse had not the slightest inkling of what was in store that afternoon and evening. First off, Press Secretary Bill Moyers informed him that the luncheon had been canceled. He explained that the President had to tour areas in the Midwest devastated by spring flooding. If Newhouse wanted a chance to talk to him he'd better come along. The two men flew all over the place, to

Pennsylvania, Ohio, and Illinois. Each time the plane put down, the President would drag his guest along with him as he made speeches and met with important local officials. Back on the plane, Johnson did his utmost to make his reluctant guest feel a welcome part of the day's activities. Newhouse hadn't been around politicians enough to realize that he was being given the "treatment."

When they returned to Washington, Newhouse was invited to sit in on a briefing by Dean Rusk and then to join the President for a skinny-dip in the White House pool. There followed a quiet dinner with Lady Bird, and before he left for home late that night, he had gotten what he came for — a promise that LBJ would travel to Syracuse on 5 August to dedicate the S. I. Newhouse School of Public Communications.

Newhouse's most pressing concern, though, was a dinner to be held in his honor by the university on the evening of 4 August — the night before the dedication ceremonies. He had been told that it would be appropriate to make a few remarks on that occasion, and the prospect of doing so before 700 or 800 people filled him with terror. "If I'd known I would have to speak," he told Florence Glickman half seriously, "I'd never have given the gift."

In January, Newhouse started assembling drafts of a speech. He didn't like the sound of the one Dean Clark had prepared and threw it away. He didn't like the one written by Casey Jones, editor of the *Herald-Journal*, either. Even a speech prepared by Phil Hochstein failed to satisfy him. So in March, he began to write his own, and as soon as it was ready, he practiced arduously.

Each Wednesday for a couple of months, he had Dean Clark and Frank Funk, dean of the university's School of Speech, meet him after lunch in the empty ballroom of the Syracuse Hotel, where the dinner was to be held. Before this select audience, he would give the speech repeatedly, changing words that didn't sound right and eagerly seeking advice on his posture and inflection, even the phrases he was using. "The first one was stumbling," recalled Clark, "but he was not ignorant or insensitive to the nuances of the English language. By the end, he knew it by heart. Even after all that, though, the night he gave it, he sweated like a pig."

The result of these months of practice was an eloquent, moving address which revealed that Newhouse had finally overcome his sense of shame about the past. "I cannot be unaware of a dramatic contrast that concerns my name," he said to an audience that included dozens of relatives and the publishers of most of his newspapers, who had traveled to Syracuse for the occasion. "The first time it appeared anywhere was on a birth certificate written in a New York tenement where I was born.

"I am proud of that.

"Tomorrow I will see my name inscribed on the wall of what is perhaps the most modern School of Communications in the world. I am proud. . . , too, . . . that I can share this pride in my lifetime, with all of you here tonight."

"In the elevator afterwards," Florence Glickman recalled, "I said to him, 'You touched me. Your speech was wonderful.' "

" 'Florence,' he asked, 'was I really good?' It was sincere."

Before dawn on the morning of the long-anticipated dedication ceremony, Newhouse received some worrisome news. The President had been up all night attempting to fashion a response to attacks on U.S. destroyers in the Gulf of Tonkin, and his advisers were urging him to cancel his visit to Syracuse. Soon a second call came in. The President wanted Newhouse to know that he had given his word and would arrive on schedule.

Greatly relieved, S. I., Mitzi, and Chancellor Tolley went out to the airport around ten o'clock to meet the presidential party. It had been arranged that Mitzi and Lady Bird would ride into town in one car, while Newhouse and Johnson would go in a separate vehicle.

Almost before the back door of that car was shut, the President set upon his host in a manner that made him extremely uncomfortable. "Sam," he said, "what can you do for me in Portland?" Though the reference was a bit oblique, Newhouse understood perfectly well that the President was asking for help with an endorsement from the traditionally Republican *Oregonian*. He did his best to dodge the question.

"How about the *Times-Picayune*?" Johnson demanded.

"Mr. President," Newhouse replied, "I wish you wouldn't ask me these things."

"Goddammit!" snorted LBJ. "Why do you think I came here?"

"That's a great newspaper," Newhouse said uneasily. "I've never meddled with it at all. I'm proud of the fact I haven't."

"Look!" directed the President. "Don't fudge!"

"I'll tell you what I'll do," Newhouse said. "We'll see what we can do about the headlines."

"That's not enough!" retorted Johnson.

Finally, Newhouse relented. "Look, Mr. President," he said, "I'll help you all I can."

A crowd of nearly 20,000 — including Governor and Mrs. Nelson Rockefeller and U.S. Senators Jacob Javits and Kenneth Keating — awaited the motorcade's arrival. Speaking from a platform set on the plaza of the brand new, cantilevered, poured-concrete School of Journalism building, Johnson made only passing references to its donor before launching into a speech about hostilities in the Gulf of Tonkin. "On August 2," the President asserted, "the U.S. destroyer *Maddox* was attacked on the high seas in the Gulf of Tonkin by hostile vessels of the government of North Vietnam. . . . The attacks were deliberate. The attacks were unprovoked. The attacks have been answered." The speech marked the beginning of direct, admitted U.S. involvement in the Vietnam War.

When her husband had finished, Lady Bird cut the bright-orange dedication ribbon with a twenty-six-year-old pair of gold-plated scissors, and she and her husband prepared to head back to the airport. Chancellor Tolley asked Newhouse if he wanted to join them for the trip to Hancock Field.

"No sir!" Newhouse informed him. "I won't go through that again."

But in that fall's election, New Orleans's *Times-Picayune* and *States-Item*, both of which had gone for Richard Nixon in 1960, endorsed Johnson. In Portland, the *Oregonian* decided not to endorse either candidate; it, too, had actively supported Nixon in 1960 and did so again in 1968. Most telling was the position of the *St. Louis Globe-Democrat*. Without interference from Newhouse, that paper would surely have supported Goldwater. Instead, it made no endorsement. Overall, only two Newhouse papers endorsed Goldwater in 1964, while thirteen supported Johnson. In the nation as a whole, less than five papers out of every ten (42.3%) endorsed Johnson that year.

Part VI
1962-1979: The Last Years

The Press closes

SUFFOLK 15th YEAR — No. 63
at 1977 L.I. Daily Press Pub. Co. Inc.

FRIDAY, MARCH 25, 1977

Entered as Second Class Matter
at Post Office, Babylon and Bay Shore, N.Y.

10 CENTS

TODAY'S ISSUE IS THE LAST

It is with great personal sadness and regret that we are forced to announce the closing the The Long Island Press. Today's issue—No. 83 of our 157th year—is the last. The Newspaper family has been associated with the Press for almost half a century. We are proud that it has been a good and respected newspaper that cared about the best interests of its readers. We are proud that it has been a leader in many campaigns to improve our schools, to build colleges, to protect the civil rights of citizens, to create parks, to enhance the arts, to nurture wildlife, to elect the best people to public office.

But a fine newspaper can do things only if it is economically secure. The hard fact is that the economic base of the Press has steadily eroded in recent years. Our costs have inexorably risen while our revenue has inexorably shrunk. We have had continuing losses for the past three years.

It is a pattern all too familiar in New York City. One by one, newspapers have disappeared in New York first the dailies in Brooklyn and the Bronx, then the Evening Sun, the Mirror, the World-Telegram, Journal American and Herald Tribune. Our sister paper, the Long Island Star Journal, suspended in 1968.

Despite the omens and despite the odds, we made a massive effort to survive. We invested almost $10 million in new equipment for The Press and we enlarged our news, advertising and circulation staffs. It was not enough. Five years ago, we appealed to the nine unions which represent Press craft employes to abandon their feather-bedding make-work rules and to permit us to use new automated machinery without increasing our costs still more. Unfortunately, the unions could not see the wisdom of our appeal at that time.

Wages and the cost of everything we bought, especially newsprint, continued to soar. Circulation dropped as the middle class fled the city. The national recession, which lasted longer in New York than the rest of the country, forced a number of stores to close and the survivors sharply curtailed their advertising in The Press.

We continued to hope for both improvement in the economy and more favorable terms from our unions. Some of the unions were prepared to help, but not all could. Our hopes are now exhausted. There is simply not enough revenue to publish a good local newspaper in Queens without incurring losses forever.

Long Island Press

'New directions' budget

★ ★ ★   ★ ★ ★

Carey gets start on less spending

By DAVID SHAFFER

ALBANY (AP)—Gov. Carey, who said he wanted the new state budget to set a "new direction" away from ever-increasing taxes and government spending, is getting only a partial start on that from the legislature.

Legislative sources reported today that the new budget of nearly $11.5 billion has been completed in all but a few details.

And as information on the final budget deal has leaked out over the past week, it has become clear that pressure-group politics in the legislature forced Carey to agree to restorations of many of the cuts he had proposed in school aid, aid to local governments, tuition assistance, drug treatment, welfare grants and other favored programs.

But the budget plan provides far fewer spending increases for favored programs than would have seemed politically possible just a year or two ago. And the budget, which is expected to be enacted next week in time for the beginning of the new fiscal year on April 1, will include the "start" on personal income-tax cuts which Carey had said he wanted, and even a reduction in business taxes below what he wanted.

• • •

IT PROVIDES for the first reduction in income-tax rates for New Yorkers in decades.

Legislative leaders of both parties met with Carey late yesterday, and emerged saying the budget agreement was essentially in place.

"All that is left now is some little nit-picking stuff," said Senate Minority Leader Manfred Ohrenstein, Manhattan Democrat. "We've got a deal."

The final bargaining produced a few enrichments in the school-aid part of the budget, which Carey had wanted to cut and for which the legislature won a slight increase. But the small increase in the $3 billion school spending was a far cry from the huge boosts which have become virtually a tradition in recent years.

UPSTATE Republican senators abandoned their fight for cuts in welfare grants yesterday, eliminating the last major obstacle to an agreement.

The major victors in the bargaining which led up to the budget agreement appeared to have been the 14 members of the Assembly in the Black and Puerto Rican Caucus. They successfully held out against Carey's proposals for cuts in basic grants to some welfare recipients in the "home relief"

program and against Republican demands for even greater grant cuts.

The minority legislators had threatened to withhold their support of the budget if the welfare cuts were left in — jeopardizing Assembly speaker Stanley Steingut's chances of mustering the 76 votes needed to pass the budget from among his 90-member Democratic majority.

Upstate members of the Republican majority in the Senate briefly revolted Wednesday night against the lack of welfare cuts. But they were forced to back down after Senate Majority Leader Warren Anderson convinced them the slight increase in their cherished school-aid program could be jeopardized if they did not yield.

• • •

AS THE BUDGET negotiations wound to their conclusion, both houses met briefly, and took these actions, among others:

● The Assembly gave final legislative approval to a bill setting this year's statewide primary elections for local offices for Thursday, Spet. 8, with a runoff for citywide offices in New York City on Sept. 19. The measure is expected to be signed by Carey, who had vetoed an earlier bill setting up a June 7 primary.

● The Senate approved and sent to Assembly a bill to require the Port Authority of New York and New Jersey to hold hearings before any future toll or fare increases on its bridge tolls or fare increases on its bridges, tunnels and mass-transit facilities.

The final welfare package includes nearly $200 million in cuts below current projections for the $1.8 billion welfare program. But the money would come from reductions in medical assistance and such things as rent allowances — not in the basic family
(Turn to Page 6)

ICE-BREAKER: Sanitationman Bob Byrnes sprinkles a shovel full of salt on Merrick Boulevard at the corner of Hillside Avenue in Jamaica after a water main break last night turned the intersection into a sheet of ice, making roadway conditions hazardous. A similar situation was reported at Hillside and Sutphin Boulevard which police had to shut down for a time until the Jamaica Water Supply Co. repaired the broken main. (Photo by Robert Kalfus)

Richard DeAngelis tells his wife, Abby, and children, Marisa, 9, left, and Richard Jr., 12, how it felt to find all that money. (Bob Kalfus Photo)

THINGS PICKING UP
★ ★ ★ ★ ★ ★
Sanitman finds 14G lost by couple

By TOM TURNER

There's an old saying that goes: things are picking up in the Sanitation Department." That certainly was

"I decided to turn it in before we got into trouble," he said.

When Foreman Robert Volpe saw what had been brought to him, he

2 court actions fight

Defeat squeeze play on porn

By GEORGE DOURIS and H. L. KLEIN

A squeeze play between public reaction to pornography and the questionable constitutionality of a "blue zone" plan delayed adoption by the Boar

30 Newhouse & Sons

IT WOULD ALL BE THEIRS. In less than twenty years, Newhouse's two sons, S. I., Jr., and Donald, would inherit control of Advance Publications, Inc., and thus of the huge communications empire their father had amassed. Each was to receive five of the ten voting shares of API stock. The remaining 990 nonvoting shares would go — free of estate taxes — to the S. I. Newhouse Foundation, whose board of directors the sons would also control. "I've built this thing up," Newhouse explained, "and I'm not about to let it go to pieces."

But were Si and Donald up to the task? For, as Newhouse himself explained, "The boys have been trained differently from myself." There were powerful reasons for him to worry. One, of which he was keenly aware, was the abject failure of the sons of other major newspaper publishers — Hearst and Pulitzer, in particular — to live up to their father's greatness. Another was Newhouse's own experiences with one of his boys.

In 1962, right after he closed the deal for New Orleans's *Times-Picayune* and *States-Item*, he turned to his older son for an explanation of an item he came across in the financial reports of one of the newspapers. Si, it appeared, had charged $11-worth of shaving cream to the family business. Not only did this violate Newhouse's precepts of how the newspapers should be run, but $11 was a lot to pay for shaving cream. At the time, Si was nearly thirty-five years old, and his father must have wondered if he would ever overcome the sense of disappointment he sometimes felt about his first child.

Beginning in early childhood, his father's inattention had been a source of discomfort for Si, especially when contrasted with the affection with which his mother smothered him. School was a particular problem. At Horace Mann, which he attended after his family moved to Manhattan, he was, in the words of a family intimate, "a rambunctious, crazy kid. He had no personality and no brains. His schooling was not satisfactory." During those early years, Si developed just one lasting friendship — with Roy Cohn, who later was to become one of America's most notorious lawyers.

After Horace Mann, he attended Syracuse University, where he met with little success. "He was a bright kid," recalled Chancellor Tolley, "but in many respects, he was not ready for college." First, Si was expelled from the journalism department for failing to maintain a sufficient grade-point average, and after three years, he quit school altogether. "Even then, there was something different about him," recalled clothing designer Donald Brooks, who roomed next door for a time while the two were in college. "When everybody else was playing Benny Goodman or Glenn Miller, the music you heard from Si's room was Mahler or Sibelius."

After Syracuse, Si put in a stint with the U.S. Army (1950–52) and then went to Portland to work for KGW, one of his father's radio stations. That, too, was not much of a success, and he soon returned to New York for an apprenticeship at the *Long Island Daily Press*. "He was a perfectly decent guy," recalled one of Si's co-workers, "but he was awfully screwed up. He'd sit around the office reading the *Daily Worker*, but then at the end of the day, he'd offer to give you a lift back to Manhattan in his Cadillac! He never wrote worth a damn and didn't seem to do much of anything."

In Washington, D.C., at the offices of the Advance News Service, Si was the object of even greater ridicule. "He was known in the bureau as Jerry Lewis," Jules Witcover recalled. "He looked like Jerry Lewis. He acted like Jerry Lewis. They'd line him up with press credentials for these big foreign trips, and he would come in with about four cameras hanging all over him. The kid was just ludicrous."

In one regard, however, Si did manage to please his parents — at least for a while. On Sunday, 11 March 1951, while on leave from the Army, he was married at the Waldorf-Astoria to Jane Franke, a fine-arts student he had met at Syracuse. Franke was, in the words of a friend of the family, "a nice Jewish girl from the Bronx." She quickly became a favorite of Mitzi's.

The couple made S.I. and Mitzi even happier when they moved back to Manhattan to start a family. By 1956, they had produced three children — S. I. III, Wynn, and Pamela. But after Pamela was born, their marriage broke up. "That was a bad time, especially for Mitzi," recalled Ernie Doepke. "She thought divorces were not part of the Newhouse family. For a couple of years, when we went to their home, S. I., Jr., wasn't there. She wouldn't have him. She practically disowned him."

During that time, Si became an unabashed playboy and jet-setter. "Both Mitzi and Sam felt this was their failure," recalled Chancellor Tolley. "That somewhere along the line, they hadn't given Si the common sense he needed." Little things like the shaving-cream incident obviously weighed on their minds, but Si's father must have been especially troubled by the frivolousness ascribed to his son in an article in the *New York Times*.

"Mr. Newhouse started life afresh last year, inspired by a movie with 'a marvelous bachelor apartment,'" the *Times* reported on 6 April 1966.

> "After I saw it, I decided to move," he says, sliding his black espadrilles over the jackal fur rug (50 skins imported from Greece) in the living room of the six-room, two-terrace apartment he describes as "very much me at the moment." Surrounded by abstract art . . . and greige-toned upholstered furniture that owes its allegiance to no period or style, he sums it all up with "I feel comfortable here."
>
> Part of the comfort is attributed to a Filipino houseboy whose cooking talents extend from spaghetti to duck, and whom Mr. Newhouse calls "one of the great luxuries of the world." Another luxury is the pale fox bed throw that challenges the monastic simplicity of the tobacco-brown bedroom with its felt-covered walls and portable television set.

This was not the sort of life-style Newhouse had ever imagined for his children. Yet, at the time of publication of the *Times*'s article, there were also signs that Si was beginning to get the knack of the business, and for these, his father was grateful. Si moved over to *Vogue*, where he seemed more comfortable, and he even started to show an interest in the affairs of the newspapers. According to Harold Martin, who for many years served as production manager of the *St. Louis Globe-Democrat*, "S. I. and S. I., Jr., would visit about every two weeks. The two of them would go through the building together, see the key people, and we'd all go to dinner.

Then S. I. would go back to the hotel, and S. I., Jr., would speak to me for hours and see the plant again."

"I know there was a lot of speculation about him," Martin concluded, "but on those visits, he listened to everything, and he asked all the right questions."

With the other son, there were never any real doubts. Not only was Donald Edward Newhouse "sober as a judge," in the words of Chancellor Tolley, but he seemed to take to the newspaper business naturally. He also bore a distinct physical resemblance to his father.

That Donald was to be the real newspaperman in the family seemed to have been understood by his parents almost from the time he was born. At Christmas in 1935, S. I. and Mitzi set up trust funds for both sons. For S. I., Jr., there was a lump sum of $100,000 in cash, provided by his mother. The interest was to be payable to him in 1948 when he attained the age of twenty-one, and the principal would accrue to him four years later. Similar arrangements were made for Donald, but his trust fund came from his father, and all but $250 of it was in the form of promissory notes made by the Staten Island Advance Company.

Like his older brother, Donald dropped out of Syracuse University after his third year, but where Si did so with no particular purpose in mind, Donald had a reason. He was so anxious to become involved in the family business that he could not see the point of staying in college for another year. While in Syracuse, he had put in long hours in the papers' classified advertising departments. Thereafter, he was trained in all phases of newspapering by his Uncle Ted at the *Long Island Press*. It was not long before Donald became production manager of the *Jersey Journal* and took his older brother's place alongside his father on business trips. Even his marriage worked out well.

Donald, who had inherited his father's short stature, was described by acquaintances as methodical and more rigorous and precise than his older brother, who, at five feet, six inches, was distinguished by curly hair and a modish style of dress. One observer noted that Donald's "brisk, no-nonsense manner gives him an uncanny resemblance to his father."

That impression was shared by many others, including Dean Wesley Clark at Syracuse University's School of Journalism. "When it came time for [Leonard Lyons's son] Douglas's bar mitzvah," Clark recalled, "it was held in a big temple on the Upper East Side in New York with at least a thousand people, including Red Buttons and Ethel Merman, and a speech by Justice Douglas. I sat next to Donald Newhouse."

"Don," Clark asked, "how does this compare with your bar mitzvah?"

"When it was time for my bar mitzvah," Don replied, "my father said, 'We're not going to spend any money on that kind of nonsense.' And we didn't."

Donald's special place in the family was underscored when S. I. arranged for him and Suzie and their three children to move into an apartment at 730 Park Avenue, just below his parents. And for weekends, Donald's family had their own private house at Greenlands.

Different as Newhouse's two sons were, it was clear by the mid-1960s that they were both capable of taking over from their father. It remained to be seen, however, when he would let them assume that responsibility. For his was a powerful personality, and as long as he remained healthy and able to supervise the affairs of his empire, he would cling to it tenaciously.

31 The Publishers of the Future

IN LATE MAY OF 1967, Newhouse attended a party held in his honor at Hinerwadel's Grove, a private resort on the north shore of Lake Onondaga, a few miles from Syracuse. Hosted by Harry Marley, this celebration of Newhouse's birthday had long been an annual event for executives from his local newspapers and radio and TV stations. Every year, they gathered to eat their fill of clams, chicken, and lobster and to honor the man who was their benefactor.

For some of the men from the *Herald-Journal* and *Post-Standard*, Harry Marley's clambake was also a chance to engage in a private sport — trying to guess the guest of honor's age. For those who didn't know, Newhouse's appearance made the question a challenge. There was a trace of grey in his hair, especially at the temples, but otherwise he exuded youthfulness. He had a full head of hair and a ready smile, and his round, unlined, pink face retained a healthy glow. To the casual observer, he could have been in his late fifties.

The truth about Newhouse's age always came as a shock, even to people who felt they were well acquainted with him, and that spring in Syracuse, the sense of surprise was as great as ever. The boss was seventy-two years old, and though he had been known to complain about his family's tendency to "blow up," he seemed to be having no difficulty keeping up with the others in the food and drink departments.

Newhouse's recent business accomplishments made it even more difficult for the men at the party to believe that he was already seven years past normal retirement age. The previous summer, only a few months after taking charge of the three newspapers in Springfield, Massachusetts, he had snapped up the morning *Mobile Register*

■ 230

(circulation 46,905) and the afternoon *Mobile Press* (71,488). The deal also netted him control of the *Mississippi Press-Register* (circulation 10,900) in nearby Pascagoula. Though the *Mobile Press* and *Register* were, journalistically speaking, some of the sorriest properties in America, they were also among the most profitable.

Soon after the Mobile acquisitions, Newhouse announced that he had finally cornered the remaining stock in Condé Nast and would merge the company with the Patriot News Company in Harrisburg. A short time later, on 7 March 1967, he dropped the real blockbuster. For $54.2 million, he had taken over the 125-year-old *Cleveland Plain Dealer*. As with his previous acquisitions in Portland, Birmingham, and New Orleans, the price set a record.

Yet, despite such successes and apparent good health, several of those who spoke with Newhouse that day at Hinerwadel's were struck by a querulous note that seemed to have slipped into his conversation. "Where," he wondered aloud in the presence of some of the men from the *Herald-Journal* and the *Post-Standard*, "are the next publishers coming from?" The question came up not once but several times, with Newhouse seeming to despair each time he returned to the subject of the men he called "the publishers of the future."

Some of his gloomy spirits may have been attributable to the nature of the event itself. And, though few of those present knew, as soon as the festivities surrounding his birthday were over, he planned to undergo surgery on painful varicose veins in both of his legs. Still, the real reasons for his depression went far deeper than intimations of mortality. The newspapers were still uppermost in his mind, and they had developed a potentially serious problem.

With the addition of the *Plain Dealer*, Newhouse owned twenty-two newspapers in sixteen cities spread throughout the U.S. Each day, they produced more than 3.2 million papers, and each year, they grossed nearly half a billion dollars. Yet, the owner of this vast empire ran it with all the finesse of the proprietor of a family store. He maintained no central headquarters and disdained the fuss and red tape of organization charts and management strategies. There were not even centralized mechanisms for planning and budgeting.

People who wanted to get in touch with the boss had to go through Miss Anne Canavan, a lavender-haired spinster who served as his personal aide and troubleshooter from an office at the *Newark Ledger*. If they didn't know it already, those making inquiries soon learned that he transacted as little business as possible by letter, preferring the telephone. For advice, he relied almost exclusively on his accountant, his lawyer, and his two brothers, frequently calling the last of these in the middle of the night. "After all," he would tell Norman and Ted, "if I can't sleep, why should you?"

The simplicity of the setup was amply demonstrated by a series of questions and answers in a deposition taken of him during the course of litigation concerning the *Denver Post*. William McClearn of the Denver firm of Holland & Hart traveled to New York City in late January of 1969 to ask the questions.

McClearn:	Would you give me your business address?
Newhouse:	I don't have an office. I just go from place to place. I use a desk, so I would have to give you twenty-odd addresses.
McClearn:	When Mr. Goldman from time to time would send you memos, what would you do with the copy you received?
Newhouse:	Destroy it.
McClearn:	You don't keep personal files?
Newhouse:	I do not have a file.
McClearn:	Do you maintain a diary or calendar?
Newhouse:	No, I do not.
McClearn:	What records do you keep to show where you are at a particular time?
Newhouse:	None at all.

If there was any model for the way Newhouse ran his affairs, it was that of a national sales operation. He often referred to his newspapers as "products," and, in describing the regular visits he and his brothers and sons paid to the various newspapers, would lapse into salesman's jargon. "We call on them regularly," he would say. Or, "Norman covers the southern territory." Within the family, these trips came to be known as "newspaper routes."

In an age when the complex, sophisticated practices taught by Harvard Business School had finally taken hold, Newhouse's operation was, in the words of one careful observer, "a management consultant's nightmare." It was also a model of efficiency, turning out profits at least twice those of the closest competitors — Time, Inc., and the Times Mirror Publishing Company of Los Angeles.

The problem with his system was that it discouraged the development of good people to run the newspapers. One of the major stumbling blocks was Newhouse's long-standing policy of allowing no one outside the family to own stock in the business. The case of Harold Martin, who started with the Newhouse organization in 1955 as an assistant business manager in Syracuse, was not unique.

"I had an agreement that I would be a publisher if I would go where Mr. Newhouse sent me," Martin explained. After Syracuse, he was production manager in St. Louis from 1956 to 1959, and for the next four years he was in charge of the back shop in Birmingham. But in 1963, he quit abruptly to work for the newspapers in nearby Montgomery, and not too long after that, he became president of the Jefferson Pilot newspaper chain.

"When I told S. I. I was leaving," Martin recalled, "he reminded me about the publisher's job. He said, 'If that's what you want, I can fix it up right away.'" But what Martin wanted was a piece of the action, and on that point, Newhouse was firm: "You know I don't let people buy in."

Newhouse's attitude about a publisher's primary responsibilities did not help things. Local autonomy notwithstanding, he made it clear to each of his top employees that their first obligation was to the bottom line. That, in turn, carried with it two tasks: making sure local advertisers remained happy, and keeping costs down. At a minimum, satisfying the advertisers meant leaving their affairs — except for events like new store openings — alone. And keeping internal costs down meant treating lower-level employees like chattel. "The guys at the top really get paid off," explained Wes Clark, who, during his tenure as dean of Syracuse's School of Journalism, became acquainted with quite a few of Newhouse's publishers. "But there's very little for the other people. Newhouse gave minimum wages to the replaceable people."

Newhouse's penchant for secrecy and his belief in the principles of nepotism only exacerbated the problem. Moreover, said one of his publishers, "He didn't like to have many grasshoppers. What he wanted was droves of ants."

From a manager's point of view, the most troubling aspect of Newhouse's system was his refusal to engage in systematic planning or budgeting. "The psychology of no budget — of making each year like the last unless special permission is granted — is intimidating," explained one man who suffered through it quietly for years at one of Newhouse's papers. "It creates puppets on strings."

Finally, Newhouse had a quirk that drove many of his best people to distraction. He made it a practice never to praise them. "If I said something was good," he once explained, "the next time I didn't say anything, they would think I didn't like it. So it's better to say nothing." "Even with his sons," Florence Glickman said, " 'very good' was lavish praise."

The result of all this was that, by 1967, management was painfully thin in the Newhouse organization. By the time of the party at Hinerwadel's, two of his favorite publishers, Mike Frey in Portland and Ernie Doepke in Harrisburg, had told him of their plans to retire. And before they could step down, there was a third shock. That September, while visiting New York, the *Globe-Democrat*'s Dick Amberg, then fifty-five years old and the publisher Newhouse most admired, suffered a fatal heart attack.

As if losing his three top publishers in one fell swoop weren't enough, Newhouse also had to contend with Thomas Van Husen Vail, the forty-year-old dandy he inherited when he acquired the *Cleveland Plain Dealer* that spring. Vail, the great-grandson of the paper's founder, had been in charge since 1963. His greatest goal was to win a Pulitzer Prize, and to that end, he hired a group of young, aggressive reporters dubbed the "Young Tigers" and gave the editorial department a $1 million-a-month budget to see that they got results. His control of the purse strings in the production shop was even laxer, with the result that staffers soon came to refer to it as "Featherbed Heaven."

In short, he was not Newhouse's type. The product of rich parents and a Princeton education, Vail seemed far more interested in what the *Plain Dealer* could do for his standing in Cleveland, New York, and Washington, D.C., than in what he could do for it.

Though Newhouse had promised to retain Vail as publisher as part of the purchase agreement, he could not accept the prospect of letting him continue to be in charge. Instead, he quietly moved in

Leo Ring, an old composing-room hand from Newark, St. Louis, and Birmingham. "Leo Ring," said Harold Martin, for whom Ring worked in St. Louis and Birmingham, "is the best foreman I ever had work for me anywhere." In Cleveland, Ring was given the title "Assistant to the General Manager" and was put in charge of dealing with the paper's unions. That much he certainly did. During his first few years in Cleveland, he negotiated the elimination of more than half the 600 positions in the *Plain Dealer*'s composing room, arranged for the installation of plenty of modern, labor-saving equipment, and regularly faced down the paper's Guild unit.

Inside the *Plain Dealer*, no one doubted Ring's control. "The line of authority for the paper's operations," explained a man in the business department, "ran from S. I. Newhouse to Norman Newhouse to Leo Ring. It totally bypassed Vail and [Business Manager Roy] Kopp." "They have the titles," Ring once said in his direct manner, "and I make the decisions."

The problem with this setup was that the man actually in charge rarely read the paper and knew even less about producing a good editorial product. During Ring's first ten years as assistant to the general manager, most of the Young Tigers left, including Joe Eszterhas (who became an editor at *Rolling Stone*) and James M. Naughton (who covered politics for the *New York Times* before becoming national editor of the *Philadelphia Inquirer*). At the same time, the *Plain Dealer* ran through five managing editors and seven city editors. Largely as a result of savings engineered by Ring, the paper's profits went up, while its journalistic quality dipped perceptibly. Fifteen years later, the *Plain Dealer* still had not won Tom Vail his Pulitzer.

The transfer of Leo Ring to Cleveland in 1967 signaled an undermining of local autonomy at several of Newhouse's newspapers. Unable to groom a satisfactory new generation of local publishers, Newhouse was increasingly forced to resort to sending loyal men from close to home out into the field. Later that same year, for example, Fred Stickel, a Newhouse-trained executive at the *Jersey Journal*, went to Portland to become general manager of the Oregonian Publishing Company. Stickel, and not newly named publisher Robert Notson, would call the crucial shots. The following year, Newhouse sent his brother Norman to New Orleans, where he could keep closer tabs on the *Times-Picayune* and the *States-Item*, as well as the Alabama papers.

Under the new arrangement, local people might retain the publishers' jobs, but their independence was no longer assured, and, more than ever, business concerns would dictate the newspapers' performance.

32 Final Exam

"You're just the man I want to see," announced Arthur H. "Red" Motley as he approached Newhouse outside a Broadway theater one night in the fall of 1975. At the time, Motley was publisher and chairman of the board of *Parade*, a tremendously successful rotogravure supplement inserted on Sundays in more than nineteen million American newspapers. He was also a great promoter, whose motto was, "Nothing Happens Until Somebody Sells Something." On that particular fall evening, Red Motley was looking to make something happen.

Though Newhouse was in the middle of his eighty-first year, he seemed, at the time of the chance encounter, as alert and active as ever. To be sure, weekends at the farm tended to stretch out longer, and he seemed to have developed great interest in his grandchildren, as well as a heightened appetite for travel. But where changes were most apparent was in his attitude toward the newspapers themselves.

After acquiring the *Cleveland Plain Dealer*, Newhouse began in earnest the job of getting his most important properties ready for the next generation. During the next eight years, he poured hundreds of millions of dollars' worth of profits back into the business. A hundred and seventy-six million dollars went into new plants in cities that most needed them — Newark, New Orleans, Springfield, and Syracuse. Though there were substantial tax advantages associated with this massive reinvestment program, its real purpose was quite different. "One of the major reasons for all the new plants," explained Len Gorman, an executive with the Syracuse newspapers, "was to avoid labor problems that were crippling the New York papers at that time."

■ 237

Another $26 million went to buy a 49-percent interest in the Bowaters, Ltd., paper mill in Catawba, South Carolina. The plant could supply more than two-fifths of the empire's total requirements for newsprint. Moreover, Newhouse set things up so that his newspapers paid market prices for the paper, thereby providing Bowaters with extra funds to invest in new timberlands.

Finally, Newhouse paid some $21 million to purchase the circulation lists of the *Newark Evening News* and the *Bayonne Times*, thus solidifying his control of northern New Jersey. The way he went about the latter acquisition, however, was bound to harm his reputation in the city where he grew up.

For years after Newhouse's forced departure from Bayonne in 1925, Judge Lazarus's younger son Herman, who served as publisher of the *Times*, swore the family paper would never be sold to Newhouse. On Herman's death in 1966, the *Times* became the property of his widow, Helen. Only five years later, on the Fourth of July weekend during which the paper was to celebrate its one-hundredth anniversary, she went ahead and sold the paper to Newhouse anyway, for $1 million. Immediately, the *Times* was merged into the *Jersey Journal*, leaving dozens of Bayonne residents out of work. And to thwart rumors that local businessmen were planning to start a local paper of their own, as soon as he took over, Newhouse had the *Times*'s equipment torn up and thrown out into the parking lot to rust.

The demise of the *Newark Evening News* was an even sadder story. Though once a great newspaper, the *News* had been severely neglected by its owners, and that September, for a measly $20 million, Newhouse was able to acquire both its plant and its Sunday edition. Less than a year later, the paper shut down for good, leaving the *Star-Ledger*, once the weakest offering in town, as the only survivor — as well as the largest daily in all of New Jersey.

Other than the *Times* and the *News*, which, basically, had folded up shop by the time he bought them, Newhouse made no major newspaper purchases during the eight-year interval that followed his acquisition of the *Plain Dealer*. In this regard, too, his attitude had changed. No longer was he interested in taking over any newspaper that was available. He now thought of himself as a collector. As such, his goal was finding what he called "gems to add to my crown."

The publication he had coveted the longest was probably the *Washington Post*. Back in 1953, Col. Robert McCormick offered Eugene Meyer, then owner of the *Post*, a chance to bid on the *Washington Times-Herald*. A bit uncertain as to how to proceed, Meyer called Newhouse. "First," Newhouse said, "I must tell you, the Colonel has invited me to bid as well. To me, it's worth $7.5 million. But it's worth more to you, because you could get the additional advantage of merging the two papers. I suggest you bid a million more."

Over the following decade, as the *Post* prospered and rose to prominence under Meyer's son-in-law, Philip Graham, Newhouse must have wished he had used the opportunity to try to get the papers for himself. He may even have made such an offer and been rebuffed. Whatever the case, within a week or two of Graham's tragic death in 1963, he traveled to Washington to discuss with Clark Clifford the possibility of going after the *Post*. Considered by many to be America's preeminent superlawyer, Clifford had been close to Graham and was on friendly terms with his widow, Katherine, who inherited control of the paper.

"He told me how he had started from nowhere and now had an extensive empire," Clifford recalled nearly two decades later. "And then he launched on it. 'I'd like to buy the *Washington Post*,' he said. 'It's a paper that interests me, and it's got great possibilities. I would like you to negotiate for me. I am willing to pay $100 million for the paper.' Flat out like that. It was an awful lot of money at the time."

Newhouse didn't have to tell Clifford that if he succeeded, there would be a healthy broker's fee, perhaps two or three million dollars. That much was understood. But he did coach Clifford on the kinds of arguments he might use: "He talked a little about how Mrs. Graham was not trained in operating a complex operation of that kind, and how the boy, Donnie, was eighteen years old, and obviously he wasn't ready." Inexperienced as she may have been at the time, Katherine Graham refused to sell.

Around the same time, Newhouse offered even more for the one paper he read regularly — the *New York Times*. According to Adolph Ochs Sulzberger, who became publisher shortly afterwards, the offer was not taken seriously at the *Times*. ("They'd never sell to a kike like me," Newhouse later told Wes Clark in Syracuse.)

After the *Times* and the *Post*, the newspaper that most interested

Newhouse was the *Philadelphia Inquirer*. "He thought it was the best and most undersold paper in the eastern United States," said Ernie Doepke. Not the least of the *Inquirer*'s attractions was its proximity to Newark and New York. Moreover, Philadelphia seemed like a terrific newspaper market. Even in the late 1960s, it was able to support the profitable operation of four newspapers — the *Inquirer* and *Daily News*, both owned by Walter Annenberg, and the *Journal* and *Bulletin*, controlled by the McLean family — at a time when few cities could maintain two. And though the afternoon *Bulletin* held the lead in both circulation and advertising revenue, Newhouse figured that it was only a matter of time before it, and others like it, were pushed under by the deadly combination of the evening news on television and the problems of delivering newspapers in densely populated urban areas during the afternoon rush hour.

Through broker Joseph Neff, who was Annenberg's brother-in-law, Newhouse made regular inquiries about the *Inquirer*. His persistence appeared to have paid off when, one weekend in 1969, Joe Fuerst, who had been put in charge of Annenberg's affairs during his tenure as Ambassador to Great Britain, called Newhouse at the farm. They arranged to meet for a cocktail later in the day at Washington Crossing. Fuerst wanted to know if Newhouse would be willing to pay $55 million for the *Inquirer*.

After agreeing to pay what would amount to yet another all-time record price for an American newspaper, Newhouse heard no more from Fuerst for some time. A few months later, when he called to confirm the deal, he was told it was still on. Additional assurances came to him via Ed Russell, who called on Ambassador Annenberg in London. Soon thereafter, the *Inquirer* was sold for $55 million, but the buyer was John Knight. Newhouse realized that his role had been simply to assure that Annenberg would get a record price from Knight.

He grew even more envious of Knight in 1974, when Knight merged his chain with that of the Ridder brothers in a deal that relegated Newhouse to second place in overall circulation. After that, Newhouse's daily readership of 3.54 million (5.8 percent of the nation's total) was several hundred thousand below the 3.725 million of Knight-Ridder (6.1 percent). Moreover, Newhouse had fallen to fourth in total newspaper ownership, behind Gannett, Thomson, and Knight-Ridder.

Thus, when Red Motley told him, "Whitcom wants to sell its stock in Booth," Newhouse was eager to pursue the matter. Whitcom was the abbreviated name of John Hay Whitney's communications corporation, and Booth was the sort of property that might make the long drought worthwhile. The eight newspapers it ran operated as monopolies in their Michigan cities — Ann Arbor, Bay City, Flint, Grand Rapids, Jackson, Kalamazoo, Muskegon, and Saginaw. "As sedate as Whistler's mother," according to a Detroit newsman, they were small to medium in size and thus more profitable than larger publications. (On revenues of $200 million in 1975, the company netted $16 million after taxes.) Moreover, Booth was well ahead of most in the installation of modern, labor-saving equipment. The papers might not be the gems Newhouse wished to add to his crown, but they were, in the words of one analyst, "the Cadillacs of the industry."

In 1973, Booth Newspapers traded 16 percent of its stock to Whitcom in return for *Parade* magazine. From the outset, Whitcom's manager, Walter Thayer, wanted to take Booth over. But when he realized that he would be opposed by the company's managers at every turn, he decided instead to attempt to sell the stock at an inflated price.

The morning after the tip from Motley, Newhouse called John Whitehead at Goldman, Sachs, the New York investment banking firm that served as underwriter for Booth Newspapers. Ordinarily, a man in Whitehead's position might have been expected to offer resistance, but he plunged right in, arranging for Newhouse to meet with James Sauter, Booth's president and chief operating officer. Over lunch in New York that January, Newhouse asked Sauter how the various members of the Booth family would respond to his buying Whitcom's stock. Sauter said he couldn't speak for them but promised to find out.

Newhouse was off to Acapulco that week and would not return until mid-February, when, it was agreed, Sauter would get back to him. Their meeting had not been unfriendly, but the plan to talk again was about the only agreement the two men had reached.

Afterwards, as Newhouse and his sons drove uptown, he asked what they thought about the idea. Both opposed the deal on the ground that it would be buying trouble. Newhouse disagreed. Though he was eighty and near the end of his career, his ability to spot golden opportunities where others could not was as keen as ever. "Besides," he told his boys, "you've got to learn in life that nothing worth getting ever comes to you without having to fight for it."

Before Newhouse returned from Mexico, Thayer demanded a decision on Whitcom's Booth stock. Newhouse directed his sons to buy it, and on 12 February, they purchased 846,823 shares for $30.5 million — about $36 a share. Sauter, who had not been consulted, was furious and raced to New York to hire merger expert Joe Flom and to do whatever else would be required to avoid a Newhouse takeover. Within a few days, he and Newhouse met a second time, with Newhouse trying to assure Sauter that he was interested only in being a silent partner in Booth, and that a takeover was the furthest thing from his mind.

"I jumped all over S. I. about the Acapulco business," Sauter recalled. " 'Why should I believe you now?' I asked, but every time you belted him over the head, he just came back with a smile. 'That's water over the dam,' he said."

Newhouse became an even more ominous figure on Booth's horizon less than two weeks later, when he got hold of 404,850 shares from the Cranbrook Educational Community. Though he had cornered almost 25 percent of the newspapers' stock, he continued to insist to Sauter and others that he had no interest in obtaining control.

Then, one night in early May, Newhouse invited Sauter and other key Booth executives to a club in New York for dinner. Newhouse sat at the head of the table with Sauter on his right. Suddenly, in a grand gesture, he pulled out a trust agreement he'd had his attorneys draw up. It purported to prevent him from buying more Booth stock for ten years and to require him to refrain from interfering in the company's operations for the same period of time.

"I couldn't react without reading it," Sauter recalled. "Afterwards, we found out it was a sham and told him so. It didn't tie his hands. It was 100 percent pure gesture."

For the next several months, Newhouse and Booth's management remained locked in a stalemate. By July, though, several Booth family members had banded together to sell their stock — just as Newhouse had expected. They first approached the huge Thomson organization, which owned scores of newspapers in the U.S. and

Canada, and soon, representatives of the Thomson interests were in touch with Newhouse.

Newhouse, of course, was in no mood to sell. But he was also aware that Roy Thomson, the chain's owner and founder, had died recently and that his estate remained in an unsettled condition. It was a chance to try to shoot the moon. Right away, he offered Thomson's heirs more than a billion dollars in cash for the opportunity to overtake Knight-Ridder and Gannett.

Because the Thomsons would not sell, Newhouse's bold offer was not made public, but it at least had the effect of scaring them off. By then, though, other interested buyers were lining up, most notably the Times Mirror Company of Los Angeles, whose bid of $40 a share was accepted by all of Booth's shareholders save Newhouse. The deal was scheduled to be completed that October.

Ignoring the trust deed he had given Sauter back in May, Newhouse immediately countered with an offer of his own. He would pay $47 a share, or $7 more than the Los Angeles company had bid. It was a master stroke, for simply to match it Times Mirror would have had to reduce its annual dividend by ten cents a share. Because Newhouse had no stockholders to worry about, it was understood by both sides that he could afford to go much higher without difficulty.

On 8 November 1976, after more than six decades in the newspaper business, Newhouse concluded his final transaction. For a total of $305 million, he acquired the eight Booth newspapers and *Parade* magazine. It was likely to remain the biggest American newspaper deal of the twentieth century.

33 Last Act

IT WAS STILL DARK outside when editor Dave Starr walked into the city room at the *Long Island Press* the morning of 25 March 1977. Most of the night staff had gone home, leaving a skeleton crew to watch as he handed the six paragraphs to night editor Al St. James.

"It is with great regret and sadness," began the announcement of Newhouse's last act as a newspaperman, "that we are forced to announce the closing of the *Long Island Press*." The newspaper that had served as the empire's flagship for nearly fifty years was going down. In the sinking lay a stunning recapitulation of its owner's greatest strengths and greatest weaknesses.

From the outset, Newhouse's choice of Queens amply demonstrated his skill at identifying newspaper markets that possessed great, untapped potential. By the end of World War II, Jamaica was already the third largest shopping center in all of New York State. At the same time, thanks to such growth and to Newhouse's careful doctoring, the *Long Island Press* was well on its way to becoming the sixth largest afternoon paper in America. By 1967, it would boast some 445,000 daily subscribers — a nearly tenfold increase from the time of Newhouse's purchase. That year, too, advertising was to reach an all-time high — 25,429,623 lines, an even greater increase than had been achieved in circulation. During "Jamaica Days" in the fall, advertising was so heavy that the *Press* had to print two special sections — of 150 pages each.

After Queens, Newhouse sensed, the next great burst of economic growth would occur a little to the east, in Nassau and Suffolk counties. There, the *Review-Star*, an unattractive and pedestrian rag, had had the entire area to itself for two decades, but, try as he might during the late 1930s, Newhouse could not convince its owner, James Stiles, to sell.

In early 1939, just after he merged the *Flushing Journal* with the *Long Island City Star*, Newhouse leased an empty automobile showroom in Hempstead and outfitted it with a printing press and five Linotype machines that he had had pulled out of the *Journal*'s then vacant plant in Flushing. Thus equipped, he began publication of the only newspaper he ever originated — the *Nassau Journal*, a four-page wrapper of news into which were inserted copies of the *Star-Journal* (for the North Shore) and the *Press* (for the rest of Nassau County). To save the cost of establishing his own carrier-boy delivery system, he arranged to have the new paper delivered by an independent dealer. However, after only a week, he and the dealer feuded over the terms of the arrangement, and Newhouse gave the project up. Then, a few months later, he sold the plant for $50,000 to Alicia Patterson and her wealthy husband, Harry F. Guggenheim. "I thought she'd see it as a toy," he later explained, "something to play with for a while, and that eventually I'd be able to buy it back from her."

Patterson published the first issue of *Newsday* on 3 September 1940, with a press run of 30,000. Wanting to appeal to transplanted Manhattanites, she made sure her new paper provided its readers with a bold, bright, and open-minded product. For the first seven years, it lost money — a total of $750,000. But by the time Newhouse got back to Patterson with an offer of $1 million for *Newsday*, she was not the least bit interested.

Still, Newhouse saw how much advertising *Newsday* was getting from the suburban outlets of Brooklyn and Manhattan department and specialty stores, and he determined to get some of it for himself. He went back to James Stiles, whose *Nassau Review-Star* was suffering at *Newsday*'s hands, and, in a secret deal consummated on 1 January 1949, Newhouse took over ownership of that paper.

It was all to no avail. As one of the *Press*'s reporters later put it, "We couldn't fight *Newsday* with the *Review-Star*. It was a shitty piece of paper. Its appearance alone would deter people from reading it." A special Nassau County edition of the *Long Island Press*, begun in 1953 after the demise of the *Review-Star*, fared little better, because it failed to cover the affairs of such booming Nassau townships as New Hyde Park, Hempstead, and Garden City. "*Newsday* just took over," recalled a *Press* reporter who worked on the Nassau County edition. "Period. We couldn't touch it."

Newhouse's decision not to make a more serious effort in Nassau County came naturally. He was in a hurry to add to his holdings, and the newspapers in Syracuse, Jersey City, and Harrisburg would get him there more quickly and with fewer risks than investing years of effort and millions of dollars in building a major new publication from scratch. But if his decision was provident at the time, it was also irreversible. Should Alicia Patterson's new paper succeed, and should enough of the residents of Queens follow the other New York City transplants to eastern Long Island, the keystone of his burgeoning empire would be in serious trouble.

The *Long Island Press*'s readers would desert Queens only if the pleasant, solidly middle-class community in which they lived deteriorated. That, in turn, could occur only if the community's major institutions — including its daily newspaper — let it.

By the mid-1950s, Newhouse must have begun to notice a change coming over Jamaica during his weekly visits. Slowly at first, and then more rapidly, poor black and Hispanic families moved into the south end of town. With the new residents, to whom Jamaica offered little work, came other changes. There were more burglaries, holdups, and muggings. There was trouble in the schools. Small shops lost business.

The *Long Island Press*, obviously, was not ignorant of all this, but counteracting the urban blight that had begun to destroy Queens first required that the paper acknowledge the problem's existence. Advertisers, however, did not want such articles in the paper. "A store would be robbed," recalled Leo Meindl, then the paper's Mr. Fix-it columnist, "and its owner would call up to ask us not to cover it. They'd say it wasn't good for business." In response to such pleas, the *Press*'s editors soon adopted a practice that must have been unique in New York journalism. No "negative" stories would be published in the *Press* unless they appeared first in other New York papers — like the *Post*, *Times*, or *Daily News*. More than journalistic competition was lost as a result of this curious practice. Because the *Press* was the only paper that followed the affairs of Jamaica closely, the new rule had the unintended effect of blacking out coverage of the borough's problems during the very period when there might have been a chance of rectifying them.

It wasn't until the mid-1960s, when Queens's fate had pretty much been sealed, that the *Press* allowed its news and editorial columns to print the truth about what was going on in the community it claimed to serve. At that late date, there was little left for the paper to do but wring its hands in public.

There was another, more insidious reason why the *Long Island Press* failed its readers. Newhouse was so blinded by his hatred of the paper's unions that he would stop at nothing to keep his employees' wages and benefits down. In the mechanical departments, Newhouse got the below average productivity he paid for, but in the editorial department there always seemed to be talented young people willing to put up with almost any indignity for a chance to write for the local paper.

And were there ever indignities! During the 1940s, for example, Newhouse supervised the creation of something called the Allied Bi-County News Service — ABC for short. To work as a reporter at the *Press*, aspiring journalists started out running errands as copy boys. Those who showed promise were assigned to ABC for a year or two. Only after that were they allowed to join the *Press*'s regular payroll. In the meantime, thanks to ABC, Newhouse could maintain a night shift at the *Press* without paying Guild wages or overtime.

ABC News, though, was nothing compared with the Queens-Nassau Picture Service. Known more familiarly as Queens-Nassau Pix, run first by Leonard Victor and later owned by Newhouse's cousin Raymond and a man named Herbie Einzig, the outfit allowed the *Press* to do without photographers altogether. It ran only wire photos and pictures from Queens-Nassau Pix. For years, the service was located in Flushing at 162nd Street and Northern Boulevard, seven miles north of the *Press* building. Later, it moved to a rat-hole office above a meat store at 16909 Jamaica Avenue (three blocks from the *Press*). And during the final years, it moved into the second floor of a building connected to the back end of the *Press* building on Merrick Boulevard. The service's full-time photographers were paid much less than the Guild contract called for and even had to pay for medical insurance out of their own pockets.

It was inevitable that these union-avoiding services would become riddled with graft and corruption, to the point that they actually cost the *Press* more than regular Guild jobs would have. Double sets of books were kept. Relatives of the owners were put on the payroll but did no work. Phony expenses were charged — most notably at Queens-Nassau Pix, where, to cite just one instance of the fraud being perpetrated, the official books showed false entries of hundreds of dollars each month for prizes supposedly given to employees for outstanding photographs.

Similar problems began to affect the *Press*'s regular managers. There were numerous freebies available just for the asking, from cameras to TV sets to tickets for sporting and cultural events. There were special license plates that provided immunity from parking citations. Young reporters were made to serve as the editors' personal chauffeurs and errand boys. Some of the editors even got paying jobs as public relations consultants for professional organizations in Queens and then made sure their clients received special coverage in the *Press*.

Perhaps the most outrageous abuse involved a Newhouse cousin who had an interest in antique cars. He somehow got permission to turn the first floor of the *Press*'s building out back into his own private vehicle storage area. Each evening thereafter, the *Press*'s night watchman was to start the cars up and let their engines idle for a while. On several occasions, he showed his friends at the news desk his new responsibility. "The dingy bowels of the *Press* building," one of the reporters recounted a few years later, "looked like Harrah's [in Las Vegas, where antique cars are shown off]. It was a private showcase. It was immense — like a football field."

Such signs of decay were not reported by the *Press*, or any other newspaper for that matter. But in 1974, three of the paper's most idealistic reporters could stand it no longer. They compiled a list of the more flagrant abuses, complete with clippings from the paper, and sent them anonymously to Newhouse at his Park Avenue apartment, with copies to Norman in New Orleans and the *Press*'s chief editor, Dave Starr. No visible changes resulted.

Newhouse's failure to respond contradicted practically everything he had ever stood for as a newspaperman. Perhaps he never received the letter. Perhaps he was shielded from the truth by his trusted associates at the *Press*. Or perhaps he was too old to care about what, at that time in his life, must have seemed minor details. More likely, he saw that something was wrong with his newspaper in Queens but was blinded to its causes by the incredible animosity he still bore toward organized labor.

Whatever the real reason for Newhouse's inaction, by the early 1970s, the *Long Island Press* was a disaster largely of its own making. In the five years between 1969 and 1974, circulation and advertising lineage were cut in half, and starting in 1974, the paper began to lose money for the first time since the Depression. Before things could deteriorate much further, Newhouse simply pulled the plug. The way he went about that final act showed that anger at the unions still burned within him.

"Five years ago," read the announcement that Dave Starr delivered to the *Press*'s editor the morning of 25 March 1977, "we appealed to the nine unions which represent *Press* craft employees to abandon their featherbedding make-work rules and to permit us to use new automated machinery without increasing our jobs still more. Unfortunately, the unions could not see the wisdom of our appeal at that time. We continued to hope for . . . more favorable terms from our unions. . . . Our hopes are now exhausted."

Newhouse didn't stop at harsh language for his people. He also did what he could to see that they got as little severance pay as possible. In final negotiations with the unions, he and his brother Ted, the *Press*'s general manager, sought to avoid paying severance or pensions to their employees, some of whom had been working at the paper for as long as thirty years. Then, when they did agree to severance pay, they exacted a promise that the unions would not try to collect retirement benefits.

Though some former *Press* people obtained newspaper work elsewhere — and were surprised at the better pay — many remained without jobs, and hardly anyone was left with fond memories of the way they had been treated.

"The *Press* made its money by scrimping on money," wrote former *Press* man Fred McMorrow that March. In his piece, published by *Newsday*, McMorrow recalled a conversation he had with noted New York newspaper columnist Jimmy Breslin in the early 1950s.

Said Breslin of the *Press*, which had provided him with his start in journalism, "This paper is doing something it's going to pay for some day. It's stepping over a dollar to pick up a dime."

34 Thirty

THE END WAS SO PATHETIC that his family did not want anyone to know. Sometime after the Booth deal and the closing of the *Long Island Press* — perhaps because of the strain they caused — Newhouse had a slight stroke. It seemed not to do too much harm; in fact, he was able to attend another of Harry Marley's parties at Hinerwadel's in May 1977. But then, with horrible suddenness, the process of deterioration accelerated.

Newhouse was all right physically, but the onset of senility caused his mind and reactions to revert to those of a young boy. So, ironically, the man who had been managing a newspaper at the age of sixteen now had something of the childhood that he had missed in his youth. In the last two years of his life, Newhouse was captivated by crayons and chalk, using them to spell out simple words in large, ungainly letters. "C-A-T," he would say as he wrote. "See? C-A-T. Cat!" And he frequently begged "to go outside and play." At other times, a black mood would come over him, and he would throw violent tantrums.

Mitzi dropped everything to be with her husband. Instead of nights at the opera or on Broadway, she would accompany him and his attendants on visits to the circus. She read to him by the hour, and when he appeared to overindulge his newfound sweet tooth, she would take the candy away. Few family intimates were allowed to see Newhouse in this state; and for the most part, he was kept away from people, especially newspaper people, with any of a number of excuses.

In July 1979, just after the disastrous fund-raising visit by the men from Syracuse University, there was a second, more serious stroke, and on 15 August, Newhouse was admitted to Doctors Hospital. He died there two weeks later. The funeral was a lavish affair, held at Temple Emanu-El on 31 August. That afternoon, his body was carried aboard the Staten Island ferry to Baron Hirsch Cemetery, where he was laid to rest within sight of Hyman Lazarus's grave.

The life of S. I. Newhouse must be regarded as one of the great success stories of our time. Despite handicaps that would have discouraged even Horatio Alger, he put together the greatest newspaper publishing empire in American history. Moreover, he did it himself — with a passion for hard work, true genius, and a tremendous sense of optimism about his business. Finally, he left the legacy of local editorial autonomy — a philosophy that seems to capture the ideal of modern newspaper ownership. Newhouse explained in press releases issued through Ray Josephs's agency:

> Whatever political interest each newspaper publisher or editor has is based on what he thinks is best for the community in which he operates, and he expresses himself fully without submitting anything to me. . . .

> Only a newspaper which is a sound business operation can be a truly free, independent editorial enterprise, able to do the best possible job for the community. . . .

> Whatever contribution I may make will be primarily in the direction of supporting the internal integrity of these great publications and assuring the present local management full freedom to make their own thinking effective.

And yet in practice, Newhouse failed to live up to the standards set by those principles and, in fact, seemed consciously to abandon them. His fierce, unyielding attention to the bottom line ultimately cheapened the lives of most of the people who worked for him. His was the type of organization that could enclose disclaimers like the following with a Christmas bonus:

> It is not to our taste to offer any expression on this occasion except our very best wishes of the season, but our lawyers insist that it is necessary

for the record to note, in respect to this and future years, that this is a wholly voluntary offering on the part of the management and not the result of any agreement or undertaking.

His was also the type of organization that could censor coverage of the accidental death of one of its employees for fear a relative might sue.

Nowhere, however, was Newhouse's attitude toward the men and women who worked for him better expressed than in his relations with organized labor. For, during the course of his career, Newhouse put more newspaper people out of work than any other publisher in history. "If S. I. Newhouse owned a National Football team," stated one of his editors, "he would try to play with ten men."

In the mid-1970s, *More*, a sprightly magazine of journalism, compiled a list of the ten worst big-circulation daily newspapers in America. It should have come as no surprise that three of Newhouse's newspapers were on it — the *Cleveland Plain Dealer*, the *New Orleans Times-Picayune*, and the *St. Louis Globe-Democrat*. Around the same time, several publications, including *Time* magazine, tried to identify the nation's ten best newspapers. People from all walks of life and all parts of the U.S. were polled, and not one Newhouse publication was included on any of the lists.

The reason for such a poor showing is simple. Newhouse began his life in newspapers with one goal — to accumulate capital. And because he continued to pursue that goal with a doggedness that was as narrow-minded as it was effective, he was never able to see a larger purpose for himself. Perhaps this is the real tragedy of his long and remarkable career: having amassed a huge communications empire — thereby acquiring the capacity to reach and inform millions of people across the country — Newhouse had absolutely no interest in communications as a means to any end other than his own profit. And unaffected by the romance of journalism or by its element of public service, he lacked the incentive that made other major publishers — like the Sulzbergers and the Grahams — strive for greatness in their news and editorial columns, as well as in their quarterly financial statements. For Newhouse, a newspaper was not a newspaper at all. It was a package whose purpose was to carry advertising.

There is, however, a more damning element to Newhouse's legacy: he "succeeded." In fact, he succeeded so well that his model of newspapering as a business, and little more, has become the dominant theme of modern journalism. When Newhouse began at the *Bayonne Times* in 1911, less than 5 percent of all American newspapers were chain-owned. But by the time he handed control of his empire to his brothers and sons in 1977, nearly two-thirds of all daily newspapers in the United States had lost their independence. During the same period, the number of cities with two or more competing newspapers dropped from more than 500 to 35. Newhouse did not cause this remarkable consolidation alone, but he certainly profited from it. And, in the end, he helped to legitimize it. The result is a journalism as bland and uninspired and unhelpful as the huge, faceless corporations that produce it. It is little wonder that today Newhouse's newspapers fail to serve their readers with distinction.

Afterword

SOMETIME AFTER NEWHOUSE arranged to buy the Booth newspapers, and perhaps after he had his first stroke, his closest advisers rewrote his will. No longer would the bulk of his estate be given to his foundation, where the proceeds could benefit the likes of Syracuse University and Lincoln Center. Instead, most of Newhouse's stock in Advance Publications Inc. was placed in trust for his six grandchildren, with the ten voting shares held in a separate trust controlled solely by his two sons. Mitzi was to receive his substantial — 44.44 percent — interest in the Newhouse Broadcasting Corporation. Finally, a portion of API stock was reserved to cover estate taxes, which, as the result of a favorable ruling from the IRS, later proved to be far lower than many close observers had anticipated.

At the same time that Newhouse's will was being redrafted, his sons were taking control of the vast empire their father had been so reluctant to relinquish. Still living within a few blocks of each other in Manhattan, but with Donald operating out of the *Newark Star-Ledger* plant in New Jersey and Si, the Condé Nast building at 350 Madison Avenue in the city, the two devised a new plan of action that kept control of their far-flung operations completely within the family. Uncle Theodore, seventy-six years old at the time of S. I.'s death, was given responsibility for the newspapers in Massachusetts and Oregon. Norman, then seventy-three and living in New Orleans, supervised the family properties in Ohio, Mississippi, Alabama, and Louisiana. A first cousin, Robert Miron, the forty-two-year-old son of S. I.'s sister Estelle, became the heir apparent to the broadcasting end of the business, while another first cousin, Gertrude's forty-five-year-old son Richard Diamond, ran the *Staten Island Advance* and oversaw the operations of the eight Booth newspapers in Michigan. That left Si with the magazines, the *St. Louis Globe-Democrat*, and the *Cleveland Plain Dealer*, and Donald with the papers in New York, New Jersey, and Pennsylvania.

Within the family, Donald, the younger son, was clearly dominant, but was willing to let it appear to the outside world that his older brother was in charge. Between them, they acted quickly, buying one magazine (*Gentleman's Quarterly*), starting another (*Self*), and selling their five TV stations to the Times Mirror Publishing Company for $82 million. A portion of the proceeds from this last transaction was used to pick up a series of cable-TV properties, and by early 1981, the Newhouse family owned and operated dozens of cable systems throughout the Northeast, South, and Midwest, with a total of 500,000 subscribers — making theirs the eighth largest cable-TV operation in the United States. Then, in 1982, Si and Donald announced the spring 1983 start-up of *Vanity Fair*, which was expected to be the most exciting — and certainly the most glamorous — new magazine venture of the year.

The most important development in the period immediately following Newhouse's death, however, was the family's purchase in early 1980 of the Random House book-publishing subsidiary of the RCA Corporation. In addition to the fifty-five-year-old Random House imprint, the publishing firm included Alfred A. Knopf, a highly respected hardcover publisher; Ballantine Books, a publisher of mass-market paperbacks; Vintage Books; Pantheon Books; and Modern Library. At the time of the $70-million purchase, Random House's best-seller was William Styron's *Sophie's Choice*, and Knopf's was John Le Carré's *Smiley's People*. And although 1979 was not a good year for the company (estimated pretax earnings on gross revenues of nearly $150 million were between $5 and $10 million), the following three years found its fortunes vastly improved, thanks to a book list containing an unusually large number of good-quality best-sellers, like Carl Sagan's *Cosmos* and Robert Caro's *The Path to Power*. Then, in March 1982, the Newhouses bought Fawcett Books from CBS, and in early 1983 announced their intention to create a new hardcover imprint, Villard Books.

Even on the newspaper side of the family's business, where revenues tended to flatten out in the early eighties, Newhouse had left his sons well positioned. With no outstanding debts and no shareholders other than themselves to satisfy, they could comfortably ride out the recession. In two cities — New Orleans and Portland — where the economy and competition from free-distribution shoppers cut into profits, the family merged morning and afternoon papers to effect substantial savings. In general, however, the newspapers have continued as before; the transition to the next generation has been carried out quietly and successfully.

Acknowledgments

IT WAS THROUGH my five-year association with *Willamette Week*, an alternative newsweekly in Portland, Oregon, and my longer friendship with that paper's founder and publisher, Ronald A. Buel, that my interest in journalism bloomed and my curiosity about S. I. Newhouse developed.

From its inception, this project was blessed by tremendous help from others. Gerry Pratt made me draw up a budget and then suggested I double it. Had he not intervened so fortuitously at the beginning, *Newspaperman* would not have been completed. Homer Williams lent me money to get started and later offered helpful suggestions on the manuscript. Terence O'Donnell encouraged me to meet Chester Kerr, who, in turn, agreed to have Ticknor & Fields take on this project.

My research, often conducted out of crowded quarters in YMCAs and in dozens of phone booths from coast to coast, was aided by scores of newspaper people like George and Mae Vecsey, who welcomed me as an honored guest in their household and were willing to sit for hours while I asked my questions. In Manhattan, fellow journalist Lynda Eklund went out of her way to help with research.

During the course of my writing, Philippa Brunsman, Alan Webber, and John Svicarovitch offered tremendous assistance with everything from choice of words to thought patterns. Susan Regan and Michael Cooke managed to turn my handwriting into a clean manuscript — twice. Elizabeth Yeats and Valerie Fisher offered thoughtful comments.

Then, when I was done, the full force of Ticknor & Fields's fine staff made itself felt. First, Paul Weaver, Katrina Kenison, and Joan and Chester Kerr made suggestions that helped turn a very rough draft into a publishable book. Katrina's subsequent editing was as sensitive and thoughtful as a writer could ask for. Jean van Altena did a fine job of copy editing, and Amy Mantell kept *Newspaperman*'s production on schedule.

From the beginning, *Newspaperman* was a collaborative effort. The person who contributed the most to that collaboration — in every way — was my wife, Ellen Rosenblum.

A Note on Sources

As MENTIONED in the introduction, I had no cooperation from Newhouse's immediate family in the preparation of this biography. Nor would any current Newhouse newspaper or magazine publisher consent to be interviewed. Likewise, the morgues of the family's publications were placed off limits. Even photos of Newhouse, especially those from his early years, had been rounded up by his family — sometimes on the pretense of borrowing — and, thus, taken out of public circulation. All this, I discovered, was rather standard treatment, which succeeded in discouraging a handful of would-be biographers before me. I realized that, in order to proceed, I would have to rely instead on the techniques of investigative reporting.

Save for the Michigan cities that are home to the Booth newspapers, I traveled at least once to those cities in which Newhouse either owned, or made serious attempts to own, newspapers. In each, I pored over microfilms of back issues of the publications involved and talked to anyone I could find who might have known Newhouse or known about him. As is inevitable in such a process, hundreds of calls proved dead ends. Hundreds more were of limited worth. Several dozen, though, led to interviews which were enormously helpful. Sadly, many of the people with whom I spoke were unwilling to be named in this book. Some were deeply afraid of reprisals from the Newhouses; others did not wish to rekindle old animosities; and still others simply wished to avoid public attention. I have complied with their wishes. But wherever I have chosen to use material from an unattributed interview, I have obtained independent corroboration.

In addition to library research and interviewing, I spent weeks in courthouses and federal records centers around the country sorting through case files of a score of lawsuits that involved Newhouse in one way or another. These voluminous records are a previously untapped source of sworn affidavits, depositions, transcribed testimony, and important business documents regarding Newhouse and his newspapers. In addition, transcripts of proceedings before the National Labor Relations Board, now warehoused in Suitland, Maryland, provided important information.

Toward the end of my research, I located in the Library of Congress in Washington, D.C., a copy of a memoir Newhouse had prepared for members of his immediate family. It is, to the best of my knowledge, the only copy of that book available to the public. Why it is there, and why more than a dozen of its pages are blank, are not immediately apparent. Entitled *A Memo for the Children* and written for him by the former managing editor of the *Long Island Press*, Newhouse's memoirs are not of much interest to the general public. They suffer greatly from the selective recall of their subject and the troublesome inattention to detail and context of their writer. Nonetheless, for my purposes they were invaluable, especially with regard to Newhouse's early years. They also serve to corroborate, occasionally by negative implication, much of the fruit of my own investigation. In those instances where my research is at variance with the memoir, I have rechecked my sources carefully before proceeding.

Certain books and publications provided background information for many phases of Newhouse's life. The most significant were Edwin and Michael Emery's *The Press and America* (Prentice-Hall, 1978), Samuel Eliot Morison and Henry Steele Commager's *The Growth of the American Republic* (Oxford, 1962), the *New York Times*, *Editor & Publisher*, the *Guild Reporter*, and N. W. Ayer & Son's *Newspaper Annual and Directory*. In addition, newspaper analyst John Morton consented to a long interview in which he provided a broad overview of the newspaper business in America.

The notes that follow list the major sources for this biography, plus material that might otherwise have been placed in footnotes. I have attempted to keep this information as straightforward and basic as possible.

1. 1895–1924: APPRENTICE

The central facts of this first section were drawn from Newhouse's memoirs and from interviews with cousins and acquaintances in Bayonne. School records, city directories, and birth, census, naturalization, and bar records made it possible to follow the movements of Newhouse's family during these early years.

Several published accounts added significant details. They were, primarily, those found in *Advertising Age* (9 May 1955, p. 42), *Business Week* (26 January 1976, cover story), *Collier's* (4 August 1951, p. 31), *Esquire* (August 1959, p. 87), *Forbes* (29 October 1979, p. 110), *Saturday Review* (8 October 1960, p. 55), the *Staten Island Advance* (21 March 1936, "S. I. Newhouse became a publisher when 18"), *Time* (27 July 1962, cover story), and the *Wall Street Journal* (12 February 1982, "Newhouse chain stays with founder's ways, and with his heirs"), as well as lengthy obituaries published in several Newhouse newspapers and in the *New York Times* and the *Washington Post*.

In addition, I had the benefit of extensive notes taken by John Lent when he interviewed Philip Hochstein in the spring of 1964. Apart from a few telephone calls and some minor correspondence, the man who served as Newhouse's chief editorial adviser for more than four decades did not assist in the preparation of this biography. He even denied participating in the 1964 interview, though Lent was able to provide ample documentation that it had, in fact, occurred.

1. First Assignment

Notes:
Leo Rifkin was the friend in whom Newhouse confided his feelings about his early years.

Interviews:
Helen Lazarus Barrett, Maurice Brigadier, Mary K. Davis, Harry Field, Sydney Lazarus, Leo Rifkin, Louis Ripps, Horace Roberson, Irving Yorysh, Nat Zinader.

Secondary Sources:
Allen, Frederick Lewis. *The Big Change.* New York: Harper & Brothers, 1952.
Gold, Michael. *Jews Without Money.* New York: Liveright, 1930.
Howe, Irving. *World of Our Fathers.* New York: Simon & Schuster, 1976.
Lent, John. *Newhouse, Newspapers, Nuisances.* New York: Exposition Press, 1967.

Newhouse, S. I. *A Memo for the Children.* New York: published privately, 1980.

Rischin, Moses. *The Promised City: New York's Jews 1870–1914.* Cambridge: Harvard University Press, 1962.

Roskolenko, Harry. *The Time That Was Then: The Lower East Side.* New York: Dial Press, 1971.

Schoener, Allan, ed. *Portal to America: The Lower East Side.* New York: Holt, Rinehart, and Winston, 1967.

Sinclair, Gladys Mellor. *Bayonne Old and New.* New York: Marantha, 1940.

Swanberg, W. A., *Citizen Hearst.* New York: Scribner's, 1961.

———. *Pulitzer.* New York: Scribner's, 1967.

2. Running the *Times*

Interviews:
Louis Adler, Joe Bodarky, Maurice Brigadier, William Feinberg, Harry Field, Nathan L. Jacobs, Edward Kukowski, Sydney Lazarus, Gertrude Lederman, Alvin Posner, Horace Roberson, Evelyn Zinader, Nat Zinader, Milton Zundell, Sarah Zundell.

Secondary Sources:
Manchester, William. *The Glory and the Dream: A Narrative History of America, Vol. I.* Boston: Little, Brown, 1973.

Sinclair, *Bayonne Old and New.*

Zinn, Howard. *A People's History of the United States.* New York: Harper & Row, 1980.

Bayonne Democrat, 1905–11
Bayonne Herald, 1905–11
Bayonne Public Opinion, 1905–11
Bayonne Review, 1905–11
Bayonne Times, 1905–11
Newark Evening News, 1905–11
New York Journal, 1905–11
New York World, 1905–11

3. Life Beyond the *Times*

Interviews:
Gertrude Lederman, Leo Rifkin, Charlotte Schoenberg, Evelyn Zinader.

4. Upstairs, Downstairs

Interviews:
John Keseday, Bill Krupkin, Leo Rifkin, Charlotte Schoenberg, Nat Zinader.

Secondary Sources:
Bayonne Times, 1911–20

5. First Acquisition

Notes:
Leo Rifkin and Eleanora West, director of the Fitchburg Historical Society, made available to me the basic material for the true story of Newhouse's first newspaper venture in Massachusetts. It is, to say the least, at odds with the version Newhouse himself told. (See the profile in *Esquire*, August 1959, p. 87.)

The story of Newhouse spending Saturday afternoons reading beside the *Times* building was recounted to me in a letter from Bill Krupkin. Nick Kenney, who worked for the *Bayonne Times* around 1920, is one person to whom Newhouse boasted of his intentions to own a chain of newspapers "just like Mr. Hearst." (See *Editor & Publisher*, 19 October 1957, pp. 62–64.)

Interviews:
Maurice Brigadier, Harry Field, John Keseday, Bill Krupkin, Sydney Lazarus, Leo Rifkin, Elliott Wellington, Eleanora West, Nat Zinader.

Secondary Sources:
Fitchburg City Directory for 1920
Fitchburg News, 1916–21
Fitchburg Sentinel, 1916–20

6. On His Own

Notes:
The unauthorized salary arrangement was explained to me by Sydney Lazarus. The original corporate charter of the *Staten Island Advance* is still on file in Borough Hall, St. George, Staten Island.

Interviews:
Louis Adler, Maurice Brigadier, Harry Field, Nathan Frankel, Sydney Lazarus, Gertrude Lederman, Loring McMillen, Leo Rifkin, Horace Roberson, Charlotte Schoenberg, Evelyn Zinader.

Secondary Sources:
Leng, Charles W., and Davies, William T. *Staten Island And Its People: A History, 1609–1929.*
Staten Island: A Brief History. Unsigned monograph in St. George Library Center, Staten Island.

Bayonne Times, 1921–22
Staten Island Advance, 1910–24

II. 1924–1933: TECHNICIAN

In preparing this section, I relied heavily on much the same material as I did in section I — the memoirs, magazine profiles, and obituaries — as well as on my interviews and John Lent's notes of his interview with Philip Hochstein.

7. Starting Over

Notes:
A lengthy profile of Henry Garfinkle appeared on the front page of the *Wall Street Journal* for 3 July 1969. Entitled "A Rough Dealer," it was prepared by *Journal* staff writer Ronald Kessler.

Interviews:
Maurice Brigadier, John Bruno, Harry Field, Emily Brown Fine, Nathan Frankel, Henry Garfinkle, Myron Garfinkle, Florence Glickman, Sidney Glickman, Walter P. Kane, Sydney Lazarus, Carol Smith Morrissey, Leo Rifkin.

Secondary Sources:
Bayonne Times, 1924–25.
Staten Island Advance, 1924–25.

8. A Lesson in Vindictiveness

Interviews:
Maurice Brigadier, Henry Garfinkle, Walter Kane, Fred McMorrow.

Secondary Sources:
Staten Island Advance, 1927–28
Staten Islander, 1925–28

9. The People's Champion

Notes:
This chapter represents one of the few instances where a Newhouse paper itself was the best source. Issues of the *Staten Island Advance* for September 1930 provided the key elements in the story of Newhouse's failed attempt to unseat David Rendt. The interviewer mentioned, but not named, at the end of the chapter was Robert Shaplen of the *Saturday Review*.

10. Acquiring the *Press*

Interviews:
Emily Brown Fine, Jackie Gebhard, Walter Kane, Mrs. Clayton P. Knowles, Carol Smith Morrissey, Walter Ridder, Leo Rifkin, George Vecsey, Mae Spencer Vecsey.

Secondary Sources:
Allen, Frederick Lewis. *The Big Change.* New York: Harper & Brothers, 1952.
Collins, Thomas. "The *Long Island Press*, 1821–1977." *Newsday*, 26 March 1977.

Long Island Press, 1929–34

III. 1934–1938: MASTER

Perhaps the most complete record of this stormy period in Newhouse's life is provided by weekly reports in *Editor & Publisher* (offering by and large the publishers' side) and the *Guild Reporter* (the reporters' side). In addition, there exist in the Federal Records Center in Suitland, Maryland, voluminous records of proceedings brought against Newhouse by various Guild members. The most comprehensive of these involved a religion reporter at the *Newark Ledger* by the name of Agnes Fahy. The hearing that dealt with her complaint covered all aspects of Newhouse's relations with the Guild between 1934 and 1938. Newhouse, Hochstein, and even Charles Goldman were called to testify.

11. Guilded

Interviews:
John Bruno, William Farson (John Lent's notes), Emily Brown Fine, Philip Hochstein (Lent's notes), Walter Kane, Frank Keating, Mrs. Clayton P. Knowles, Carol Smith Morrissey, Bertram Powers, George Vecsey, Mae Spencer Vecsey.

Secondary Sources:
Broun, Heywood. *New York World-Telegram* column, "It seems to me." 7 August 1933, p. 21.
Crosby, Alexander. "I was the Guild's first striker." *Guild Reporter*, 23 October 1959.
Leab, Daniel J. *A Union of Individuals: The Formation of the American Newspaper Guild, 1933–1936.* New York: Columbia University Press, 1970.
National Labor Relations Board. Case No. II-C-2168. Re: Long Island Press Publishing Company.
Newspaper Guild of New York. Agreements between the Newspaper Guild of New York and the Long Island Daily Press Publishing Company. Unpubl.
————. Letters to Guild officials from Hochstein, Hofmann, Newhouse, and Goldman. Unpubl.

Editor & Publisher, 1933–34
Guild Reporter, 1933–34
New York Herald-Tribune, 1933–34
New York World-Telegram, 1933–34

12. Newark

Notes:
This chapter relies primarily on court records of the lawsuits that transpired between Newhouse and Russell, bankruptcy proceedings, and testimony taken during the hearing of Agnes Fahy's NLRB complaint.

Interviews:
Philip Hochstein (John Lent's notes), Edwin F. Russell, Richard Scudder.

Secondary Sources:
Fiester, Kenneth. "Newark vet recalls the *Ledger* of old." *Guild Reporter*, 13 January 1959.
"L. T. Russell dies in West." *Newark News*, 14 June 1948.
Swanberg, *Citizen Hearst*.

Newark Evening News, 1934–36
Newark Ledger, 1934–36
Newark Star-Eagle, 1934–36

13. Smashing the Opposition

Notes:
The first half of this chapter (getting rid of L. T. Russell) is based on newspaper accounts of testimony by Newhouse, Russell, and others at the various court proceedings involving the two antagonists. See especially the *Newark Evening News* for 7–26 October and 5–7 December 1938, also for 4 April–27 May and 19–26 June 1939.

For the part of the chapter that deals with smashing the Guild, the voluminous records of the National Labor Relations Board are the best source. Particularly helpful were transcripts of testimony by Charles Goldman, S. I. Newhouse, and Philip Hochstein, as well as a copy of the NLRB trial examiner's final report. The *Newark Evening News* provided regular coverage of the lengthy NLRB proceedings and subsequent appeals, as did *Editor & Publisher* and the *Guild Reporter*.

14. The Final Battle

Interviews:
Ernest A. Doepke, William Farson (John Lent's notes), Jackie Gebhard, Philip Hochstein (Lent's notes), Frank Keating, Theodore Kheel, Mrs. Clayton P. Knowles, Bertram Powers, A. H. Raskin, George Vecsey, Mae Spencer Vecsey.

Secondary Sources:
Leab, *A Union of Individuals*.
National Labor Relations Board. Case No. II-C-2168. Re: Long Island Press Publishing Company.

New York Newspaper Guild. Arbitration agreement of 10 April 1937. Unpubl.

————. Letters of Hofmann, Hochstein, and Goldman. Unpubl.

U.S. Supreme Court opinion. Watson v. AP.

Long Island Press, 1934–38
New York Herald-Tribune, 1934–38
Queens News, 1934–37

15. The Chief

Notes:
The basis for this incident is Newhouse's own account in the memoirs. No other record exists of this meeting between the two newspaper giants. By the time research for this book began, Hearst and Block were dead, and Berlin was incapacitated by illness and old age.

IV. 1939–1955: OPPORTUNIST

16. Syracuse

Notes:
This chapter makes use of court records of antitrust proceedings filed against Newhouse by the Syracuse Broadcasting Corporation, owner of station WNDR. Included in the files is a lengthy deposition by Newhouse, in which he discussed his early involvement in the Syracuse newspapers. Newhouse, WSYR, the *Syracuse Herald-Journal*, and the *Syracuse Post-Standard* defended themselves successfully.

Interviews:
Howard Carroll, Wesley C. Clark, Joe Ganley, Florence Glickman, Len Gorman, LeRoy Keller, Robert Peyer, Lawrence Sovik, William P. Tolley, E. R. Vadeboncoeur, Jerome Walker.

Secondary Sources:
Chamberlin, Anne. "America's unknown press lord." *Esquire*, August 1959.

Rogers, Stephen. "S. I. Newhouse." *Syracuse Herald-Journal*, 30 August 1979.

Syracuse Herald, 1937–39
Syracuse Herald-Journal, 1939–45
Syracuse Journal, 1937–39
Syracuse Post-Standard, 1938–45

17. The Good Life

Notes:
A lengthy profile of Leonard Lyons appeared on the front page of the
Wall Street Journal for 30 April 1968.

Interviews:
Abe Beame, Wesley C. Clark, Henry Garfinkle, John Gerald, Florence
Glickman, Nat Goldstein, LeRoy Keller, John Lindsay, Jeffrey Lyons,
William Tolley.

Secondary Sources:
Kessler, "A rough dealer."
Manhattan, Reverse Telephone Directory.
Rogers, "S. I. Newhouse."
Starr, David. Introduction to *A Memo for the Children*. New York: pub-
lished privately, 1980.

18. Jersey City

Notes:
An important source of information for this chapter is a bound volume of
highlights of the *Post-Standard* v. *Evening Journal Association* litigation.
The collection, located in the Newark offices of the law firm Carpenter,
Bennett & Morrissey, contains transcripts of court testimony by New-
house, Charles Goldman, Walter Dear, and Albert Dear.

Interviews:
Cyrene Dear, Katherine Dear, Richard Scudder.

Secondary Sources:
Jersey Journal, 1915–50

19. Harrisburg

Notes:
Dauphin County court records of the administration of Vance McCormick's estate were helpful in the preparation of this chapter.

Interviews:
Karl F. Achenbach, J. Kenneth Beaver, Meade Detwiler, Ernest A. Doepke, Milton Jacques, W. D. Lewis, Marie Ridder, Edwin F. Russell, Jim Smith, Paul Walker.

Secondary Sources:
Harrisburg Evening News, 1946–55
Harrisburg Home Star, 1948–54
Harrisburg Patriot, 1946–55
Harrisburg Telegraph, 1946–55

20. Portland

Notes:
Toward the end of his life, E. B. MacNaughton submitted to a series of taped interviews in which he discussed, among other subjects, the circumstances surrounding the sale of the *Oregonian* to Newhouse. The tapes are located in the archives of the library of Reed College in Portland, Oregon.

Interviews:
Ernest Doepke, Harold Helms, Ray Josephs, Robert C. Notson, Jerome Walker.

Secondary Sources:
Forrester, Steve. "How Newhouse did it." *Willamette Week*, 19 July 1976.
Liebling, A. J. *The Press.* New York: Ballantine, 1961.
MacColl, E. Kimbark. *The Growth of a City: Power and Politics in Portland, Oregon.* Portland: The Georgian Press, 1979.
Notson, Robert C. *Making the Day Begin: A Story of The* Oregonian. Portland: Oregonian Publishing Company, 1976.

The *Oregonian*, 1940–53
Oregon Journal, 1940–53

21. Meeting the Press

Interviews:
Anne Chamberlin, Wesley Clark, Philip Hochstein, Ray Josephs, John Lent, Mort Reichek, Edward Uhlan, Jerome Walker.

Secondary Sources:
Chamberlin, "America's unknown press lord."
Forrester, "How Newhouse did it."

Lent, *Newhouse, Newspapers, Nuisances.*
Small, Collie. "Little publisher, big empire." *Collier's*, 4 August 1951.
Staten Island Advance, 21 March 1936. "S. I. Newhouse became a publisher when 18."
Walker, Jerry. "S. I. Newhouse buys *Oregonian.*" *Editor & Publisher*, 16 December 1950.

22. Local Autonomy

Interviews:
John Bloomer, Elzey Burkham, Turner Catledge, Montgomery Curtis, Ernest Doepke, Ray Jenkins, Ray Josephs, Harold Martin, John McDowell, Robert Notson, Harrison Salisbury, Wallace Turner, E. R. Vadeboncoeur, David Vann, Jerome Walker.

Secondary Sources:
Bass, Jack, and Devries, Walter. *The Transformation of Southern Politics: Social Change and Political Consequence Since 1945.* New York: Basic Books, 1976.
Bayley, Edwin R. *Joe McCarthy and the Press.* Madison: University of Wisconsin Press, 1981.
Corley, Robert Gaines. *"The Quest for Racial Harmony: Race Relations in Birmingham, Alabama, 1947–1963."* Ph.D. dissertation, University of Virginia, 1979.
Hanson, Clarence B., Jr. "Influence of S. I. Newhouse Upon the Editorial Content and Local Management of the *Birmingham News.*" Affidavit on file with Federal Communications Commission.
―――. *The Story of the Birmingham News, A Good Newspaper.* New York: The Newcomen Society, 1967.
Hart, Jim Allee. *A History of the* St. Louis Globe-Democrat. Columbia: University of Missouri Press, 1961.
MacNaughton, E. B. Tapes in Reed College Archives.
Salisbury, Harrison. *Without Fear or Favor: An Uncompromising Look at the* New York Times. New York: Times Books, 1980.
Shaplen, Robert. "The Newhouse phenomenon." *Saturday Review*, 8 October 1960.

Birmingham News, 1950–61
Chicago Tribune, 1961
Huntsville Times, 1955–61
Newark Evening News, 1945–60
Newark Star-Ledger, 1945–62

The *Oregonian*, 1950–57
St. Louis Globe-Democrat, 1954–56
St. Louis Post-Dispatch, 1954–56

V. 1955–1962: EMPIRE BUILDER

By this point in his career, Newhouse was a major public figure, so that his business activities were covered more carefully by the press. Thus, I have relied heavily on *Time, Newsweek, Editor & Publisher, Business Week*, and the *New York Times* for basic details of the major transactions during this period. The citations are too numerous to list here, but anyone wishing more information need only look in the *Reader's Guide to Periodical Literature* and the *New York Times Index* for the year in question.

23. In Vogue

Interviews:
Ernest Doepke, Henry Garfinkle, Myron Garfinkle.

Secondary Sources:
Citizen Kane. Film directed by Orson Welles. 1941.
Kessler, "A rough dealer."

Charm, 1957–59
Glamour, 1957–65
House & Garden, 1957–65
Living for Young Homemakers, 1959–61
Mademoiselle, 1957–65
Vogue, 1951–62
Young Bride's, 1957–62

24. Coming Out

Interviews:
Henry Garfinkle, John Gerald, Nat Goldstein, Vincent Sardi, William Tolley.

Secondary Sources:
Amory, Cleveland. "The beautiful people." *New York Times Encyclopedic Almanac*, 1970, pp. 617–18.

Curtis, Charlotte. "Nes-Café society." *New York Times Encyclopedic Almanac*, 1970, pp. 409–10.

Healy, George W., Jr. *A Lifetime on Deadline*. Gretna: Pelican, 1976.

Vogue, 1957–70

25. The Solid-Gold Pyramid

Notes:
The best sources of information concerning the corporate structure of Newhouse's empire are transcripts of depositions taken of him for lawsuits in Denver and Syracuse. The former names Newhouse as plaintiff; files on it can be found in the Federal Records Center just outside Denver. The latter lawsuit was brought by radio station WNDR in 1951; its files are available to researchers at the Federal Records Center located in the military terminal in Bayonne, New Jersey.

Newhouse himself raised the issue of where the money was coming from in an interview with Carl Spielvogel in the *New York Times*. ("Advertising: A builder in the fourth estate," 29 March 1959: "I know there has been a lot of talk about people who are supposed to be my backers.")

The matter of using the Foundations's funds is described by Newhouse himself in his deposition in the Denver lawsuit, taken in New York by Bill McLearn on 29 January 1969, at the offices of Pual, Weiss, Goldberg, Rifkind, Wharton & Garrison.

Interviews:
Ernest Doepke, James Sauter.

Secondary Sources:
Reichek, Mort. "S. I. Newhouse and Sons: America's most profitable publishers." *Business Week*, 26 January 1976.

26. Striking It Rich

Notes:
The details of the secret agreement between the *Post-Dispatch* and *Globe-Democrat* in St. Louis were revealed in a letter from Newhouse attorney Charles Sabin to U.S. Senator Philip Hart in 1965 during the course of testimony on a bill that came to be known as the Newspaper Preservation Act of 1967. Sabin's "Statement relating to the agreement between Pulitzer Publishing Co. and the Herald Co.," dated 26 February

1965, may be found starting at page 3441 of the record of S. 1312. It went unreported in St. Louis for more than a decade.

Jack Rosenthal, a sportswriter for the *Oregonian* when the Portland strike began, filled a large box with clippings, news releases, and the like during the months immediately following the walkout. He was kind enough to cart it into his office at the *Times* and allow me to spend the better part of a day going through it. He was equally generous with his recollections.

Interviews:
Elzey Burkham, Ernest Doepke, Rollin Everett, Lon Hocker, Milton Jacques, Gene Klare, Robert Notson, Jack Rosenthal, Ed Sehon, Jim Smith, Charles Stark, Robert Steinke, Wallace Turner, Jerome Walker, Paul Walker.

Secondary Sources:
Forrester, "How Newhouse did it."
Hart, *St. Louis Globe-Democrat.*
MacColl, *Growth of a City.*
Notson, *Making the Day Begin.*

Daily Strike Bulletin (Portland), 1959–63
Harrisburg Evening News, 1949–55
Harrisburg Patriot, 1949–55
Oregon Journal, 1959–63
Oregon Labor Press, 1959–63
The *Oregonian*, 1955–64
Portland Reporter, 1961–63
St. Louis Globe-Democrat, 1958–62
St. Louis Post-Dispatch, 1958–62

27. On Top

Interviews:
Turner Catledge, Walter Cowan, Thomas G. Fitzmorris, Shelby Friedrichs, James K. Glassman, Charlotte Hays, LeRoy Keller, Dan McCoy, Jerry Nicholson, Ken Weiss.

Secondary Sources:
Breed, Warren. "Evaluating the Role Performance of the *New Orleans Times-Picayune*." Paper read at a meeting of the Southern Sociological Society, 12 April 1969, at Tulane University.

Healy, *A Lifetime on Deadline.*
"He's a new kind of press lord." *Business Week,* 23 June 1962.
"The newspaper collector." *Time,* 27 July 1962.
Wilds, John. *Afternoon Story: A Century of the New Orleans States-Item.*
  Baton Rouge: Louisiana State University Press, 1976.

Figaro, 1975–80
New Orleans States-Item, 1957–65
New Orleans Times-Picayune, 1957–70

28. Disgruntled Heritors

Notes:
The best sources for Newhouse's experiences in Denver and Springfield
are court records of the litigation Newhouse brought in both places. The
Denver material can be found at the Denver Federal Records Center, in
the plaintiffs' index under Herald Company, Newhouse, and Rippey.
Fred Lane of Nutter, McLennen & Fish in Boston was kind enough to let
me spend several days in his firm's offices sifting through the six-foot-
thick transcript of the proceedings of Newhouse's actions against Sid
Cook and the other trustees of the pension funds. The public library in
Springfield has assembled in its periodicals department photocopies of
the many newspaper articles that resulted.

Interviews:
Medill Barnes, Sid Cook, Arthur Goldberg, Struve Hensel, William
McLearn, Robert Meserve.

Secondary Sources:
Beauregard, George N. Final report on Newark Morning Ledger v. The
  Republican Company et al. February, 1964.
Forrester, "How Newhouse did it."
Hosokawa, Bill. *Thunder in the Rockies: The Incredible* Denver Post. New
  York: Morrow, 1976.
Liebling, *The Press,* p. 7.

Cervi's Rocky Mountain Journal, 1959–73
Denver Post, 1955–73
Rocky Mountain News, 1955–73
Springfield News, 1960–67
Springfield Republican, 1960–67
Springfield Union, 1960–67
Straight Creek Journal, 1975–80

29. The Living Monument

Notes:

Much of the source material pertaining to Omaha can be found in the Federal Records Center in Kansas City, Missouri, under the heading of *Joseph A. Neff* v. *World Publishing Company*, a lawsuit in which Neff attempted to be paid a finder's fee for the deal that fell through for the *Omaha World-Herald*. The file includes the transcripts of lengthy testimony by Neff and W. Dale Clark.

The complete files of Chancellor Tolley in the archives at Syracuse University were made available to me. They contain documentation of the phony research program, as well as letters and records outlining another, grander tax-avoidance scheme that was not carried out. It was also Tolley who sat in the car with Newhouse and President Johnson and told me of what happened that day.

In mid-1983, four years after Newhouse's death, his foundation finally made a major gift to the Portland area — $2 million for a college scholarship fund.

Interviews:

Wesley Clark, Florence Glickman, I. M. Pei, Edgar Allan Poe, William Tolley.

Secondary Sources:

Hammer, Alexander R. "Newhouse buys paper in Omaha." *New York Herald-Tribune*, 30 October 1962.

Limprecht, Hollis. *The Kiewit Story*. Omaha: *Omaha World-Herald*, 1981.

Omaha World-Herald, 1960–62
The *Oregonian*, 1962–64
St. Louis Globe-Democrat, 1962–64
Syracuse Herald-Journal, 1957–64
Syracuse Post-Standard, 1957–64

VI. 1962–1979: THE LAST YEARS

Here, again, *Newsweek*, *Time*, *Business Week*, *Editor & Publisher*, and the *New York Times* provided the central details, and again, the citations are too numerous to list.

30. Newhouse & Sons

Notes:
Records of the original trusts created for S. I., Jr., and Donald are on file at Borough Hall in St. George, Staten Island.

Interviews:
Ernest Doepke, Harold Martin, Fred McMorrow, William Tolley, Jules Witcover.

Secondary Sources:
Grigsby, Jefferson. "Newhouse, after Newhouse." *Forbes*, 29 October 1979.
Machalaba, Dan. "Newhouse chain stays with founder's ways, and with his heirs." *Wall Street Journal*, 12 February 1982.
Reichek, "S. I. Newhouse and Sons."
Shaplen, "The Newhouse phenomenon."
Trachtenberg, J. A. "The Newhouses: Publishing's private empire," *W*, 19–26 December 1980.

31. The Publishers of the Future

Interviews:
Roldo Bartimole, Wesley Clark, Ernest Doepke, Robert Duvin, Shelby Friedrichs, Florence Glickman, Steve Hatch, LeRoy Keller, Harold Martin, William McLearn, Philip Porter, Leo Ring, Michael Roberts, James Sauter, Terence Sheridan, William Tolley, Herman Vail, Jerome Walker.

Secondary Sources:
Bartimole, Roldo. *Mediacrity*. Cleveland: Point of View, 1973.
Diedrichs, Gary. "The Beautiful and the Damned." *Cleveland*, November 1974.
Osborne, Richard. "Vailed Threats." *Cleveland*, June 1980.
Porter, Philip W. *Cleveland: Confused City on a Seesaw*. Columbus: Ohio State University Press, 1976.
Sheridan, Terence. "The Firing of a PD Reporter." *Cleveland*, June 1972.

Cleveland Plain Dealer, 1965–75
Cleveland Press, 1965–75
Mississippi Press-Register, 1966
Mobile Press, 1965–70
Mobile Register, 1965–70

32. Final Exam

Notes:
Newhouse's memoirs recount the story of meeting Red Motley and also detail the billion-dollar offer to the Thomsons.

John Morton provided me with copies of extensive coverage he prepared on the Booth deal for a newsletter he published at the time.

Interviews:
Walter Annenberg, Helen Lazarus Barrett, Joe Bodarky, Wesley Clark, Clark Clifford, Ernest Doepke, Len Gorman, Ed Kukowski, James Sauter, Richard Scudder, Theodore Sorenson, Adolph Ochs Sulzberger.

Secondary Sources:
Kupferberg, Herbert. "Parade's anniversary: Remembering 40 years." *Parade*, 23 August 1981.

Philadelphia Bulletin, 1967–75
Philadelphia Daily News, 1967–75
Philadelphia Inquirer, 1967–75
Philadelphia Journal, 1967–75
Wall Street Journal, 1975–78

33. Last Act

Notes:
Former *Press* photographer Joe DeMaria provided the basic details of the abuses at the *Press*. Other former *Press* employees confirmed DeMaria's account.

Interviews:
Joe DeMaria, Jackie Gebhard, Fred McMorrow, Leo Meindl, George Vecsey.

Secondary Sources:
Collins, "The *Long Island Press*, 1821–1977."
Gorman, Nancy. Affidavit re: ABC News Service. Unpubl., on file with Federal Communications Commission for WAPI.
Kranes, Marsha, and Carpozi, George, Jr. "*L. I. Press* dies at 156." *New York Post*, 26 March 1977.
Lent, *Newhouse, Newspapers, Nuisances*.

McMorrow, Fred. "Remembering the *Long Island Press*." *Newsday*, 28 March 1977.

Portnoy, Sandra Margolin. "Workers meet to mourn the *Press*." *New York Times*, 9 April 1978.

Rainie, Harrison. "How an ex-farm journal became a cropper." *New York Daily News*, 26 March 1977.

Stetson, Damon. "The *Long Island Press* shuts down." *New York Times*, 26 March 1977.

Long Island Press, 1970–77

34. Thirty

Notes:
Jules Witcover supplied me with the language of the disclaimer he received with his Christmas bonus at the Newhouse News Service one winter.

The woman whose accidental death received so little coverage was named Parker. She was a receptionist at the Harrisburg newspapers who drowned during the June 1972 floods that inundated central Pennsylvania.

This chapter also makes use of obituaries in the Newhouse newspapers.

Interviews:
Ben Bagdikian, John Gerald, William Tolley.

Afterword

Notes:
The Newhouses did not purchase the Florida property, photos of which Mitzi showed the men from Syracuse University in the summer of 1979. Instead, they set about constructing a place of their own on Chateaux Drive in Palm Beach. A special room was designed for S. I., but he died before the house could be finished.

After her husband's death, Mitzi held onto the Park Avenue duplex, but as soon as the Chateaux Drive home was completed, she began to spend most of her time there. Then, on 29 April 1980, she sold her major asset — 105 shares of stock in the Newhouse Broadcasting Corporation (46.66 percent of the total shares outstanding) — back to the company, leaving its ownership split equally between her sons. The deal left her well fixed for life.

On top of the 5 shares of NBC stock Mitzi owned already, she had received 100 more from her husband's estate on 31 March 1980. The total price for the stock was to be its fair market value as determined by the Chemical Bank of New York — estimates placed the figure at between $30 million and $60 million. In the meantime, Mitzi received $2 million down, the remainder to be paid in installments with interest over the next fifteen years.

A Note on the Map, "Newhouse's America"

As explained in this biography, many of the publications listed on the endpapers are no longer in existence. Some, like the *Jersey Observer* in Hoboken, New Jersey, were merged out of existence as part of Newhouse's basic strategy. Two others, the *Long Island Star-Journal* and the *Long Island Press*, failed.

At the time of Newhouse's death in August 1979, his newspapers boasted a total daily circulation of 3,214,437. Readership of the Condé Nast magazines and *Parade* totalled 27,555,192.

Index

ABC. *See* Allied Bi-County News Service (ABC)

Abraham & Strauss, 37

acquisitions, 123, 138, 158, 187; after Newhouse's death, 256; *Bayonne Times,* 238; *Birmingham News,* 167, 192; Booth newspapers, 2, 241–43; Bowaters, Ltd., paper mill, 238; *Cleveland Plain dealer,* 231, 234, 237; Condé Nast, 181, 187, 231; *Denver Post* (partial interest), 204–8; Evening Journal Association (Jersey City), 202; *Fitchburg News,* 29–33; *Flushing Journal,* 123; *Harrisburg Patriot* and *Evening News,* 141–48; *Harrisburg Telegraph,* 144–45; *Huntsville Times,* 167; *Jersey Journal,* 131–38; *Jersey Observer* (Hoboken), 132–33; last, 243; *Long Island City Star,* 123; *Long Island Press,* 67–73, 139, 145; magazines, 177–801; *Mississippi Press-Register* (Pascagoula), 231; *Mobile Press,* 231; *Mobile Register,* 230–31; *Nassau Review-Star,* 245; *New Orleans States-Item* and *Times-Picayune,* 200, 202, 225; *Newark Evening News,* 238; *Newark Ledger,* 89–95; *Newark Star-Eagle,* 130; *Oregon Journal,* 196, 199, 202; *Parade* magazine, 243; *Portland Oregonian,* 149–55, 157–58, 159, 160, 162, 164–65, 187, 189, 202; properties squeezed to provide cash for, 189, 190, 193–95; Random House and affiliated companies, 256; record sales prices, 154, 155, 164, 167, 189, 200, 231, 243; *St. Louis Globe-Democrat,* 166–67, 189, 214; speculation re financing of, 187; Springfield (Mass.) newspapers, 208, 209, 210–12, 230; *Staten Island Advance,* 35–39; Street & Smith, 178; *Syracuse Herald* and *Journal,* 113–22, 130, 162; *Syracuse Post-Standard,* 118–19, 130, 162; *see also* newspaper properties

Advance News Service, 226

Advance Publications, Inc. (API), 188, 225, 255

advertisers: role of, 233, 246

advertising: *Bayonne Times,* 14–16, 26, 27; Harrisburg Sunday papers, 146, 147; *Long Island Press,* 72, 81, 82, 244, 249; *Newark Ledger,* 90, 91, 92, 93, 94; *Portland Oregonian,* 165; radio challenging newspapers for, 95; revenues, 66, 68–69, 119, 140; *Staten Island Advance,* 35, 36–37, 38, 54, 55, 59–60; *Syracuse Herald,* 113; *Syracuse Herald-Journal,* 117–18; women's magazines, 178

Advertising Age, 154, 159

Aetna Life Insurance Company, 212

Allied Bi-County News Service (ABC), 247

Amberg, Richard Hiller, 191, 234

American News Company, 179

American Newspaper Guild, 88, 107, 160; in Cleveland, 235; at *Long Island Press,* 77–84, 101–6, 114, 158; and *Newark Ledger,* 96, 99–100, 114; at *St. Louis Globe-Democrat,* 191, 192; at *Staten Island Advance,* 84–87

American Newspaper Publishers Association (ANPA), 28, 67, 148, 195, 205

American Weekly, 89

Ancorp National Services, Inc., 179

Ann Arbor News, 241

Annenberg, Walter, 240

anti-Semitism, 31, 68, 158

API. *See* Advance Publications, Inc. (API)
Arenfeldt, Rose. *See* Newhouse, Rose Arenfeldt
Associated Press: American Newspaper Guild unit of, 101–2; wire service, 30, 98, 158
Audit Bureau of Circulation, 30, 97
Ayer, N. W., Advertising Directory, 152

Baldwin, William H., 209–10
Ballantine Books, 256
Baltimore Sun, 198
Bar Harbor, Me., 140, 141, 142, 143
Barnum, Jerome, 67, 68, 115, 116, 118, 126
Bausch, Frank, 71
Bay City Times, 241
Bayonne, N.J., 11, 13, 15, 16, 17, 19, 25, 30, 32, 38, 48; Lazarus's activities in, 12; Newhouses in, 9–10; Newhouse's reputation in, 238: strike-breaking in, 17
Bayonne Democrat, 15
Bayonne Herald, 15
Bayonne Review, 15
Bayonne Times, 12–13, 21, 22, 24, 30, 41–42, 52, 189; acquired by New-house, 238; Lazarus's widow in-herited, 48; Newhouse running, 14–20, 25–27, 28–29, 34, 36, 38, 42, 47, 50, 52, 131, 253; Newhouse's plan to buy, 132–33; and sale of *Fitchburg News,* 32–33
Bayonne Times Company, 30, 34
Belinkoff, Rose, 24
Belluschi, Pietro, 150
Bergoff, Pearl (called Red Demon), 17, 105
Berlin, Richard, 107, 108, 109
Berry family, 177–78
Berryman, Clyde, 204
Birmingham, Ala., 167, 200, 233, 235; Newhouse's acquisitions in, 231; race relations in, 171–73, 174
Birmingham News, 2, 189; acquired by Newhouse, 167, 192; effect of local autonomy on, 171–74
Block, Paul, 90, 94, 108–9, 122, 130, 142
Boggs, Hale, 219
Bolter, Jack, 197
Bonfils, Belle, 203
Bonfils, Frederick, 202–3
Bonfils, Helen, 203–8
Bonfils, May. *See* Stanton, May Bonfils

Booth family, 241–42
Booth newspapers (Mich.), 116; ac-quired by Newhouse, 2, 241–43, 255–56
Bowaters, Ltd., 238
Bowles, Francis, 210
Bowles, Sherman Hoar, 209
Brenner, Alfred, 19, 47
Breslin, Jimmy, 249
Bride's, 2
Brigadier, Maurice, 16–17, 29
Brooklyn, N.Y., 36, 49
Brooklyn Times, 49
Brooks, Donald, 226
Brown, Heywood, 77–78, 79, 82–83, 84, 86
Brown, James Wright, 157
Bruno, John, 78
Burstein, Rabbi Abraham, 42
Business Week, 159, 161, 200, 201

cable-TV systems, 3, 256
Canavan, Anne, 231–32
Capote, Truman, 183
Carpenter, James, 136–37
Case, Clifford, 171
Catawba, S. C., 238
CBS, 197, 256
Chamberlin, Ann, 162
Charlottesville Observer, 198
Charm, 178; incorporated into *Vogue,* 178
Chemical Bank (New York City), 68, 150, 189, 190
Chicago Tribune, 173
circulation: *Bayonne Times,* 26; *Harris-burg Patriot* and *Evening News,* 140; Harrisburg Sunday paper, 146–47; *Long Island Press,* 68–69, 70–71, 72, 244, 249; *Mississippi Press-Register,* 231; *Mobile Press* and *Register,* 231; *New Orleans States-Item* and *Times-Picayune,* 200; *Newark Ledger,* 90, 91–92, 93; Newhouse newspaper properties, 88, 200; *Portland Ore-gonian,* 149, 165; ranking of, 240; *Sta-ten Island Advance,* 35, 36, 38, 48–50, 87; *Syracuse Herald,* 113; *Syracuse Herald-Journal,* 118
Citizen Kane, 177
civil rights movement, 171–74
Clark, W. Dale, 217
Clark, Wesley, 125, 160, 215, 218, 220, 228–29, 233, 239
Cleveland, Ohio, 235

Cleveland Plain Dealer, 2, 256; acquired by Newhouse, 231, 234, 237; on list of ten worst papers, 252
Clifford, Clark, 239
Cohen, Octavus Roy, 13
Cohn, Henrietta, 3, 23–24
Cohn, Roy, 226
Cohn, Stella, 23–24, 42
Collier's, 159, 162
comics (*Newark Ledger*), 93
Condé Nast publications, 177–79, 180, 255; acquired by Newhouse, 181, 187, 231; assistance from Henry Garfinkle, 180; merger with Street & Smith, 178; Mitzi Newhouse on board of directors of, 182; owned by Patriot News Company, 188, 231
Condé Nast Press: shut down, 179
Connor, Theophilus Eugene "Bull," 173, 174
consolidations: in newspaper industry, 95; in small and medium-sized cities, 31–32; *see also* mergers
Cook, Sidney R., 209, 210–12
Cosgrove, Thomas, 60, 63, 64
Cosmopolitan, 177
Crosby, Alexander, 84, 85, 86, 87
Curtis, Cyrus H. K., 29
Curtis Publications, 177

Daily Journal of Commerce, 67
Dallas Times Herald, 208
Davies, Jessica, 182
Davies, Marian, 108
Davis, Edward Michael ("Tiger Mike"), 206
Davis, Smith, 113, 114, 115, 116, 205; at *Portland Oregonian*, 151, 153, 162
Dear, Albert, 132, 133–34, 135–38, 202
Dear, Cyrene, 133, 135, 137
Dear, Joseph A., 132
Dear, Katherine, 134–35
Dear, Walter, 28, 131–38, 202
Dear Publications, Inc., 137–38
delivery systems. *See* distribution
Denver Children's Hospital, 203, 205–6
Denver Post, 202–4; Newhouse's suit against, 207–8, 232; sold to Times Mirror Company, 208; struggle for control of, 204–8
Denver Post Company, 203, 205; struggle for control of, 206, 207–8
Detwiler, Meade, 144
Diamond, Gertrude Newhouse (sister of S. I. Newhouse), 255

Diamond, Richard, 255–56
Dierdorff, John, 197
distribution, 48–50, 55–56, 92, 179–80, 240
Doepke, Ernie, 143, 146, 147, 155, 177, 189, 227, 240; relationship with Newhouse, 147–48; retirement, 234
Dreimuller, John, 162

Editor & Publisher, 68–69, 107, 108, 117, 138, 143, 154, 157, 159; on *Portland Oregonian* acquisition, 152; pressure on, by Newhouse for favorable press, 160; "Principal Newspaper Chains of the United States," 122
editorial content, 37, 201; effect of Newhouse's cash needs on, 190, 194, 197; local autonomy and, 166, 167–74
Eggers, Melvin, 1
Einzig, Herbie, 247
Elizabeth, N.J., 18, 41, 93
Elizabeth Times, 41–42
employee firings, 114, 116–17, 130, 133, 145–46, 235, 238, 252
employee pension funds, 191, 192; Springfield newspapers, 209, 210, 211, 212
employee relations, 26–27, 78, 106, 126, 249, 252
Epstein, Judith, 40, 41, 58, 62, 67, 86
Epstein, Mitzi. *See* Newhouse, Mitzi Epstein
Epstein, Sam, 40, 41; death of, 58; failure of business, 58, 123
Esquire, 162
Eszterhas, Joe, 235
Evans (né Epstein), Hugo, 185
Evans (né Epstein), Walter, 185
Evening Journal Association (Jersey City), 132, 134, 188; acquired by Newhouse, 202; asset sale, 137
Everett, Rollin, 191

Fach, Albert, 56–57
Farkas family, 123–24
Farrell, Eugene, 145
fashion, 181, 182; *see also* Newhouse, Mitzi Epstein, interest in fashion
Fawcett Books, 256
Feinberg, Jack, 19
Fine, Emily Brown, 71
Fitchburg, Mass., 29–31, 89, 162
Fitchburg Daily News, 29–33, 162
Fitchburg (Mass.) Daily News Company, 30, 31

Fitchburg Sentinel, 30, 32–33
Flint Journal, 241
Flom, Joe, 242
Flushing, Queens, 114, 245, 247
Flushing Journal: acquired by New-
house, 123; merged with Long Island
City Star, 245
Fortune, 179
Francke, Jane. See Newhouse, Jane
Francke
Frey, Mike, 154, 194, 195, 196; retire-
ment of, 234
Fuerst, Joe, 240
Funk, Frank, 220

Gaffney School (New York City),
10–11, 12
Gannett, Frank E., 29, 122, 141, 158;
local autonomy principle, 166
Gannett, Guy, 29, 122
Gannett newspapers, 240, 243
Garfield News Company, 128, 179
Garfinkle, Henry, 87, 123, 207; business
relationship and friendship with New-
house, 49–50, 55–56, 128–29, 179–80;
business success of, 128; control of
distribution by, 179–80; on Mitzi
Newhouse, 185; personal characteris-
tics of, 179
Garfinkle, Myron, 180
Gebhard, Jackie, 103, 105
Gelwick's News Agency (Jamaica,
Queens), 77
Gentleman's Quarterly, 2, 256
Gerald, John, 124, 184, 185
Glamour, 2, 178, 188
Glickman, Florence, 53, 126–27, 220,
221, 234
Glickman, Louis, 53, 66, 94, 121,
188–89, 232
Glickman & Company, 134, 145
Goldberg, Arthur, 207–8
Goldman, Charles, 53, 99, 103, 105, 131,
145, 185, 188–89, 198, 217, 232
Goldman, Sachs (firm), 241
Goldwater, Barry, 222
Gorman, Len, 237
Gottlieb, Eddie, 71
Graham, Donald, 239
Graham, Katherine, 239
Graham, Philip, 239
Graham family, 252
Grand Rapids Press, 241
Greater Boston Distributors, 179
Greenlands (estate), 124–25, 128, 147,
229

Greenville, N.J., 9, 11, 162
Guest, C. Z., 183
Guest, Winston, 183
Guggenheim, Henry F., 245
Guild. See American Newspaper Guild,
New York Newspaper Guild
Guild Reporter, 85, 107

Hager, Phil, 197
Hague, Frank, 38, 132
Hanson, Clarence B., Jr., 167, 173
Hanson family, 167
Harbourton, N.J., 124, 125
Harrisburg, Pa., 138, 139–40, 142, 143,
154, 155, 231, 234; economy of, 146;
Newhouse personnel in, 145; New-
house's papers in, 151, 158, 190, 246;
newspapers in, 140; Patriot News
Company, 188; Sunday paper for,
146–47
Harrisburg Evening News, 140, 147, 188,
218; acquired by Newhouse, 141–44;
merged with Telegraph, 147
Harrisburg Home Star, 144
Harrisburg News-Telegraph, 145
Harrisburg Patriot, 188, 218; acquired
by Newhouse, 140, 141–44, 147; cuts
at, 190
Harrisburg Sunday Patriot-News,
146–47
Harrisburg Telegraph, 140, 147; acquired
by Newhouse, 144–45
Hartford Courant, 208
Hearst, William Randolph, 2, 29, 122,
150, 166, 174, 200, 202; buying out,
shutting down newspapers, 32; chain
of newspapers, 88–89; mergers by,
177; Newhouse's meeting with, 107–9;
portrayal of, in Citizen Kane, 177;
press treatment of, 158; purchased
New York Journal, 8; selling unprofitable papers, 115; and Syracuse Journal, 113–14; used P. Block as front,
142
Hearst Corporation, 115
Hearst family, 225
Hearst magazines, 107
Hempstead, Long Island, 245
Herald Company (Syracuse, N.Y.), 188
Hinerwadel's Grove (resort), 230, 231,
234
Hirsch, Harold, 185–86
Hobby, Oveta Culp, 199–200
Hochstein, Phil, 52, 137, 145, 158, 159,
160, 219, 220; at Long Island Press,
71–72, 79, 80, 82, 83, 101, 104; at

Hochstein, Phil (*cont'd*)
Newark Ledger, 92, 93, 101; on New-
house, 201; and Newhouse's relation-
ship with the press, 158, 159, 160, 161;
prepared drafts of Newhouse's public
statements, 219, 220; visiting Harris-
burg papers, 145
Hofmann, William, 68, 69, 70, 72, 98,
121, 130–31, 132
House & Garden, 2, 178; incorporated
Living for Young Homemakers, 179
Houston Post, 199–200
Hoyt, E. Palmer ("Ep"), 204, 205
Hoyt, Frank L., 32
Huntsville, Ala., 167
Huntsville Times, 167

independent news dealers, 48–49, 56,
245
International Typographical Union, 105

Jablons, Naomi (sister of S. I. New-
house), 9, 14, 88; working at *Staten
Island Advance*, 51
Jackson Citizen Patriot, 241
Jackson family, 202
Jamaica, Queens, 69, 116, 119; civic pro-
test groups in, 70–71, 72; demographic
change in, 246; as newspaper market,
244
Javits, Jacob, 222
Jefferson Pilot newspaper chain, 233
Jenkins, Mary, 116, 117
Jersey City, N.J., 8, 11, 15, 28, 131, 132,
202, 246; *see also* Evening Journal As-
sociation
Jersey City Journal, 28
Jersey Journal, 235; acquired by New-
house, 131–38; Donald Newhouse
manager of, 228; *Newark Times*
merged into, 238
Jersey Observer, 137; Newhouse's plan
to buy, 132–33
Johnson, Lady Bird, 220, 221, 222
Johnson, Lyndon Baines, 219–20,
221–22
Jones, Casey, 220
Jones, Ed, 55, 197
Josephs, Ray, 157–58, 159–60, 174, 218,
251
Josephs, Ray, Public Relations Agency,
200

Kalamazoo Gazette, 241
Kander, Allen, 198, 199–200
Kane, Michael, 54–56, 57

Kane, Walter, 56
Keller, LeRoy, 199
Kiewit, Peter, 217
King Features Syndicate, 89
Kislack, J. I., 137
Knight, John S., 113, 122, 141, 158;
merged his chain with that of Ridder
brothers, 240
Knight-Ridder newspapers, 240, 243
Knopf, Alfred A., 256
Knowles, Clayton P., 71, 80
Kopp, Roy, 235
Krajewski, Henry, 169

labor disputes, 114, 133; *Long Island
Press*, 77–85, 101–6, 107; *Newark Ledger*, 107; *Staten Island Advance*,
84–87, 107; *see also* strikes
labor productivity, 26, 191, 194
labor relations, 153, 158; *see also* employee relations; unions
La Guardia, Fiorello, 82–83, 104
Lambert, Bill, 168, 197
Lauder, Estée, 183
Lazarus, Helen, 238
Lazarus, Herman, 48, 50, 238
Lazarus, Hyman, 54, 126, 251; and acquisition of *Fitchburg News*, 29–30,
31, 32, 33; and acquisition of *Staten
Island Advance*, 35–36, 37, 38, 43;
death of, 43; personal difficulties of,
42–43, 47; relationship with New-
house, 11–13, 14, 16, 18, 26, 34–35,
41; sold Newhouse his share of *Staten
Island Advance*, 41
Lazarus, Margaret Connolly, 48, 50
Lazarus, Sydney, 48, 50
Lazarus & Brenner (law firm), 11, 16,
19, 24, 25, 29
legal advertisements, 59–60, 67–68
Lent, John, 160–61; *Newhouse, Newspa-
pers, Nuisances*, 161
Lent, Rudy, 135
Lerner, Sam, 48
Lewis, W. D., 143
Liebling, A. J., 149, 202
Liebowitz, Mike, 71
Lindsay, John, 127
litigation, 135–37, 207–8, 211–12, 232
Living for Young Homemakers, 178–79
local autonomy, policy of, 150, 164–74,
221–22, 233, 251; decisive in New Or-
leans acquisitions, 200; undermining
of, 235–36
Long Island, 114, 158, 246
Long Island City, 114, 116, 119

Long Island City Star: acquired by Newhouse, 123; *Flushing Journal* merged with, 245

Long Island Daily Press, 226

Long Island Daily Press and Farmer, (later *Long Island Press*), 70

Long Island Daily Press Publishing Company, 68, 71, 188; Newhouse acquired Hofmann's stock in, 130–31

Long Island Daily Star, 114

Long Island Democrat, 70

Long Island Farmer, 69–70

Long Island Press, 92, 114, 135, 161, 189, 193, 245; acquired by Newhouse, 67–73, 123, 139, 145; American Newspaper Guild at, 77–84, 101–6, 114, 158; civic activism of, 72; closing of, 244–49, 250; Donald Newhouse trained at, 228; labor relations at, 77–85, 114; Nassau County edition, 245–46; profitability of, 88, 91, 94; reorganization of, 71–72; suspended publication during strike, 105–6

Long Island Star-Journal, 114, 131, 145, 147, 245

Los Angeles Times, 2, 197, 208

Lynch, John, 38, 59, 60–61

Lyons, Douglas, 228–29

Lyons, Jeffrey, 129

Lyons, Leonard, 129, 184, 215–16, 228

Lyons, Sylvia, 215–16

"Lyons Den, The" (column), 129

McCarthy, Joe, 170–71, 174

McCarthyism, 171

McClean, St. John, 38, 41–42, 51–52

McClearn, William, 232

McCormick, Annie (Mrs. Vance), 140–43, 147

McCormick, Col. Robert, 239

McCormick, Vance, 140, 143, 147, 158

McCormick family (Chicago), 140

McCoy, Dan, 200

McCoy, Leo, 195

McDowell, Blake, 198

McDowell, John, 169, 171

McLean family, 240

McMorrow, Fred, 249

MacNaughton, E. B., 150, 151, 153, 165

Mademoiselle, 2, 178, 188

magazine properties, 2, 177–80, 181–82, 256; profitability of, 178–79

M.A.N. machine, 194

management (Newhouse organization), 2, 78, 79, 117–18, 154, 231–36

Manhattan, 9, 10, 11, 36, 43, 109, 123; Lower East Side, 7–8

Manhattan News (company), 179

Manno, Vincent, 151

market surveys, 92, 93

Marley, Harry, 215, 216, 230, 250

Marley, Suzie. *See* Newhouse, Suzie Marley

Martin, Harold, 227–28, 233, 235

Martin, Herbert L., 27

Meadowbrook Dairy (Staten Island), 55

Meier Newhouse & Co., 162

Meindl, Leo, 246

mergers, 32; Condé Nast with Patriot News Company, 231; employees dismissed in, 130, 133, 145–46, 238 (*see also* shutdowns); *Flushing Journal* with *Long Island City Star,* 245; *Harrisburg Evening News* and *Telegraph,* 144–45, 147; Knight-Ridder chains, 240; magazines, 178; New Orleans and Portland papers, 257; *Newark Star-Eagle* with *Newark Ledger,* 130; *Newark Times* with *Jersey Journal,* 238; *North Shore Journal* with *Long Island Daily Star,* 114; planned, 132–33; Street & Smith into Condé Nast, 178, 180; *Syracuse Herald* and *Journal,* 115–18

Meserve, Robert, 211

Meyer, Eugene, 239

Miami Herald, 113

Miron, Estelle Newhouse (sister of S. I. Newhouse), 255

Miron, Robert, 255

Mississippi Press-Register, 231

Mobile, Ala., 230–31

Mobile Press, 231

Mobile Register, 230–31

Modern Library, 256

More, 252

Morning Ledger Company (Newark, N.J.), 188

Morrish, Bill, 194

Morrissey, Carol, 79, 80–81

Motley, Arthur H. "Red," 237, 241

Moyers, Bill, 219

Munsey, Frank, 29

Muskegon Chronicle, 241

Nassau Journal, 245

Nassau Review-Star, 244–45

Nast, Condé, 177–78

National Labor Relations Board, 102

national news service: owned by Newhouse, 177

Naughton, James M., 235
Neff, Joseph, 240
Neuhaus, Becky, 7, 20, 22
Neuhaus, Devorah, 7
Neuhaus, Frieda, 7
Neuhaus, Joe, 7
Neuhaus, Louis, 7
Neuhaus, Meier. *See* Newhouse, Meier
(father of S. I. Newhouse)
Neuhaus, Nachman, 7, 88
New Jersey College of Law, 18
New Orleans, 185; Newhouse acquisitions in, 200–201, 202, 231, 257; new Newhouse plants in, 237
New Orleans States-Item: acquired by Newhouse, 200, 202, 225; endorsed Johnson (1964 election), 222
New Orleans Times-Picayune, 2, 219, 236; acquired by Newhouse, 200, 202, 225; endorsed Johnson (1964 election), 221, 222; on list of ten worst newspapers, 252
New York City, 11, 41, 66, 92, 107; Newhouse's excursions to, 22–23; Newhouse's papers in, 256; society in, 181, 182; *see also* individual boroughs
New York Daily News, 103, 179, 246
New York Herald, 48
New York Herald Tribune, 81, 82, 103
New York Journal, 15, 48; Hearst interviewed Newhouse for publisher position at, 107–9
New York Newspaper Guild, 85; *see also* American Newspaper Guild
New York Post, 129, 246
New York Shakespeare Festival, 185
New York Times, 15, 48, 103, 154, 159, 166, 197, 235, 246; article on Si Newhouse in, 227; distribution arrangement with Garfinkle, 179; "Fear and Hatred Grip Birmingham," 172–73; Newhouse's attempt to purchase, 239
New York Tribune, 48
New York University, 22, 35, 162
New York World, 8, 15, 48, 70
New York World-Telegram, 77
New Yorker, 161, 179, 202
Newark, N.J., 18, 36, 89, 91, 94–95, 119, 158, 237
Newark Evening News, 15, 90, 91, 92, 93, 130, 137, 169, 170; demise of, 238
Newark Leader, 97
Newark Ledger, 107, 119, 141, 231–32; acquired by Newhouse, 89–95, 123; American Newspaper Guild at,

99–100, 114; merged with *Star-Eagle,* 130; rebuilding of, 96–98
Newark Morning Ledger Publishing Company, 97–98, 188
Newark Newspaper Guild, 90; *see also* American Newspaper Guild
Newark Star-Eagle, 90, 91, 92, 108–9; acquired by Newhouse, 130
Newark Star-Ledger, 2, 130, 137, 238, 255; effect of local autonomy on, 169–71, 174
Newhouse, Ada (sister of S. I. Newhouse), 9, 14, 21, 198
Newhouse, Donald (first cousin of S. I. Newhouse), 193–94, 195, 196
Newhouse, Donald Edward (son of S. I. Newhouse), 3, 58, 225, 228–29, 241–42; education of, 125; married Suzie Marley, 215; special place in family of, 229; taking control of Newhouse's empire, 255–56; trust fund for, 228
Newhouse, Estelle (sister of S. I. Newhouse), 21, 35
Newhouse, Gertrude (sister of S. I. Newhouse), 21, 35
Newhouse, Jane Francke, 226–27
Newhouse, Louis (brother of S. I. Newhouse), 9, 14, 21, 26, 36, 88, 198; personal characteristics of, 102
Newhouse, Meyer (father of S. I. Newhouse), 7–9, 12, 19–20; business failure of, 9–10, 16, 162; death of, 133, 198; illness of, 10, 20; left home, 20, 22
Newhouse, Mitzi Epstein (Mrs. S. I. Newhouse), 3, 62, 67, 128, 129, 215, 216; on best-dressed personalities list, 184; decorating homes, 57, 184; at dedication of School of Public Communications, Syracuse University, 221; as a director of Samuel I. Newhouse Foundation, 185; effect on Newhouse, 185–86; interest in fashion, 40, 86, 125, 181, 184; at Newhouse's illness, death, 2, 250–51; in Newhouse's will, 255; reaction to Si's marriage, divorce, 226–27; social ambition of, 123–24, 181–85; *see also* Newhouse, Samuel I. and Mitzi
Newhouse, Norman (brother of S. I. Newhouse), 4, 14, 21, 79–80, 88, 148, 235; education of, 22, 34–35; at *Long Island Press,* 102–3, 106; Newhouse relied on, 232; Newhouse's fa-

Newhouse, Norman (*cont'd*)
vorite, 21–22; at *Staten Island Advance*, 60, 63, 69, 71, 85, 88; supervision of family properties by, 255; supervision of New Orleans and Alabama papers, 236, 248
Newhouse, Pamela (granddaughter of S. I. Newhouse), 226
Newhouse, Pat, 145
Newhouse, Rose Arenfeldt (mother of S. I. Newhouse), 8–9, 10, 14, 21, 198
Newhouse, Samuel I. (Solomon): allowed no one outside family to own stock, 233; altering events of his life, 161–62, 182; annual celebration of birthday of, 230, 231, 234, 250; attention to detail, 51, 94; attitude toward publisher's responsibility, 233; attitude toward/relationship with press, 156–63, 180; aversion to borrowing, 189; background of, 3, 7–10; business acumen of, 32–33; called "journalist chiffonnier" by Liebling, 149; depressed about publishers of future, 231; disliked flying, 153; drinking, 148, 187; education of, 9, 10–11, 18, 162; effect of early poverty on, 7, 10, 124–25, 221; effect of Lazarus's death on, 47, 48; explanation of his success, 180; facility with numbers, 12, 16; failure to live up to standards he set, 251–52; financial affairs: general, 129, 130, 174; financial affairs: business, 65–66, 79–80, 113, 114, 118, 151, 180, 187–89, 193, 212, 233, 237; financial affairs: funding donations to Syracuse University, 218–19; financial affairs: salaries, earnings, 18, 34–35, 47, 88, 95, 103; friendships, 3, 23, 24, 50, 128–29, 139–40, 157, 180; getting his properties ready for next generation, 237, 238; goal of owning chain of newspapers, 29, 35, 40, 66, 88–89, 109, 114, 177, 186, 198–99, 200–201; going back on deals, 83–84, 100, 105, 242–43; grandchildren of, 255; honorary degree from Syracuse University, 214; illness, death of, 1–2, 250–51; impact on newspaper business, 4, 122, 251–53; interference with editorial content (1964 elections), 221–22; interviews with, 156–57, 158–60; Jewishness, 23, 31, 142, 158, 165; as lawyer, 18, 19, 162; life-style, 123–29, 130; "living monument" to, 216–22; management style of, 2, 78, 79, 117–18,

154, 231–36; meaning of newspaper to, 252–53; met, courted Mitzi Epstein, 39–41, 42; move from Bayonne to Staten Island, 50–51, 52, 57; name of, on masthead, 39, 90; newspaper price/worth formula, 151–53, 167; penchant for secrecy, 3, 117, 119, 143, 187, 233; personal appearance, 10, 18, 20; personal characteristics of, 3, 16–17, 24, 25, 34, 40, 125–29, 148, 158, 187; personal correspondence of, 31; personality of, 199; press criticism of, 174; rarely read his papers, 166, 174; reading trade journals, 28–29, 31–32, 72, 92, 121, 127; recreational interests of, 125–26, 139, 157; referred to his papers as "products," 232; relationship with his sons, 58, 124, 225, 227; relationships with people, 126–28, 134, 135; ruthless business practices, 16, 54–57, 78, 98, 135, 158; shift in approach to newspapers with acquisition of *Portland Oregonian*, 154–55; skill at identifying newspaper markets, 244; social life, 21–24, 39, 58, 109, 127, 180; speech at dedication of School of Public Communications, Syracuse University, 220–21; trustee of Syracuse University, 216; will, 254–55; work schedules, 30, 38, 51, 69, 90–91, 119–22, 147
Newhouse, Samuel I., Jr. (Si) (son of S. I. Newhouse), 3, 58, 225–28, 229; education of, 125; life-style of, 227; taking control of Newhouse empire, 255–56; trust fund for, 228
Newhouse, Samuel I. and Mitzi, 39–41, 57–58, 124, 185–86; move to Park Avenue, 123–24; properties acquired by, 123–25; and Si's marriage, family, 226–27; social life of, 125; trips, travel, 85, 86, 89, 125; trust funds for sons, 228; wedding anniversary, 181–82
Newhouse, Samuel I., III, 226
Newhouse, Suzie Marley, 215
Newhouse, Theodore (brother of S. I. Newhouse), 4, 9, 14, 88, 148, 195; general manager, *Long Island Press*, 249; home of, picketed, 85; Newhouse relied on, 232; and *Portland Oregonian*, 153–54; and publishing of Lent's *Newhouse, Newspapers, Nuisances*, 161; responsible for Newhouse papers in Massachusetts and Oregon, 255; trained Donald Newhouse in newspapering, 228; working at New-

Newhouse, Theodore (cont'd)
house newspapers, 36, 51, 69
Newhouse, Wynn (grandson of S. I.
Newhouse), 226
Newhouse Broadcasting Corporation,
255
Newhouse News Service, 177
Newhouse, Newspapers, Nuisances
(Lent), 161
Newman, Thomas, 53
Newsday, 208, 245–46
newspaper brokers, 113, 132, 198,
199–200, 202, 205, 240
newspaper business (U.S.), 95; anti-
Semitism in, 158; competition in, 158,
164; concentration in, 29; failure to
command big purchase prices,
164–65; family-run affairs, 149, 164;
Newhouse's biggest deals in, 2, 154,
155, 164, 167, 189, 200, 231, 243;
Newhouse's influence on, 4, 122,
251–53; Newhouse's mastery of,
187–89
newspaper chains, 29, 137–38, 150, 253;
local autonomy in, 166
newspaper families, 149, 209–12, 225;
Newhouse pursued acquisitions
among, 202–12; selling properties,
164–65, 167
newspaper features syndicates, 89, 92,
117
newspaper properties, 2–3, 119, 121,
122, 130, 149, 199, 238, 256–57; corporate structure of, 188–89; and funding arrangement for Newhouse's gifts
to Syracuse University, 218–19; management of, 231–36; monthly reports
re, 121; Newhouse preparing for next
generation, 237; originated by Newhouse, 245; pursuit of, by Newhouse,
89, 198–201, 202, 239–43; quality of,
252; ranking of, 240; reinvestment
program for, 237; secrecy re ownership of, 117, 119, 143; squeezed to
provide cash for other acquisitions,
189, 190, 193–95; Sunday editions,
117; supervision of, by members of
family, 255–56; supporting Johnson
(1964 election), 222
newspapers: afternoon, 115–16; effect of
Depression on, 66; formula for judg-
ing price/worth, 131, 151; independence of, 253; Newhouse model of,
became dominant, 253; profitable, 88;
role of "people's champion," 59;
worst, 252

Newsweek, 154, 158, 179
NLRB. See National Labor Relations
Board
North American Newspaper Alliance,
92
North Shore Journal (Flushing), 114
Northwestern University, 92
Notson, Robert, 166, 196, 235

O'Hara, E. A., 116, 117, 121–22
Omaha, Neb., 217
Omaha World-Herald, 217–18
Oregon Journal, 152, 160, 195; acquired
by Newhouse, 196, 199, 202
Oregonian Publishing Company, 235
Outcault, Richard F., 8
Owen, Ernest L., 118–19

Pantheon Books, 256
Parade, 2, 237, 241; acquired by
Newhouse, 243
Parsons, Louella, 115
Parsons School of Design, 40, 183
Pascagoula, Miss., 231
Patcevitch, Iva S. V., 177–78
Patriot News Company (Harrisburg,
Pa.), 140–41, 144, 145, 147, 188; ac-
quired by Newhouse, 142; Condé
Nast merged with, 231
Patterson, Alicia, 245, 246
Pearson, Drew, 170
Philadelphia Bulletin, 197, 240
Philadelphia Daily News, 240
Philadelphia Inquirer, 235, 240
Philadelphia Journal, 240
picketing, 81–82, 85–87; see also strikes
Piersall, Gilbert, 56
Pittock, Henry, 149
Pittock family, 202
Plotkin, Rabbi, 43
Poe, Allen, 219
Port Richmond, Staten Island, 35, 36,
85, 119
Portland, Oreg., 138, 150, 153, 154–155,
166, 167, 177; corruption investigation
by Oregonian in, 168; economy of,
152; Newhouse acquisitions in, 202,
231, 234, 257; Newhouse's union bust-
ing in, 195, 196–97; S. I. Newhouse
Foundation grants in, 219; F. Stickel
to, 235
Portland Oregonian, 2, 204, 205, 218; acquired by Newhouse, 149–55, 157–58,
159, 160, 162, 164–65, 187, 189, 202;
attacked by McCarthy, 171; did not
oppose Johnson, 221, 222; effects of

Portland Oregonian (*cont'd*)
cuts on, 190, 193–97; local autonomy policy at, 167–69; Pulitzer Prize, 168; reputation of, 149, 154; staff losses to, 197; strike of, 193–97
Portland Reporter, 197
Preble, Blanchard M., 36, 39
press: coverage of Newhouses, 154; Newhouse's attitude toward, relationship with, 156–63: *see also Editor & Publisher*
Pulitzer, Joseph, 8, 29, 70, 166
Pulitzer family, 225; Newhouse's dealings with, 192, 193
Pulitzer Prize(s), 168, 197, 234

Queens, N.Y., 43, 67, 244, 246–47
Queens-Nassau Picture Service, 247–48
Quigley, William, 54, 57

radio, 95, 115, 164
radio and television stations, 3, 177
Raidy, William, 183
Random House, 256
Ratner's (restaurant, New York City), 22–23
Ray, E. Lansing, 167, 191, 192
RCA Corporation, 256
Reader's Digest, 179
Reichek, Mort, 161
Reinfeld mob, 187
Rendt, David, 59, 60–63, 64
Retail Display Allowance, 180
Ridder, Marie, 139
Ridder, Victor, 67–68, 115, 139–40, 145
Ridder, Walter, 139
Ridder brothers, 68, 70, 122, 139, 145, 158; merged chain with John Knight's, 240; sale of Patriot Company, 141, 142
Rifkin, Leo, 22–23, 31, 35, 39, 40–41, 50–51, 67, 127; best man at Newhouse's wedding, 42
Rifkin, Rose, 50, 51
Ring, Leo, 235
Rinne, Clarence, 116–17, 121
Rippey, Helen Crabbs, 203, 205–6
Rockefeller, Nelson, 222
Rockefeller family, 124
Rodgers, Dorothy, 123, 184
Rodgers, Richard, 123
Rogers, Steve, 125, 129
Rolling Stone, 235
Rosenthal, Jack, 197
Runyon, Damon, 115
Ruppell, Louis, 159

Russell, Edwin, 96, 98, 134, 147, 148, 240; fronted for Newhouse in purchase of Patriot Company, 141–44, 145
Russell, Lady Sarah Spencer-Churchill, 141
Russell, Lucius T., 89–90, 141; forced out of *Newark Ledger,* 96–98, 158

S. I. Newhouse Foundation, 185, 189, 218, 219, 225, 255
S. I. Newhouse School of Public Communications (Syracuse University), 220–22; *see also* Syracuse University
Saginaw News, 241
St. George (Staten Island), 35, 49, 50, 85
St. Louis, Mo., 167, 185, 233, 235; effects of Newhouse on newspapers of, 190–93, 195, 197
St. Louis Globe-Democrat, 2, 185, 227, 256; acquired by Newhouse, 166–67, 189, 214; did not oppose Johnson (1964 election), 222; effects of Newhouse's cash needs on, 190–93; on list of ten worst newspapers, 252; strike of, 190–93, 197
St. Louis Post-Dispatch, 191–92, 193
salaries, working conditions, job security, 78, 81, 100, 233; *Long Island Press,* 103, 104, 247–48; *Portland Oregonian,* 194; promised by American Newspaper Guild, 78–79; *St. Louis Globe-Democrat,* 191
Salisbury, Harrison, 172–73, 174
San Simeon, Calif., 89, 107, 108, 109
Sander, Seymour, 55
Sardi, Vincent, 184
Sardi's (restaurant, New York City), 129, 184–85
Saturday Evening Post, 13, 177
Saturday Review, 174
Sauter, James, 241, 242, 243
Scheck, Emanuel P., 89, 90
Scherer, Harry, 27
Schine, J. Myer, 213
Schrunk, Terry, 196
Schwartzwalder, Ben, 215
Scientific American, 179
Scott, Harvey, 149
Scott family, 202
Scripps, E. W., 29
Scripps-Howard, 174, 199, 200
Scudder family, 90, 94, 130, 137
Self, 2, 256
Shaplen, Robert, 174
Sheppard, Eugenia, 182

Sherman Bowles Airport (Agawam, Mass.), 210
shutdowns, 32, 179, 192
Silk, Abe, 22
Singer, Maurice, 102
Small, Collie, 159, 162
Smith, Danny, 49, 92
Somnes, George, 203
South, the: Newhouse newspaper acquisitions in, 165, 166–67
Spencer-Churchill, Lady Sarah. See Russell, Lady Sarah Spencer-Churchill
Springfield, Mass.: Newhouse's acquisitions in, 208–12, 230, 237
Springfield Daily News: acquired by Newhouse, 208, 209, 210, 212
Springfield Sunday *Republican,* acquired by Newhouse, 208, 209, 210
Springfield Union, 2, 208, 209, 210, 212
Springfield Weekly Republican, 209
Staats Zeitung Und Herold, Der, 67, 68
Stackpole, A. H., 144
Stackpole, E. J., 144
Stackpole family, 140, 144
Stanton, Ed, 204
Stanton, May Bonfils (Berryman), 203–8
Stanton, Thomas J., 137
Starr, Dave, 126, 244, 248, 249
Staten Island, 35–36, 37, 38, 43, 48, 162; land speculation in, 52; political corruption in, 59–63, 64
Staten Island Advance, 42, 47, 48, 92, 119, 130–31, 188, 255; acquired by Newhouse and Lazarus, 35–39, 123; building up of, 51–53; competition to, 55–56; distribution of, 48–50; effect of Depression on, 66–67; labor relations at, 84–87; Newhouse total ownership of, 41, 52; political involvement of, 59–64, 162; profile of Newhouse in, 156–57, 158; profitability of, 88, 91, 94; salaries, working conditions at, 78
Staten Island Advance Corporation, 41–42, 66, 228; sued for libel by Rendt, 61–63
Staten Island Herald, 60
Staten Islander, 54–56, 60
Steinbaum, Evelyn, 24
Sterne, Ed, 101, 102
Stickel, Fred, 235
Stiles, James, 245
Street & Smith, 178, 180
strike insurance, 195
strike newspapers, 197

strikes, 90; against *Long Island Press,* 104–6; against *Portland Oregonian,* 194–97; against *St. Louis Globe-Democrat,* 192, 195; against *Staten Island Advance,* 85–86, 87
Sucher, Leonard. See Lyons, Leonard
Sulzberger, Adolph Ochs, 239
Sulzberger family, 252
Syracuse, N.Y., 113, 115, 116, 119, 162, 177, 185, 233; economic conditions in, 114; new Newhouse plants in, 237; Newhouse's newspaper control in, 118–19, 214, 246; Newhouse's trip to, with V. Ridder, 67–68; newspaper business in, 119, 130
Syracuse Herald: acquired by Newhouse, 113–22; merged with *Journal,* 115–18
Syracuse Herald-Journal, 2, 117–22, 150, 152, 230; acquired, merged by Newhouse, 162
Syracuse Journal, 113–14, 189; acquired by Newhouse and merged with *Herald,* 115–18
Syracuse Post-Standard, 67, 114, 115–16, 118–19, 150, 152, 191, 230; acquired by Newhouse, 118–19, 130; owned by Herald Company, 188; sued by J. McCarthy, 171
Syracuse Sunday American, 117
Syracuse University, 250, 255; Donald Newhouse attended, 228; football, 215, 216; Newhouse's association with, benefaction of, 1–2, 160, 213–22; School of Communications, 216–19, 220–22; School of Journalism, 160, 215–16, 222; Si Newhouse attended, 226

Tammen, Harry, 202–3
tax laws, 138, 151; Newhouse's mastery of, 66, 187–89
television, 164, 240
television stations, 256
Thayer, Walter, 241, 242
Thomson, Roy, 243
Thomson organization, 240, 242–43
Tiernan, Judge, 60
Time, Inc., 233
Time magazine, 154, 158, 159, 179, 192, 201, 252
Times Mirror Publishing Company of Los Angeles, 2, 208, 233, 243; Newhouse TV stations sold to, 256
Tolley, William, 1–2, 127–28, 221, 222; on Donald Newhouse, 228; relation-

Tolley, William (*cont'd*)
  ship with Newhouse, 213–16, 218, 219; on Si Newhouse, 226, 227
trade journals, 28, 31, 92, 154
Turner, Wallace, 168, 194, 197

Uhlan, Edward, 160–61
Union News Company, 179
unions, 190; at *Cleveland Plain Dealer*, 235; of editorial workers, 77–79, 84; Newhouse's animosity toward, 106, 195, 197, 247, 249, 252; at *Portland Oregonian*, 194; of reporters, 101–2; *see also* American Newspaper Guild, International Typographical Union, New York Newspaper Guild
United Press International, 199
Universal (wire service), 89
University of Missouri School of Journalism, 214

Vail, Thomas Van Husen, 234–35
Vanity Fair, 256
Vecsey, George, 71, 102, 106
Victor, Leonard, 247
Villard Books, 256
Vintage Books, 256
Vogue, 2, 178, 188; incorporated *Charm*, 178; Mitzi Newhouse and, 181–84; Si Newhouse at, 227

Vreeland, Diana, 183
Vreeland, Reed, 183

Wagner Labor Relations Act, 102
Walker, Jerome, 152, 157, 159, 160
Walker, Paul, 145–46
Wall Street Journal, 179, 197
Washington Post, 239
Washington Times-Herald, 239
Watson, Morris, 101–2
Webb, David, 182
Webster, Mrs., 71
Whitcom: sale of Booth stock in, to Newhouse, 241–43
Whitehead, John, 241
Whitney, John Hay, 241; *see also* Whitcom
Winchell, Walter, 115, 154, 157
Winston, Harry, 204
Wise, Rabbi Stephen, 22
Witcover, Jules, 226
Wolfe, William, 42, 51–52

yellow journalism, 8, 59
Young Bride's, 178
"Young Tigers" (*Cleveland Plain Dealer*), 234, 235

Zinader, Moe, 22, 23–24, 38

Newhouse's

PORTLAND

DENVER

Newspapers

BIRMINGHAM, ALA.
News
HUNTSVILLE, ALA.
News
Times
MOBILE, ALA.
Press
Register
DENVER, COLO.
Post (Partial)
NEW ORLEANS, LA.
States—Item
Times—Picayune
FITCHBURG, MASS.
News
SPRINGFIELD, MASS.
News
Republican
Union
ANN ARBOR, MICH.
News
BAY CITY, MICH.
Times
FLINT, MICH.
Journal
GRAND RAPIDS, MICH.
Press
JACKSON, MICH.
Citizen Patriot
KALAMAZOO, MICH.
Gazette
MUSKEGON, MICH.
Chronicle
SAGINAW, MICH.
News

PASCAGOULA, MISS.
Mississippi Press—Register
ST. LOUIS, MO.
Globe—Democrat
BAYONNE, N.J.
Times
HOBOKEN, N.J.
Jersey Observer
JERSEY CITY, N.J.
Jersey Journal
NEWARK, N.J.
Ledger
Star—Eagle
LONG ISLAND, N.Y.
Flushing Journal
Long Island City Star
Long Island Press
Nassau Review—Star
STATEN ISLAND, N.Y.
Advance
SYRACUSE, N.Y.
Herald
Journal
Herald—American
Post—Standard
CLEVELAND, OHIO
Plain Dealer
PORTLAND, ORE.
Oregonian
Oregon Journal
HARRISBURG, PA.
Evening News
Patriot
Telegraph

PAPER MILL • *49 percent of plant operated by Bowaters, Ltd., at Catawba, S.C.*

Broadcast

BIRMINGHAM, ALA.
WAPI AM, FM, TV
ST. LOUIS, MO.
KTVI—TV
ELMIRA, N.Y.
WSYE—TV
SYRACUSE, N.Y.
WSYR AM, FM, TV
PORTLAND, OREG.
KGW AM
KOIN AM, FM, TV (
HARRISBURG, PA.
WTPA—TV
WTTA—FM

CABLE TV • *System
Pennsylvania, and N*